'The vastness and beauty of the Gobi form a spectacular backdrop to John Hare's terrific story of wild camels, Kazakh migrations, ancient mummies, lost cities, gold miners and oil speculators. *Mysteries of the Gobi* is an exciting and important account of modern-day exploration, revealing much about the past and future of this extraordinary region.' **Sir Ranulph Fiennes**

'This is just a fantastic piece of writing. It's travel-writing, it's story-telling, it's a camp-fire tale of memorable characters and unforgettable places, packed with thrills and spills. This is an adventure story – and this is what will surely grab you – every word of it is true . . . by the time you've read it there will also be kindled within you a spark of enthusiasm for John Hare's magnificent quest in a daunting but achievable cause.' **Matthew Parris**

'*Mysteries of the Gobi* describes a series of journeys into the heart of the most remote, harsh and unforgiving deserts on the planet; it also reveals the desperate plight of the magnificent wild Bactrian camel as it struggles to survive in its increasingly exploited world. John Hare, cast in the mould of the heroic explorers of the past, is an adventurer with a mission – to save these camels from extinction. He brings to the table his power as a writer, his love for the desert, his understanding of the Chinese people and his diplomatic skills. If anyone can save the Bactrian camels, he can.' **Jane Goodall, DBE**

The Lost Camels of Tartary: A Quest into Forbidden China

'John Hare has seen deeper into the Central Asian wilderness than any other recent Western traveller. These adventures are told in raw and unpretentious form.'
John Man, *Literary Review*

'His account of his journey into the heart of the Gobi and of his dealings with his Chinese hosts is stirring stuff, as rich in human as in natural scenery.'
Max Davidson, *Daily Telegraph*

'Hare brings to his account of a hair-raising adventure not only dedication and adventure, but a sense of humour.'
Peter Somerville Large, *Irish Independent*

'John Hare is always keen to indulge his passion for remote places. His story has all the elements of tough desert travel you'd expect.'
Condé Nast Traveller

'Rich in adventure, filled with fascinating historical facts and legends, shrewd observations about the people encountered and their way of life.'
Jane Goodall, DBE

Shadows Across the Sahara: Travels with Camels from Lake Chad to Tripoli

'A sparkling and witty story of camels, sands, corruption and camaraderie . . . told with ever greater charm and humour as he whisks his willing readers off on an outlandish but wonderful journey. He succeeds in conveying the wonder of the desert.'
Vanora Bennett, *TLS*

'This is travel writing at its adventurous best.'
The Good Book Guide

For Christian, Benjamin, Lucy and Rory —
the cameleers of the future

Mysteries of the Gobi

*Searching for Wild Camels and Lost Cities
in the Heart of Asia*

John Hare

I.B. TAURIS

LONDON · NEW YORK

Published in 2009 by I.B. Tauris & Co Ltd
6 Salem Road, London W2 4BU
175 Fifth Avenue, New York NY 10010
www.ibtauris.com

In the United States of America and Canada
distributed by Palgrave Macmillan, a division of St Martin's Press
175 Fifth Avenue, New York NY 10010

ISBN 978 1 84511 512 8

A full CIP record for this book is available from the British Library
A full CIP record is available from the Library of Congress

Library of Congress Catalog Card Number: available

Typeset by JCS Publishing Services Ltd, www.jcs-publishing.co.uk
Printed and bound in India by Thomson Press India Ltd

Contents

List of Illustrations		ix
Map		x
Foreword by Matthew Parris		xiii
1	The Call of the Wild	1
2	Beyond the Dunes	26
3	Sweet as Eden is the Air	37
4	Take Flight and Follow	75
5	Hie to the Deserts Wild	88
6	Death's Shadow at the Door	118
7	Over the Unknown Pass	139
8	The Desert's Dusty Face	155
9	The Secrets of the Sands	173
10	Greater Than Anyone Thinks	185
Appendices		
1	The Current Situation of the Uighurs in Xinjiang	202
2	The First Published Account of the Wild Bactrian Camel by Colonel Nikolai Mikhailovich Przhevalsky	206
3	Spies Among the Kazakhs	213
Bibliography		225
Acknowledgements		229
Index		231

Illustrations

1 The author standing next to the second-century Buddhist shrine at Miran

2 Our injured camel on the road between Hongliugou and Miran, after the black sandstorm

3 Travelling east in the foothills of the Arjin Mountains with Tibet in the background

4 Descending from the Kum Tagh sand dunes with our camels

5 The footprint of a Tibetan bear, mistaken at first by Leilei as the footprint of a 'yeti'

6 One of two wild Bactrian camels encountered in the Kum Tagh

7 Usuman leads us towards the two unmapped valleys

8 A wild Argali ram at the Kum Su spring

9 One of our Kazakh herdsmen

10 The 'Professor', Yuan Guoying

11 The skull of an Argali ram, shot by miners, at Kum Su

12 One of the many drums of potassium cyanide found at Kum Su. It reads 'Deadly Poison'

13 Mr Mamil with some of the potassium cyanide drums at Kum Su

14 The late Tsoijin, a legendary ranger in the Mongolian camel reserve

15 Tsoijin using twenty-one stones to divine the whereabouts of Dovchin

16 Wild Bactrian camels at Tsoi Spring

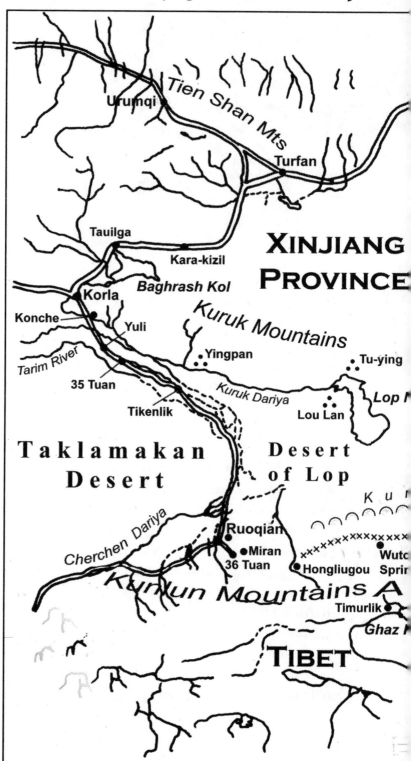

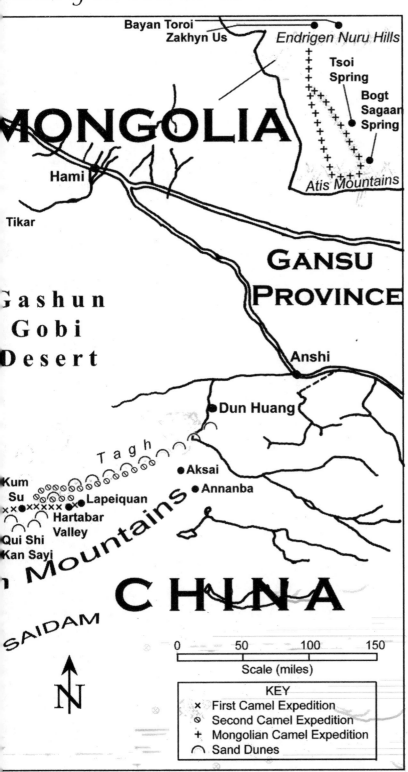

Bayan Toroi
Zakhyn Us
Endrigen Nuru Hills
Tsoi Spring
Bogt Sagaan Spring
Atis Mountains

MONGOLIA

Hami

Tikar

GANSU
PROVINCE

Gashun
Gobi
Desert

Anshi

Dun Huang

Tagh

Aksai
Annanba

Kum Su
Lapeiquan
Hartabar Valley
Qui Shi
Kan Sayi

Mountains

SAIDAM

CHINA

| 0 | 50 | 100 | 150 |

Scale (miles)

N

KEY
× First Camel Expedition
⊙ Second Camel Expedition
+ Mongolian Camel Expedition
⌒ Sand Dunes

Foreword

Long before he completed this book, John Hare asked if I would contribute a short preface. I readily agreed. I didn't even need a sample. Having made John's acquaintance years ago and tremendously respected his work for the protection of the wild Bactrian camel, I was confident that anything this brave, dogged, capable idealist put on paper would be well-informed, written from direct experience, and published in the worthiest of causes: rescuing the wild camel from the very brink of oblivion. John Hare has given the second half of his life to this great purpose and I (I thought) would chip in with my three ha'pence-worth of a preface. It would be my own little contribution.

John is nothing if not precise in his instructions. 'Your preface should, if possible, highlight our attempts to save the wild Bactrian camel from extinction,' he had written, in an email to me.

He knew I sympathized. He knew that from the comfort of the green valleys of Derbyshire I'd followed his expedition crossing the Sahara with camels, to raise funds for his Wild Camel Protection Foundation. He knew how I admired his energy: his personal efforts to collect money for his cause in any way he could – from talks to every kind of audience, small and large, all across Britain, to laboriously assembled and academically backed pitches for funding and sponsorship from governments and international bodies.

He knew, too, that in Derbyshire I kept the South American cousins of his beloved camels: llamas. He knew I'd enough knowledge of that eccentric and characterful branch of the animal kingdom, the camelids, to understand what John has worked so hard to explain and publicize: that the wild Bactrian camel is not a feral version of the domestic Asian camel, but a genetically distinct breed that has roamed the plains of Asia for millennia yet is now confined, in small and dwindling numbers, to only the most desolate parts of the planet: places human beings shun.

He knew I shared his exasperation that if you're an endangered species in need of political endorsement, state protection and charitable donations, you need to be fluffy, huggable and preferably useless, with soulful eyes; and that the noble camel, brave, stoical and self-reliant — from whose stock has been bred the friends and helpers of humanity in the harshest of conditions for thousands of years — has never graced a bumper-sticker, inspired a range of soft toys, or moistened the eyes of delegates to a political party conference.

And he knew I'd walked alongside the thousands of camels and camel-men that bring salt in great blocks up to the African highlands from that furnace of a desert, the Danekil Depression in Ethiopia. He knew I had some inkling of the thrill of waking after midnight under a starry heaven to load before dawn a train of camels; the smells; the noises; the stomach-rumblings; the soft pad-pad and metre-long strides of a racquet-sized leather foot on sand.

In short, John Hare knew how strongly I supported his work both to explain his cause — nothing less than throw into reverse a long march towards extinction — and to achieve it.

And so last night, almost a year later, I picked up the manuscript John had sent me, finalized at last — and prepared to write this preface. I started to read.

And you know what? I'm hardly going to bother highlighting the author's attempts to save the wild Bactrian camel from extinction, because there's something else the reader needs to know right away, before you turn another page.

This is just a fantastic piece of writing. It's travel-writing, it's story-telling, it's a campfire tale of memorable characters and unforgettable places, packed with thrills and spills. This is an adventure story – a whole series of adventure stories – with bandits, ambushes, breakdowns, wild desert sandstorms, wise and funny Chinese professors, lost cities, remote places, dunes, drunken assistants, dry rivers, wolves, dog-bites and rabies panics, dying camels, camel trains, dusty days and snowy nights . . . and – and this is what will surely grab you – every word of it is true.

So don't read this book because you want to help save the wild Bactrian camel from extinction. Read it because it's a great book. But by the time you've read it there will also be kindled within you a spark of enthusiasm for John Hare's magnificent quest in a daunting but achievable cause.

For this is a battle John Hare is going to win. 'Hare the Dreamer' (he writes) is what some friends have called him. Well, maybe, but we can all of us dream, and most of us do, and what then? Do we blink, smile ruefully, pour a cup of instant coffee and reach for the crossword puzzle?

Or do we make contact with the Chinese government, get an expedition together and head for the deserts of Central Asia? It's not dreaming, it's turning a dream into real life that distinguishes John Hare. This story – his own gripping story – is real. And because the author's cause is both noble and all-consuming, the story has soul.

Matthew Parris

1

The Call of the Wild

... A voice as bad as Conscience, rang interminable changes
On one everlasting Whisper day and night repeated – so:
'Something hidden. Go and find it. Go and look behind the Ranges –
Something lost behind the Ranges. Lost and waiting for you. Go!'

Rudyard Kipling, 'The Explorer'

As I stared at the travel-stained map spread out in front of me, I experienced an all too familiar surge of excitement. We were planning yet again to enter the Gashun Gobi and the Desert of Lop, one of the remotest and most inhospitable regions of China, where over previous years we had had so many adventures, experienced so many near disasters and yet had made ground-breaking discoveries. This was the desert described by Marco Polo as 'fearful' and the scholar and traveller, Hsuan-tsang, as the 'haunt of poisonous imps and fiends'. Marco Polo wrote of lost souls who wandered these desert wastes enticing travellers to follow them into seemingly unending, rolling sand dunes. A siren call that invariably ended in death.

The map set out in detail the dry, sheer-sided, rust-coloured slopes of the Kuruk (Dry) Mountains, riven with gullies that we'd explored one by one in a fruitless search for a sighting of the wild Bactrian camel. I recalled the sobering thought that one area we had crossed on foot was only twelve kilometres north-west of the Chinese underground nuclear test site, where wits and cynics had advised us to look out for the three-humped wild camel. I could see the seemingly endless expanse of pebble-strewn desert that we'd crossed with domestic camels and the wild, isolated mountain pass where the elusive snow leopard had left his tracks in the snow.

I remembered one camp pitched in the dark on the edge of a drop of 400 feet, and another on a pebble-strewn, azure-coloured slope exposed to a bitterly cold, westerly wind where we calculated that we were 220 miles in any direction from the nearest person. There was a night in the Arjin Mountains at 12,000 feet where our tea froze solid ten minutes after it had been poured into our cups. I had memories of our discovery of Tu-ying, a look-out post on the Middle Silk Road that had been overlooked by earlier explorers and the dramatic finds that we had made when we dug deep into the outpost's rubbish pit; of how we courted disaster when our truck was grounded on an endless expanse of razor-sharp rock salt that surrounds the 180-mile-long dried-up lake of Lop Nur. And lastly, I recalled how we had recovered our run-away camels when they had fled in a devastating sandstorm, leaving us marooned on the edge of Lop Nur, only hours before the time we had set ourselves to attempt a 300-mile walk across featureless desert to our vehicles and safety.

Yet even after all these experiences, my adventurous spirit was still not satisfied. It was once again leading me towards the unknown — only this time it really was the unknown. The details of our journey could only be surmised, for the maps spread out in front of us revealed an area, tucked between the Arjin Mountains and the Kum Tagh sand dunes, that had never been accurately mapped.

Both the sand dunes and the mountains stretch from east to west for almost 400 miles. Running on parallel lines approximately thirty miles apart, they meet at only one point where ferocious winds have whipped the dunes high up against the southern side of the 15,000-foot mountain range. This was the barrier of sand that we were attempting to reconnoitre with twenty camels and high hopes.

'Hare the Dreamer', some call me. Perhaps they are right. So is any person a dreamer whose active imagination pictures the possibilities of discovery beyond the bounds of accepted scientific knowledge. It is the dreamer who is the investigator, and the investigator who becomes the pioneer.

'Has anyone ever crossed those dunes, Lao Zhao?'

Professor Yuan Guoying accentuated the word 'ever' as he pointed to a series of brown, worm-like squiggles representing sand dunes on an otherwise blank map. The Professor, a short, rotund, vigorous-looking man with sharp, bright eyes that twinkled behind rimless spectacles, radiated suppressed energy. He was a patriot who believed that everything produced in China, including its political system, was superior to the product of any other country. The map was Russian and the Professor was mildly piqued that it was more accurate than recently published Chinese maps that covered the same area.

The office of the Xinjiang Environmental Protection Bureau into which four of us were crowded was dominated by the skull of a wild Bactrian camel, mounted on a plinth halfway up the wall. Three-quarters of the skull was covered in sand-coloured hair that had been ravaged by moths. The other quarter had been bleached white by the desert sun. This was fitting. The purpose of our expedition, in addition to the goal of old-fashioned exploration, was to define the southern boundary of a vast new nature reserve that would protect the critically endangered wild Bactrian camel.

Mr Zhao Ziyung, or Lao Zhao, chain-smoking zoologist, ex wild-camel hunter, exterminator of the last Przhevalsky horse in the wild, gold medal-winner as 'the ninth all-time explorer of China' and our expedition guide, was in his early sixties. He had dyed black hair, knowing eyes, a lop-sided grin and a surprisingly soft handshake. He was wearing a gabardine raincoat and his flies were done up on the wrong buttons causing his trousers to bunch at the top. The thick, woollen sweater underneath the raincoat had holes in both elbows. He was a likeable rascal, a survivor who had lived off his wits, dodging and twisting through the turbulence of China's previous four decades. In addition, he had managed to slip illegally in and out of a no-go nuclear test area since the early 1960s. This audacity had come at a price; for the last three years he had entered Urumqi hospital on an annual basis to have his blood, as he put it, 'changed'.

Lao Zhao studied the map intently, sucked hard on the damp end of a cheap cigarette and then let it dangle on his lower lip as he opened his mouth to speak.

'No,' was his emphatic reply.

It was revealing to learn that there was still an area in the proposed 155,000-square-kilometre wild camel nature reserve where Lao Zhao had not set foot.

Yuan Lei or Leilei, the Professor's six-foot, 30-year-old son, who like his father had been with me on three previous expeditions into the Desert of Lop, pointed to a narrow valley on the map that led into a steep-sided fissure in the Arjin Mountains. It lay just to the west of the dunes.

'That's Qui Shi Kan Sayi,' he said. 'If we set off with twenty camels from Hongliugou valley following a line along the foothills, it will take us thirteen days to get there.' He turned to his father, 'You could travel in our jeep to Qui Shi Kan Sayi, meet us there and re-equip the expedition before we set off with our camels over the dunes. You could then travel along the old disused Chinese Nationalist road through the mountains and meet us at Lapeiquan spring. When we reach Lapeiquan we will have crossed 300 miles from west to east.'

Leilei had inherited his father's enthusiasm and vast appetite for both food and adventure. It was only the Professor's inexhaustible capacity for watching television that had not been passed on through his genes. Tall by Chinese standards and good-looking, he had a bright and open nature that endeared him to many of his colleagues and to me.

The Professor looked up at his son and shook his head. 'It's too dangerous. There's no track and we have no idea how long it will take to get camels over the dunes. They're constantly shifting, and if the sand is soft and the going is difficult it could take six or seven days or even longer. There's no record of anyone having crossed those dunes with or without camels and the Russian map tells us nothing.'

The 59-year-old Professor of Zoology was no stranger to risk. Three years earlier we had together undertaken a tough round trip on foot of forty-four miles to reach the ancient city of Lou Lan, which lay 400 miles north of the sand dunes near the northern tip of the dried-up lake of Lop Nur. On a moonless, pitch-black night, that walk had nearly ended in disaster when we almost missed our base camp at three o'clock in the morning. We had shared many tight corners but it was thanks to the Professor that the Chinese government was seriously considering the application to establish a nature reserve for the wild camel in their former nuclear test site.

'What do you think, John?'

I looked up at the Professor. Inwardly I was thrilled that we at last had the chance to enter a part of China that had never been properly mapped. I also knew that the Professor, in spite of his initial caution, would find the lure of entering unknown territory tempting.

'This is the last unsurveyed sector of our reserve and we can't just leave it blank. I think we should try to cross the dunes.'

The Professor was wavering. 'Can you raise money for such an expedition?' He looked at me intently. 'Without money we can do nothing.'

'I can't promise, but I'll try. It might interest National Geographic but they will want a reassurance that the Chinese will put in money too.'

Fortunately, it did interest the National Geographic Society. Three months later, after two visits to their headquarters in Washington, I managed to secure most of the funding for the expedition and persuaded the Xinjiang Environmental Protection Bureau to put up the rest. However, in the process, I squandered the chance of taking their magazine photographer with us. The *National Geographic Magazine* section of the Society had provided funding for the expedition. This meant that we might benefit from a full-length feature story in a magazine, whose circulation of over nine million copies a month makes it one of the largest monthly journal sales in the world.

The head of the highly professional photographic division asked me for the precise dates when the expedition would begin and end and I had replied that I could not give an exact answer. We were crossing unknown territory, with imperfect maps and along no known route. How could I be precise?

My initial impreciseness was compounded when they asked me how many wild camels we would see on the expedition. This was another question that was impossible to answer. 'We might see none or we might see fifty,' I had replied. 'There are only about 650 camels in an area which is bigger than Texas.'

I should have given them a definite number, just as I should have spelt out exact dates. The end result was that they agreed to pay for the expedition, but would not send along their photographer.

Sadly, my naivety lost us the chance of gaining potentially valuable publicity for the wild Bactrian camel, an animal more critically endangered than the giant panda. And what an animal. No other mammal can survive on water containing such a high percentage of salt – not even the domestic Bactrian. While Chinese scientists were testing nuclear bombs – over forty of them – the wild camel was wandering through clouds of radioactive fall-out and surviving; not only surviving, but reproducing. This remarkable creature has sought refuge in the harshest, most hostile and hauntingly beautiful desert in China. Like one of Marco Polo's lost souls, the enigmatic wild Bactrian camel has led our expedition team into the very depths of the wilderness, into a Martian landscape that even in this age of satellite images is, in some places, unknown and undiscovered. We were preparing to travel to this lost country one more time.

Three months later we set out in two jeeps and a truck, leaving Urumqi, Xinjiang's capital city, in a steady downpour. Our destination was the Hongliugou valley where we had arranged for our twenty hireling camels and their herdsmen to meet us.

Our party consisted of the Professor, his son Leilei, guide Lao Zhao, Li Weidong, a naturalist from the Xinjiang Environmental Protection Bureau and a burly, bearded cameraman from Chinese Central Television called Qi Yun who had come with us to take still pictures of the wild Bactrian camel in the absence of a *National Geographic* photographer.

Qi Yun was from southern China and had the look of a man who had been plucked out of a tropical forest and deposited rather abruptly in the desert – which indeed he had. A man of very few words, his widely appreciated accomplishment was an ability to play his native tunes on a hand-made wooden flute. Its haunting, melancholy notes drifted over the night air of many an evening campfire, spreading a feeling of security and well-being.

By contrast, 35-year old Li Weidong was an old hand who had been with us on a previous expedition to Lop Nur. Of slight stature and meticulously neat and tidy, he was taciturn, knowledgeable and an excellent team member. Apart from being a highly competent scientist, he was also an excellent cook. A species of pika, a hamster-like mammal that he discovered in the Tien Shan or Heavenly Mountains south of Urumqi, had been named after him. Unfortunately, as the expedition progressed it became obvious that Li Weidong regarded Leilei as a non-scientific upstart who had only managed to get onto the expedition by virtue of his father's good standing. This occasionally led to him making pointed comments on the behaviour of the unfortunate Leilei, who adequately made up for any lack of scientific qualifications by the wholehearted way that he threw himself into every task.

Of our three vehicles, the truck, which looked to my unmechanical eye distinctly unsound, was wooden-sided with two balding tyres and had been clearly hired at a cut-price in the name of cost cutting. Besides carrying all our food, water, petrol, tents and other kit it also carried Mr Qi and his flute.

As we left central Urumqi, with its fast-rising tower blocks and air of vibrant activity and prosperity, the unrelenting rain had reduced mud on either side of the road to thick, black sludge. Mud-brick Uighur slums, enveloped in a thick haze of industrial smog, were surrounded by acres of sodden litter. Some of these slum houses had been demolished, and rusty, broken window frames and doors were piled up for sale by the side of the road. As the road wound into countryside, strips of plastic sheeting used by farmers to protect their seedlings from late frost festooned the wayside poplar trees.

This was similar to the Urumqi that the redoubtable Mildred Cable and Francesca French, missionaries in Xinjiang in the middle years of the last century, had described:

The town has no beauty, no style, no dignity and no architectural interest. During the winter there are constant heavy snow-storms, but the snow must not be allowed to lie on the flat mud roofs, lest at the first thaw the water should leak into the houses. It is therefore shovelled wholesale into the streets, and trodden by the traffic to a hard, slippery surface, which makes walking extremely difficult for several months of the year. Householders find it convenient to throw all sorts of rubbish into the street, where the constant falls of fresh snow cover up the garbage, but when the thaw sets in the mess is indescribable, and the town stinks. For one month of the spring, and one of the autumn, the mud-pits in the road are such that beasts are sometimes lost in them, and only the most athletic men can go on foot, as progress involves leaping from one stepping stone to another. The summer heat is even worse than the winter cold, and the dirty, dusty roadways are filled with jaded, unhealthy-looking people . . . For such reasons as these no one enjoys life in Urumqi, no one leaves the town with regret, and it is full of people who are only there because they cannot get permission to leave and may not leave without permission.

We stopped for lunch eighty miles from Urumqi at a truck drivers' café that nestled snugly beside three or four competitors in a long, rectangular single-storey construction covered with party slogans and white bathroom tiles. Lao Zhao chose the meal of mutton and noodles, and coated it liberally with black vinegar. Our expedition guide had remarkably unreconstructed table manners, which became starkly evident as he picked at his yellowing teeth with a knife. Later, as a signal to us that he had finished eating he swept discarded mutton bones and unwanted food off the table and on to the floor for the proprietor's cheerful, young and uncomplaining daughter to sweep up.

When unwittingly I blew my nose into a red-and-white spotted handkerchief and returned it to my pocket Lao Zhao curled up his nose in disgust.

'It's better that it goes on the floor than in your pocket,' he said with a laugh as he enveloped those of us who had not finished eating in a cloud of cigarette smoke.

To reach the Arjin Mountains and the Hongliugou valley involves a drive of over 1,800 miles from Urumqi. In this wide valley, with its fresh spring water and ample vegetation, we had arranged for twenty domestic camels to graze and fatten in preparation for the thirteen-day trek through the mountain foothills and the six- or seven-day journey across the dunes. Initially, the motor road winds through the Tien Shan and runs on to the semi-industrial county capital city of Korla, the second largest city in Xinjiang.

Explorers such as Sven Hedin, the renowned Swedish explorer, and Aurel Stein, the eminent British archaeologist who visited Korla in the early years of the twentieth century wouldn't recognize the city today. Surrounded by haphazard industrial flotsam, the old mud-walled city has long since been bulldozed to make way for a large, concrete, people's square, surrounded by garish, nondescript, tiled buildings and high-rise office blocks. The Tien Shan form an impressive, snow-capped backdrop, though barely visible through the foul-smelling, industrial smog that envelops the city during all seasons of the year.

In the people's square, children frolicked like spring lambs or crashed into each other in battery-powered kiddie-cars. A squatting Uighur policeman, the first one that I'd seen, proudly showed me a naked woman displayed on the back of a crumpled playing card that he kept screwed up in his tightly clenched fist. How odd that it was the queen of hearts.

My journal records the night spent in Korla: '*In a seedy, flea-bitten doss house near a very noisy main road. All my kit is in both the expedition truck and the second jeep which appear to have been held up. Having blocked my ears with lavatory paper, I crash out in what I stand up in.*'

Next day the truck arrived. Apparently a rope had snapped and some of our equipment had been strewn along the mountain road, including a tent that was never recovered. In addition, the jeep's engine kept boiling over and regular halts had had to be made to cool it down. This was déjà vu with a vengeance. All my previous trips by truck and jeep into the Chinese Gobi had been dogged by numerous mechanical failures. This was one of the main reasons I had decided that any future expeditions into the Gobi desert would be undertaken with camels – but first you have to find them.

Five miles outside Korla the road deteriorated into an unusually constructed, narrow, yellow brick-built road. This had been built using forced labour many years earlier and deserted brick kilns popped up on either side of the road at intervals of about fifty miles. With the brick kilns long abandoned, the road was suffering from a woeful lack of maintenance. It wound its way to the Uighur town of Yuli, then through 'old soldier camp' or 35 Tuan (Regiment), and finally after a long stretch of 800 miles into the dilapidated but strategic township of Ruoqian, or as the Uighur people who live there call it, Charkhlick.

'If we spend a night at 35 Tuan we can visit Ordek's grave on the way,' the Professor suggested. 'Then next day we can look at the site for a proposed reserve check-point at Yingpan ancient city and go on to Tiger River which is close by.'

Just as Lao Zhao was our expedition guide, so Ordek, a local Uighur, had been the senior guide to Sven Hedin. Hedin had criss-crossed and mapped much of the Gashun Gobi, the dried-up lake of Lop Nur and the Taklamakan desert in the early twentieth century and had made intriguing discoveries ranging from mummies dating from 2500 BC to the ancient city of Lou Lan.

It was Lou Lan's discovery that brought fame to Ordek. He had unwittingly mislaid the expedition's spade and was sent back by Hedin to look for it on his own. Precious though the spade must have been, having trekked to Lou Lan and through the arid and intensely inhospitable surrounding area, it seems a strange decision. However, Ordek not only found the missing spade but also the partially buried ancient city, and became the first person for 1,600 years to have done so. The Professor had put forward this interesting proposal to visit his final resting place.

There are over one hundred Tuans in Xinjiang and 35 Tuan lies just south of Yuli. Some were constructed as settlements for ex-soldiers, compulsory or otherwise. Others were former correction camps for victims of the Cultural Revolution. Yet others, more ominously, are not shown on official maps at all, so one cannot be certain what goes on there today.

After 36 Tuan, the map marks 39 Tuan. Any enquiry as to the whereabouts of 37 Tuan and 38 Tuan leads to an uncomprehending stare.

I once managed to repay inquisitive questioning in kind when in 1995 my interpreter, anxious to discover if I had a second agenda asked me what my views were on Taiwan. I gave him a blank, vacant stare and asked, 'Taiwan? Who is Taiwan?'

The question was not asked again.

35 Tuan was originally an army agricultural colony and, like all the old soldier settlements, strategically positioned to quell discontent. It is a very ancient Chinese military strategy that retired soldiers are compulsorily settled in far-flung provinces in case non-Han Chinese natives become restless. In the 1960s, 35 Tuan was converted to a camp where dissidents were re-educated. I had already spent a night at 35 Tuan in 1997 where we marvelled for the first time at the startling tail of comet Halle-Bopp.

On that occasion, we had been woken by martial music at 7 a.m. and listened to stirring exhortations booming out through loudspeakers on every street corner. So a night at 35 Tuan was not exactly a novelty, but the other items on the Professor's agenda were intriguing.

Next morning we breakfasted at Yuli and then sought out Ordek's grandson Abdu Sadik and his granddaughter Niazhan, who lived in a hamlet to the south of the city. They were a delightful old Uighur couple, Abdu dressed in a long flowing burka topped with a straw hat emblazoned with the words, 'World Cup 1966'. Niazhan conservatively dressed in brown woollen stockings, an ankle-length floral skirt and a black cardigan. A white headscarf was tied tightly around her head. They were clearly very touched that we had come to pay our respects to their grandfather.

I had bought a bunch of carnations in Yuli and we drove over soft sand to the well-built, mud and cement-lined mausoleum about three miles from the hamlet. I laid the flowers on Ordek's grave, said a brief prayer and after photographs all round we set off on a very rough road in a strong wind and swirling dust. The dust became thicker and thicker until by the time we reached 35 Tuan at 7.30 p.m. visibility was down to ten yards. There must have been a terrific sandstorm in the desert to activate this degree of dust. The roadside loudspeakers in 35 Tuan were blaring out propaganda but there was no one in sight, not that one could see very far. After thirty minutes we checked in at the barrack-like doss house.

The washroom was reached after a walk across two courtyards and through two iron gates. However, the indescribable condition of the lavatory, where previous occupants appeared to have missed the hole with an unerring frequency, made me long for open fields.

'Don't make love to a person in this room who is not your wife,' the notice on the wall above my bed proclaimed. In the room next door, a baby yelled all night.

Yingpan ancient city and Tiger River are not far from each other and are a three-hour drive from 35 Tuan. Yingpan is over 2,000 years old and the ancient wall round the city is largely intact. When we reached it I could see immediately that mounds of mud indicated where buildings had once stood. But it was not the city wall and muddy hummocks that caught my attention − it was the ransacked graves. Strewn at the foot of a large mound about a mile from the city was wood from coffins that had been flung about like driftwood littering a beach after a terrible storm. Deep cavities in the mound indicated where these coffins had come from and scattered among the wooden detritus were bones, skulls and a rib-cage, mostly in fragments, but one skull was complete with ginger hair and two rows of teeth.

'What happened here?' I asked the Professor incredulously. 'Who did this?'

'First Muslims ransacked these Buddhist graves, and secondly they were vandalized during the Cultural Revolution,' replied the Professor impassively.

I can usually sense when the Professor does not want to discuss something unpalatable. I knew that he was old enough to have been a participant in the Cultural Revolution so I chose my words carefully.

'Why has no one bothered to tidy it up?'

'What for? They are only old bones. They do not mean anything to anybody.'

I decided to question no more.

We looked at a site for a check-point near a track that entered the proposed reserve. Two years previously the Professor had seen two wild Bactrian camels in this area and so was keen to establish a check-point at Yingpan. Tracks and roads into the vast reserve are few and a check-point is a useful control for apprehending potential hunters or illegal miners.

However, part of Professor Yuan's unyielding financial philosophy is that budgets expand according to need and not to available resources, especially if the architect of the budget is a foreigner. I knew that a check-point at Yingpan, though sensible, would cost over $10,000 and there were no funds available to build one.

We drove on in our jeep to Tiger River, which flowed through a picturesque tree-lined valley about two miles from Yingpan. It was uninhabited and unspoiled apart from a newly constructed irrigation pipe that drained river water away to irrigate the farms of Yuli. It was difficult to imagine that the Bengal tiger roamed here for thousands of years until they were finally exterminated in 1935.

The next day, we left 35 Tuan and resumed our journey down the yellow-brick road to Ruoqian. The dust was as thick as ever and the wind howled from west to east, sending cascades of swirling sand spiralling upwards.

'It's a black storm,' said Lao Zhao gravely. 'A big one and a bad one.'

Sandstorms are frequent in the Gobi desert during the months of April, May and June. They can blow up extraordinarily quickly. One moment the sky is clear and blue, then an ominous dark patch appears on the horizon. This patch spreads with phenomenal speed and about thirty minutes later the increasing velocity of the wind heralds the onset of a storm. Normally the sandstorm is what is called a yellow storm, which allows the sun to percolate through the swirling clouds of sand so that everything is turned yellow. Occasionally a black sandstorm blows up, turning day into darkest night. Pebbles and small rocks are hurled through the air. Paint has been known to be stripped off a vehicle, turning it to silver. It would not be pleasant to be travelling with our camels in such a storm. I prayed fervently that our domestic camels grazing in the valley of Hongliugou were all right.

Further down the road, our vehicles slowed to pass vertical wooden poles that had been planted in the sand in a seemingly haphazard fashion.

'What is that?' I asked.

Lao Zhao gave a wily smile as he flicked cigarette ash through the open window of the jeep. 'They wanted to make a TV programme about Lou Lan and asked me to be the consultant,' he said. 'However, the Korla government refused to allow us to go there to make the programme so I built Lou Lan for them here.'

'You built Lou Lan? By the side of the road?'

He laughed. 'Why should we make it difficult for ourselves? We could get here easily by jeep, they could make their film, I would be paid my fee and everyone would be happy.'

'Did they think this collection of timber really was Lou Lan?'

Lao Zhao grinned and gave me a knowing wink. 'I didn't tell them that it was Lou Lan.' He paused. 'On the other hand, I didn't tell them that it wasn't.'

At one point, the dead and dying remains of mature desert wild poplars lined either side of the yellow-brick road and were a depressing testimony to the drying of the desert and the spread of desertification. For long periods, sand dunes in both the Gashun Gobi and Taklamakan deserts towered on either side of the road to the east and to the west, seemingly poised to spill over and link those two immense deserts. In other places, drifting fingers of deep sand had been blown across the road, forcing us to halt and extract ourselves with planks and shovels.

We passed a spot where four twelve-foot branches had been stuck in the ground. Black cloth had been tied to their tops and these rags were flapping violently in the wind. The whole scene had an eerie appearance and I asked what it was.

'That's where a Uighur herdsman's family; his wife, two sons and a girl, perished in a sandstorm while looking for their lost flock of sheep,' said Lao Zhao impassively.

Later that day we arrived in Ruoqian, where branches of trees and sheets of corrugated iron littered the streets, evidence of the great wind that had been stirring up the clouds of sand all the way from Korla.

The city of Ruoqian (Charkhlick, on the old maps) seemed down-trodden and depressed, as though its ancient, pulsating Uighur heart had been ripped out and replaced by a socialist-style substitute. The market-place was a slab of concrete covered in debris and broken glass surrounded by empty decaying stalls. A mustard-yellow post office with peeling paint, a large, half-occupied hotel and a few other indeterminate buildings dominated the empty, joyless streets that radiated away from them. As a crossroads to Korla to the north, Tibet to the south, Kashgar to the west and Miran and the Desert of Lop to the east, it should have been as full of bustle and life as it was when Przhevalsky, Hedin, Stein and other explorers visited it at the start of the last century. But it was lifeless, and the wind, the tail-end of the black sandstorm that howled through its dispirited streets and shredded the emerging, tender leaves of its poplars, was an appropriate backdrop for this grey, dusty, soulless town.

We stayed in a dank and damp caravanserai in Ruoqian, as the government hotel charges for a foreigner were extortionate. One-storey, mud-brick buildings – each containing ten hovels that sported a bed, a basin and a wooden table – surrounded a pock-marked, rubbish-strewn rectangular courtyard on three sides. The pervading smell of engine oil made it feel that we had bedded down in a garage. This damp and dirty doss house was our home for two nights while additional food was sought out and bought by the Professor, including two sheep that were hoisted alive onto the back of the truck together with sacks of maize for our camels. There was general relief when these administrative details were finally accomplished and we headed east towards Hongliugou, our springboard into the Gobi.

36 Tuan was less regimented than 35. There was no early morning martial music nor political harangues. Cheerful, ever-smiling Mama Feng and her bashful daughter ran the Tuan caravanserai. Mama Feng

had endeared herself to me two years earlier when we had first put up in her mud huts. I had urgent need of the lavatory and when I asked her where it was her sunburnt face creased into a huge smile. She squatted down on her hunkers, pointed to the open countryside and majestically swept her hand from side to side.

'China is our toilet,' she said. 'Go where you like.' She spluttered with laughter. 'But make sure you do something good for our farms, Mister Tuzi (Hare).'

Mama Feng now confided with great pride that her daughter, who turned crimson whenever a man spoke to her, was going to be married in two weeks' time. She patted her ample stomach.

'Babies soon,' she said and started to hum quietly to herself. 'No "one baby only" system in 36 Tuan,' she whispered. 'Many babies will come.'

Suddenly she looked embarrassed and put her hand to her mouth. With a sharp intake of breath she waddled off into her tiny bedroom. I heard a key turn in a lock and the scrape of a wooden drawer as it was wrenched open. There was a rustle of paper. She emerged moments later, clutching two letters, both of which had my handwriting on them. When we had stayed there two years previously, I had given Mama Feng the letters to post. Now she handed them back to me.

'The post office wouldn't accept them,' she said apologetically. 'They didn't know how many stamps were needed to send them to England.'

The dining-room boasted the inevitable TV. Having been deprived for many days of his staple diet of undiluted television, the Professor was soon firmly ensconced in front of the box, flicking contentedly from channel to channel. Sadly, he could not find a programme that showed the Chinese military knocking hell out of Japanese soldiers. These black-and-white cameos were, I had discovered, his staple television diet.

My mud hut bedroom was five star compared to Ruoqian and contained a tin bowl, a metal bed, a thermos full of hot water and a thick over-rug. Overlooked by a beaming Mama Feng, I downed an enormous, tummy-warming plate of noodles, mutton and vegetables, went to my hut, lay down on my bed and immediately fell asleep.

Foreigners are charged an additional fee on leaving 36 Tuan on the assumption that they will visit the ancient city of Miran, which is situated in the desert three miles to the east. Miran lay on our route to Hongliugou and, to dodge the fee, the Professor decided that Leilei and I should walk there, avoiding the police check-point on the road. He and the rest of the team would then pick us up near Miran's ancient mud wall.

The first to mention the ancient city was the Russian explorer Colonel Nikolai Mikhailovich Przhevalsky. Nominally in search of a route to Lhasa, he was more concerned with geography and general information-gathering than with archaeology. In 1876, he left Korla and reached Lop Nur in December, thereby proving its long-doubted existence. Przhevalsky settled to winter at Ruoqian and among his detailed observations of plant and animal life there was a note mentioning three ruined sites in the vicinity. From the entry on his map it is certain that Przhevalsky's large city was Miran. It is also certain that the colonel never actually set foot in it. Not only was Przhevalsky the first foreigner to identify Miran, he also discovered the wild Bactrian camel. On his return to Russia he had shown two wild Bactrian camel skins and a wild Bactrian camel skull to incredulous scientists in St Petersburg.

It was Przhevalsky who opined that 'three things are necessary for the success of long and dangerous journeys in Central Asia – money, a gun and a whip.' During his 1880 ground-breaking expedition to Tibet, each of his companions carried a Berdan carbine, two Smith and Wesson revolvers, a bayonet and forty rounds of ammunition. For Przhevalsky, these arms were 'our guarantee of safety in the depths of the Asiatic deserts, the best of all Chinese passports.'

In 1906 Stein stayed for two days in Miran identifying a Tibetan fort from the eighth century. Only when he returned in January 1907 did he realize the importance of the site. He came upon a series of

Buddhist shrines, the earliest in Chinese Central Asia, decorated with wall paintings and filled with sculptures. Under extreme weather conditions – the temperature never rose above freezing – he extracted a large quantity of materials and in early February dispatched a convoy of six camels loaded with antiquities to Kashgar. He later returned in 1914 and unlocked more secrets of this ancient city. Stein concluded that Miran was strategically important during the Han Dynasty and later during the five-century supremacy of the Shanshan and Khotan kingdoms that bordered the Gashun Gobi and Lop Nur. The city fell under Tibetan rule during the eighth and ninth centuries AD and the artefacts, paintings and Buddhist constructions identified by Stein reflect each of these different cultures.

One of the outstanding pieces to be found today in New Delhi's museum is called 'Garland Dado', located by Stein in a shrine at Miran. Painted in tempera, in frail reds, greens and yellows, and outlined in dark brown, busts of men and women smile serenely from an undulating garland carried by small boys. Local beauties, similar in dress and hairstyles, appear alongside men of various origins: an Indian prince, a bearded man in Parthian-style costume, another with cropped hair, representing the multitude of nationalities engaged in travel and trade along the Silk Road. In addition, there is the 'Angel Dado'. With their shaven heads and large wings, it is difficult to believe that these other-worldly beings come from the very borders of China.

Miran today remains a crumbling, partially walled city. Outside the walls are stupas – Buddhist dome-shaped temples – all of which have had their paintings and treasures removed over the years by Stein and others. The stupas stand about eight feet high, looking like enormous pepper-pots and rise seemingly haphazardly and rather surprisingly out of the desert sand. Some of them are still intact but most have collapsed and fallen into decay.

When Leilei and I eventually reached the crumbling mud ruins we waited three hours for our truck and the two jeeps to arrive, mostly crouching behind a stupa to gain protection from the howling wind and swirling sand. Apparently the authorities had attempted to charge the Professor and the rest of the team a huge amount to leave 36 Tuan. Telephone communication is difficult from such a remote place and it took three hours before the necessary clearances were given from Ruoqian. They never discovered that a foreigner was part of the team. If they had, the charge would have been much higher.

Once Miran is left behind, there is no further settlement at all, ancient or modern, as the rocky, sandy, bleak terrain cannot support the flocks of the semi-nomadic Kazakhs who inhabit this region. The 150-mile drive from 36 Tuan to the Hongliugou valley crosses innumerable rocky and tortuous gullies, which in high summer carry the snowmelt from the Kunlun Mountains into the desert.

Any tyre marks are swept away in the summer floods. In between these riven landforms are sandy stretches where a line of wooden telegraph poles stretches out from west to east. These poles mark the track but in many places the sand had piled up into mini dunes so that our jeeps were forced to zigzag tightly left to right and right to left to avoid becoming bogged down in soft sand or slamming up against partly concealed rocks.

During a relatively quiet interlude Professor Yuan Guoying peered and then pointed into the hazy distance.

'Look over there. It's a camel,' he muttered.

We drew closer and found a camel lying on the ground with a broken shoulder. As the jeep slithered to a stop a man appeared from behind a mound of sand. It was one of our Kazakh herdsmen who had been designated to mind the domestic camels waiting for us at Hongliugou.

'The big wind was so strong that the camels broke loose and scattered,' he explained. 'We were unable to stand upright, let alone look after them. When I left our camp we'd managed to recapture four. I set off after this one and have been following its tracks for two days.'

The Professor knelt down and examined the stricken camel. 'It will never recover. We'll have to cut its throat,' he said.

After a hard winter, camels have to be fattened in the spring on emerging fresh grass and greening shrubs. The whole point of taking the camels to Hongliugou had been to fatten and rest them for the rigorous journey that lay ahead. It would have been foolhardy to attempt to cross treacherous sand dunes with camels that were not fit. Three weeks was a very short time to get them ready to undertake an arduous desert journey. Now that they had run off in all directions, any strength that they had acquired would have disappeared. When they were all rounded up we would have to wait at least a further two weeks at Hongliugou to condition them for the journey all over again.

As these thoughts ran through my mind, I grimly recalled the answer that I had given to the National Geographic Society when they had asked me for the exact dates when the expedition would begin and end.

The poor camel that lay on the track looked up at us with its large luminous eyes. It would never recover. We were miles from Hongliugou. The only option was to put it down as humanely as possible, which, with the aid of a sharp knife, we did.

Camels are the ultimate stoics. They never complain, they neither whimper nor whine. Phlegmatic and intensely brave, they work until they drop. The only time I had witnessed real distress in a domestic Bactrian camel and its total recognition of the instigator of its misery was when the cruel wooden nose plug which is fitted through a camel's nostril by Central Asian cameleers was ripped through its nasal membrane. This happened because Lao Zhao, a knowledgeable guide but no animal lover, had refused to detach the rope that joined the unfortunate camel to a camel in front of him. Both were at the time negotiating a steep and tortuous slope. The camel in the rear slipped and the camel in the lead walked on. The result was an appallingly bloody muzzle. The camel survived but it could no longer be tethered to carry a load. Little wonder that whenever it saw Lao Zhao it would break into a deafening bellow.

When we eventually arrived at Hongliugou we found that seventeen of the twenty camels had been rounded up. Two were still missing.

Two of our three Kazakh herdsmen were out looking for them and the remaining herdsman, Usuman, and his wife were looking after the others at the camp. Usuman, a leathery, sinewy man in his early forties with a lifetime's experience of the area, proved to be a valuable asset. Six of our camels that had run nearly 100 miles during the sandstorm were considered too weak to undertake such a rigorous expedition. Usuman agreed to hire us six of his own animals, which were not only in top condition but were also biddable and even tempered.

Camels, both Dromedary and Bactrian, suffer from a bad press. The general impression is that they are nasty, spiteful animals that spit and bite and blow undigested food over a handler when they are angry. All true, but this invariably applies to camels that have been badly trained or mistreated. Usuman's camels had been intelligently and humanely reared and looked after. His young, attractive wife amused us by showing us how her favourite camel would kiss her on the lips when encouraged to do so. Her camels stood up and sat down at her gentle command and were some of the most obedient and well-behaved domestic Bactrian camels that I had ever seen. She also had an angora goat that followed her everywhere like a devoted dog. We stayed in the valley surrounded by Usuman's large flock of sheep and goats for ten days while our camels struggled to get fit for the journey.

Hongliugou in the spring is plagued by large non-malarial white mosquitoes, which can give the most enormous bite. After two days, my ears, eyes and even the back of my hands looked as though I had just spent ten unequal rounds in a boxing ring. We yearned to leave Hongliugou and its bloodthirsty insect life. On the day before we were due to depart I discovered that it wasn't only mosquitoes that were after my blood.

In the late afternoon, Usuman's black Tibetan guard dog hurtled towards me down the side of the hill, scattering sheep and goats in all directions. I spun round and, in the same instant, it sank its teeth deep into my left shin. Up went its head and off came the leg of my corduroy trousers. There was no warning bark or gesture and to this day I carry the scars of its teeth on my leg. To a cacophony of bleating sheep I stared vacantly as blood dripped onto my boot.

Moments later, Usuman, with shouts of rage, was holding his dog by its ears and shaking it vigorously. I turned away and limped back down the Hongliugou valley towards my tent.

For the very first time I thought that maybe we should abandon this ill-starred trip. Earlier negative portents had been unmistakable: a badly twisted ankle three weeks before I was due to leave England for China, the devastating black sandstorm that had blown up without warning and scattered our domestic camels in all directions. If it hadn't been for the storm, I wouldn't have been idly watching herdsmen packing up their tents and been bitten by the dog. We would already have set out on our expedition and been well on the way to surmounting the barrier of sand dunes.

I arrived back at my tent to find the ebullient Professor busily sticking nine-inch needles into Lao Zhao's knees who squealed as each needle entered a sensitive area of his knee joint. On my arrival, the Professor laid down his acupuncture kit and peered at the dog bite with great concern. 'You must clean it up quickly. One tooth has pierced very deep. You are lucky. If it had bitten you from behind and in the leg muscle you might not be able to walk.'

That evening Usuman's young wife came to my tent. Her head and lower part of her face were covered in a black cloth covered in rosebuds and she clutched a small package of wrapped newspaper. She held it out for me without a word and I took it and unwrapped the packet. To my amazement it contained hair — the hair of the dog that bit me. Leilei was moving about outside the tent and I called him in.

'Please ask her what I should do with this, Leilei.'

'Put it on the wound straight away,' he explained. 'It will cure everything, even dog sickness.' He meant rabies.

I am aware of the usage in English of 'the hair of the dog' as a cure after an evening of over indulgence. Here was another, more literal meaning. If this phrase was common knowledge in the wilds of Central

Asia, there must be some justification for the use of dog's hair as an antidote to the dog's bite. Is it possible that in medieval England the same meaning applied? I put the dog's hair in a bandage smeared with Savlon and tied it to my leg.

'You'll be all right, now,' she said softly. 'You won't get the sickness.'

She had a confident smile and I believed her. Having seen Usuman's wife work her magic with her husband's camels and her goat, I took heart from her conviction that all would be well. I am no stranger to rabies, having seen its horrifying and dire effects on a victim in Africa and I am sure that medical opinion would deride tales of a dog-hair cure. Whatever the reason, the bite did not fester. As for the trousers, the bottom half was recovered by Usuman and the Professor did a highly professional job of stitching the leg back together. It is not only with a needle and thread that the Professor excels. Lao Zhao claimed that the Professor's other needles made his knee joint mobile and able to scale the tallest dune.

Next day, our camels were deemed fit and ready to leave. To a certain extent this decision was dictated by the amount of food we had available. Too many days at Hongliugou could mean privation in the dunes, especially if we were held up by another sandstorm.

Li Weidong expertly cooked a celebratory farewell dinner planned by the Professor, to the lilting accompaniment of Qi Yun's flute. One of Usuman's sheep was slaughtered and prepared in a variety of delectable ways; even the head was cooked by the fearsome blast of a petrol-fired blowlamp. Tinned sardines – a rare delicacy – tinned sausages and boiled eggs supplemented the sheep. Evil-smelling Chinese spirits and a precious bottle of whisky were opened. Sweet Chinese wine completed the feast. Later that night, songs of three nationalities, pitched excruciatingly off-key as a consequence of too much whisky and *mao-tai*, floated down the valley to a backdrop of the Professor's celebratory, 'jumping jack' firecrackers. Amid the songs, mirth and a fire – which scattered the mosquitoes and the gremlins that had dogged the earlier part of the trip — we all inwardly rejoiced that our expedition would at last begin. Next morning, after making numerous adjustments to our kit and feeling slightly the worse for wear, we prepared to set off.

2

Beyond the Dunes

Go softly by that river-side or, when you would depart,
You'll find its every winding tied and knotted round your heart.

Rudyard Kipling, 'The Prairie'

During the first stage of the expedition, Leilei and I were to travel with the camels together with Usuman and Lao Zhang, a Chinese herdsman and camel owner, who claimed to know the route to Qui Shi Kan Sayi.

Lao Zhang had been with us on a previous expedition and was an interesting character. His wife ran a hairdressing salon in Ruoqian and he had set himself up as a shamanistic seer who could predict the future. When some years earlier our camels had fled during a sandstorm and left us marooned, it was Lao Zhang who had foretold that our runaway camels would be caught and that we would return safely to base. He had got this right even though his timings were somewhat muddled.

We planned to meet the Professor at Qui Shi Kan Sayi. He would bring fresh food and water to re-equip the camel caravan before it set off over the dunes. Lao Zhao and Li Weidong would join us for this second phase, leaving the Professor and Qi Yun to take the two vehicles to a rendezvous point near Lapeiquan spring, 300 miles to the east.

Lapeiquan, an isolated freshwater spring on an abandoned road, had vivid memories for me besides its clear, sweet water. Some years earlier, we were driving towards it from the east when there was a loud crash as something metallic hit the door of our jeep. I ducked as another missile hit the window by my side. The window cracked but didn't splinter. We were holed up in the centre of a washed-out culvert. Our driver accelerated. He spun the wheel, and set the jeep at a rocky incline in a desperate attempt to get us up on to the fragmented track.

A blunt instrument was hurled at the back of the jeep. Suddenly, on either side of the culvert, groups of men jumped up; screaming, shouting, faces contorted under brightly coloured headscarves. One of them slashed at the jeep's tyre with a razor-sharp kitchen chopper. I ducked again as an axe handle struck the windscreen with a resounding thud. Our driver managed to get over the top of the culvert. He accelerated and drove at speed along the remains of what once had been a road. The Professor was shouting to Leilei, who grappled in the back of the jeep for our shotgun. We drove off the track and parked on the top of a mound of gravely sand.

Our other vehicle was lumbering along behind us. I'd recently christened the track 'the road of a thousand wash-outs'. Built by the Chinese nationalists, it had been abandoned in the late 1960s. The culverts, which were encountered roughly every 50 yards, had been systematically washed away by the torrents of water that streamed down the gullies of the Arjin Mountains when the snows melted in July.

We jumped out of the jeep. The bandits, who numbered about twenty, were definitely no longer concerned with the jeep. They had regrouped to lay siege to our provisions truck as it slowed to reconnoitre the wash-out. The Professor ran towards them, shotgun raised. He stopped, took aim, fired high above their heads and fired again.

In spite of their numerical superiority, they hesitated when the first shot was fired. When the second shot rang out, they gave way to our firepower and ran off in the direction of the mountains, their pale blue, pink, purple, green and yellow headscarves disappearing and reappearing as they zigzagged over the broken landscape. One of them stopped to give a defiant shout.

'Who are they?' I had asked the Professor when our team's excited chatter had died down. 'What are they doing here?'

'I don't know,' Professor Yuan had replied as he put the shotgun back into its case. He was excited and beads of perspiration were dripping from his face. 'They could have been illegal miners or plant-hunters. The new market economy has brought back many bad habits to China.'

I wondered somewhat apprehensively what Lapeiquan had in store for us on our return visit.

We finally set off on a bright, early May day. The dust from the sandstorm had settled, the air was clear and the sky was a brilliant blue. Usuman's family grouped themselves on either side of our camel caravan and gave us a rousing send-off. Within two hours we were negotiating the tortuous foothills of the Arjin Mountains and the intricate and numerous gullies that carry the summer snowmelt down into the desert along both wide and narrow channels.

These channels have forged their own twisted paths over countless years, and our route resembled a switchback. One moment the camels were surmounting rounded, steep-sided hillocks, the next they were struggling across a rock-strewn, dried-up riverbed. It would have been instructive to follow the same route during the height of summer when the channels were full of fast-flowing fresh water, but with temperatures reaching over 50 °Celsius in August it would also have been extremely foolhardy.

Temperatures can plummet to -40 °Celsius in January and February in this part of the Gobi and it is a tribute to the remarkable versatility of the wild Bactrian camel that it survives at all, especially in places where the only water that bubbles up from under the ground has a salt content that is greater than that of seawater. No other large mammal in the world, not even the domestic Bactrian camel, can tolerate such a high salt content. This is why we had to carry water for our domestic camels.

On the second day out after leaving Hongliugou we had made good progress. However, one of the camels was already lagging behind, even though it was walking untethered and without a load. We stopped on top of some large boulders near a steep-sided gully to allow it to catch up and as I had been on my feet most of the day I lay down on my back, pushed my hat over my eyes and started to doze.

I was abruptly woken by Leilei tugging at my sleeve and whispering urgently, 'John, John, wake up. Look over there – wild camels.'

I sprang up and turned around. Leilei was pointing to the entrance of a valley that must have been about half a mile away. I took out my field glasses and scanned an area where the valley disappeared from view. Then I saw them. A thickset wild bull camel was leading a group of females out of the valley. One by one they emerged until I had counted sixteen females and seven young camels, all under two years old. This was remarkable. I had thought that a bull Bactrian camel in the wild kept a harem of no more than nine females. I had to take a photo, preferably with the video camera.

It is an axiom for anyone setting out on any expedition or field survey to master all of your kit before you set out. National Geographic had provided me with an excellent little video camera that fitted neatly on my belt and which could take pictures of broadcast quality. But I had not taught myself how to use it before leaving Hongliugou. As I aimed the camera and zoomed in on the group of camels, they obstinately remained out of focus. I pushed several buttons but nothing altered. I started to perspire with frustration.

Then all at once the bull spotted us. Immediately he turned about and at a fast trot led his females and their calves back into the valley and out of sight. Once they had disappeared I understood what I was doing wrong. Stupidly, I had not altered the focus from manual to automatic. I was angry with myself, particularly as it was a most unusual sighting. I knew from my experience during our last camel trek, that these might be the only wild Bactrian camels that we encountered on the whole expedition. We did see many, many more but this does not alter the situation in retrospect.

Leilei and I were enjoying ourselves. Freed from our guide, the Professor and other scientists, we made our own decisions and followed our own stars. Leilei's English had greatly improved and communication was not difficult. My three previous expeditions in the Chinese Gashun Gobi had all been made with Lao Zhao and the Professor, who frequently held long conversations with each other in Chinese. It is intrusive and irritating constantly to ask if I could be told what was being said, but it was of course necessary to know when vital decisions were being made, especially as we had been in situations of extreme difficulty on a number of occasions.

This was different. Leilei and I only had with us Usuman and Lao Zhang. The two of us talked about every aspect of the wild camel expedition and decisions were made jointly and in total harmony. This proved to be important when, on the seventh day out from Hongliugou, we reached Wutong or Wild Poplar Spring.

Nestled against the backdrop of a sheer, jet-black ridge in the Arjin Mountains, Wutong Spring is an Eden where, in the spring, ancient wild poplars sport stunning tufts of light pink flowers.

Having spent days tramping over a stark, barren, rock-strewn landscape, the sight of any tree was magical and the sight of a flowering tree was breathtaking. Wutong is a Chinese word associated with sadness and sorrow because the wild poplar is the first tree to change colour and shed its leaves in the autumn. It is also unusual in that it bears one narrow-shaped leaf on its new growth and another that is serrated and broad on its old growth. But there was neither sadness nor sorrow at Wutong when we arrived there. In addition to the pink flowers, the gnarled and twisted trees were tinged with light green, indicating that spring had at last arrived in the desert.

However, every Eden has its serpent and Wutong Spring had them in abundance in the form of ticks. The size of a five-pence piece, they

live in the saltpans and by the salt springs of the Gobi and respond
to vibrations. An unwary intruder walking near a saltwater source can
awaken a mighty army of ticks that has lain dormant for months or even
for over a year. They emerge quickly and move determinedly towards a
potential source of blood.

The migratory wild Bactrian camel has to endure ticks as well. After
a possible 100-mile trek to find water it might eventually arrive at an
unappetizing salt spring. More often than not, it will then have to break
through a hard, salty crust before it can slurp up the unpalatable slush.
While doing this it has to withstand an invasion by bloodthirsty ticks
whose life-cycle depends on the camel's arrival. If the animal's luck
has really run out, it will be shot by an equally bloodthirsty hunter or
illegal gold miner lying in wait by the spring. The Mongolian Gobi with
its freshwater springs, lack of ticks and comparative freedom from
poachers is a paradise in comparison.

On our arrival, Usuman waded through five-foot-tall brittle *fragmitis*
grass that extended to a black rocky slab, to look for a waterhole. He
returned to report that fresh water trickled out of the rock in front of
us and flowed into the *fragmitis*. This fresh water was a big find; it meant
that we could fill our water containers as well as ensuring that our
camels had enough to drink.

'The whole area is swarming with ticks,' Usuman said, 'The camels
will get infested if they go in there. We must burn the grass to kill the
ticks. Otherwise the camels will refuse to drink.' Usuman noticed my
hesitation. 'The fire won't spread far,' he added.

Within minutes, red flames shot up into the air, smoke billowed and
Eden was shrouded in a dense black haze.

After a further ten minutes the flames had died down. Usuman and
Lao Zhang had waded through the black ash surrounding the waterhole
and were sweeping it from side to side with long sticks to clear a path
for the camels. Smoke spiralled slowly upwards as the camels were
led one by one to the place where the water from the black rock had
collected. Some had to be hand watered from a bowl, others summoned

up the courage to stick their heads into the charred ash to suck up the liquid. As for the ticks, they had disappeared completely. However, the smoke from the fire had revealed something very interesting.

'Look,' shouted Usuman, 'wolves.'

Close to the burnt clump of grass was a mound of clay and rock. This had been obscured before the *fragmitis* was burnt but now a wolves' den surrounded with black ash was revealed. What a formidable place to site a lair. As wild Argali sheep, the wild Tibetan ass, or a wild camel came down to Wutong to drink, the wolves must have looked out and selected their menu for the night. Usuman peered into the large black hole and then abruptly withdrew his head and stood up.

He burst out laughing as one by one three very bleary-eyed wolf cubs emerged. They were the size of plump, six-week-old Alsatian puppies.

'Keep an eye open for the adult wolves,' said Usuman. 'They must be nearby and they could become dangerous when we kill those cubs.'

'Kill them?'

'Yes, aren't you going to kill them, John?' asked Leilei. 'If you let them go they will grow up to be camel killers.'

I was presented with a dilemma, one that has divided naturalists in both China and Mongolia. The wolf is indeed a wild Bactrian camel killer, preying on the young camel before it can fend for itself and indeed, as we found in Mongolia, capable of bringing down an adult bull camel when hunting as a pack. The wolf's range does not extend into the heart of the Gashun Gobi and the Desert of Lop, where there are only saltwater springs. But in Mongolia, where the springs are nearly all fresh, the wolf is one of the wild camel's biggest threats, especially as domestic flocks on which it used to prey have been banned from the Mongolian Reserve. Some naturalists argue coherently that wildlife should be left to find its own balance and the wolves should not be touched. Others affirm that they should be culled so that their numbers can be controlled and monitored.

'No,' I said after a few moments' thought. 'This expedition has been organized to protect the environment. Let them go.'

Usuman, Lao Zhang and Leilei looked at me as though I were crazy. But the plump little wolf cubs, so beguiling at this stage in their lives, were allowed to waddle away in different directions to safety, even though I could see that Leilei strongly disagreed with me.

However, now I hold a different view. I have seen the depredations wolves do and have stumbled across many dead wild Bactrian camels and other animals that wolves have killed. Unfortunately, it is man that has pushed the wild camel into the most inhospitable parts of Central Asia. It is man's activities that should be actively prevented from harming the wild Bactrian camel and its fragile environment. The wolf population has to be controlled because man has put nature's balance out of kilter.

Shortly after we left Wutong Spring, something occurred that I had never seen before. We were passing through a steep-sided valley and stopped near the skeleton of a dead wild Bactrian camel. It had, I suspect, died of natural causes.

I got down from my camel to inspect the carcass and as my camel stood up, he bent his long neck over and picked up the wild camel's skull. Then he started to crunch it up. I looked on in amazement at my cannibal. He was loath to let it drop and as the skull was old and brittle he managed to munch on huge chunks. I later discussed this with camel expert Jasper Evans, who keeps 300 Dromedary camels in Kenya. He told me that it is not uncommon for camels to chew the bones of dead animals when they are short of calcium and he had seen it occur on a number of occasions.

As we headed towards Qui Shi Kan Sayi we came to yet another valley. To the south lay the towering Arjin Mountains and in front of us was a steep drop down to a riverbed. We had been travelling high up in the foothills for some hours and the panoramic scene that unfolded in front of us was spectacular.

We looked down on a long section of sand river valley hemmed in by steep-sloped, black shale rocks on either side. As we positioned the camels to negotiate the dangerous downward slope that fell away directly in front of us, Usuman called out to us to stop.

'Wild camels ahead!' he pointed out excitedly.

Advancing down the river valley was a group of twelve wild Bactrian camels, four adults, a bull camel and seven females with four young calves no more than twelve months old.

They were well within photographic range and we snapped away as they sauntered unconcernedly down the dry rocky surface that spread beneath us. They had nearly disappeared from our view when something – a flash of sunlight on a camera, the movement of one of our own camels – caught the attention of the adult that was bringing up the rear. It stopped, stared, and then wheeled about and started to trot back up the valley in the direction whence it had come. The others followed their leader.

Many months later when I was having my video film of this encounter edited, I looked in amazement as I saw those camels first walk and then trot, but always in the same direction.

'I am sure it didn't happen like that,' I remarked to the editor. 'They went in two different directions. First they went one way, then they turned round and went in the other.'

'I thought that it would be easier on the eye if we watched them all travel in one direction,' the editor replied nonchalantly.

We were by now on the last leg before we met up with the Professor. After three more days of travelling, averaging about sixteen miles a day, we turned south into the narrow entrance of Qui Shi Kan Sayi, a steep-sided valley whose towering sides were home to screeching ravens. About five miles beyond the valley's eastern cliffs, the Kum Tagh sand dunes swing abruptly south and pile up against the Arjin Mountains. Then some miles later, they veer back into the desert, leaving – as we surmised from satellite pictures – an unexplored region in the centre of an elongated V. No one knows what is there, and no foreigner in recorded history had, as far as is known, been inside the gap. First of all, however, one has to cross over the dunes, no easy task for camels if the sand is soft.

We were greeted with hugs and cheers when we met Professor Yuan and the rest of the expedition team at the saltwater spring two miles from the entrance to Qui Shi Kan Sayi. They had brought with them the provisions and fresh water that we would need for the second leg of our journey. Li Weidong did us proud that evening and we hunkered down to eat our most tasty meal for days.

Exhausted, Leilei and I bedded down for an early night, but at 3 a.m. our orderly campsite descended into chaos. At first, with my vivid memories of Lapeiquan, I thought we were under another attack from a group of marauding bandits. Wooden poles thumped onto tents and Chinese imprecations mingled with the bellows of a frightened camel. I jumped out of my sleeping bag and saw that one of our camels had become entangled in the dangling radio aerial that the Professor has strung up on stakes.

It began to run upstream, dragging twisted wires and our weighty radio receiver behind it. A switch on the ancient machine had been thrown and the bulky box was emitting piercing, strangulated screams, heightening the drama. Bellows and wails echoed and re-echoed down the valley and in the bright moonlight the effect was like a Chinese *Midsummer Night's Dream*.

The ever-alert Leilei sprinted after the poor camel and eventually slowed it down by clinging onto the radio receiver. It was quite something to see a camel pulling a bulky metal box and a spirited young man over the rocky surface of Qui Shi Kan Sayi. After an hour, order was restored and one by one the team members crawled into their sleeping bags.

When asked whether I think that a camel is more intelligent than a horse, I cite the case of the camel at Qui Shi Kan Sayi. When a horse spooks badly, all its equine companions charge away in terror from the object that has caused the original animal to shy. In contrast, when a camel spooks or as in this case gets caught up in wire or some other impediment, the other camels in the herd just turn their long necks and stare at their discomfited travelling companion.

In 1997 when Jasper Evans joined our camel expedition to Lop Nur, he taught our domestic camels the commands to 'sit' and 'get up' in English in under a week. It's an intelligent animal that can learn a foreign language so quickly. I tried teaching my horse Chinese, but after a week it was no wiser and had started to question my sanity. At least that showed intelligence.

The aggressive white mosquito that had been so prevalent in Hongliugou was even more voracious in Qui Shi Kan Sayi. Our blood seemed to be a particular and unexpected treat. Accompanied by a vicious little brown midge, they bit and gorged and buzzed around us. After three days of rest we left Qui Shi Kan Sayi pursued by clouds of these bloodthirsty mosquitoes. We walked slowly out of the mouth of the valley and when we were at last in the desert and free from our winged assailants we turned due east.

Ahead of us lay the shimmering line of sand dunes that form the point where the Kum Tagh embrace the Arjin Mountains.

3

Sweet as Eden is the Air

Deep in the veins of Earth,
And, fed by a thousand springs
That comfort the market-place
Or sap the power of Kings,
The Fifth Great River had birth,
Even as it was foretold –
The Secret River of Gold

Rudyard Kipling, 'Song of the Fifth River'

Scrambling up and over sand dunes can be relatively easy or extremely difficult. It all depends on the firmness of the sand. Where the Kum Tagh sand dunes meet the Arjin Mountains the dunes are very soft. The Uighur people call this type of sand *yaman kum* – hateful sand – and not without reason.

As we climbed, the surface shifted and sank around us. A few feet from a dune's peak, a pinnacle of sand with its finely turned edge would invariably collapse. I would be left floundering and threshing about in the *yaman kum*. This was tiring, as was the effect of the sand continually filling my boots. Exasperated at having to stop, unstrap and empty them, I took them off, tied them around my neck and continued the climb in bare feet. This provided temporary relief, but not for long. That evening the soles of my feet were blackened where the hot sand had burnt them.

I now understood, somewhat belatedly, why these dunes had not been crossed in recorded history. I remembered Leilei, the Professor and I planning this expedition in the Professor's office in Urumqi. I had looked at a map and casually run my finger along the base of the Arjin Mountains where they were linked to the Kum Tagh. I recalled my earlier enthusiasm. It's easy to be brave and bold when planning an expedition, but as I lay on my back for the umpteenth time gasping for breath, the reality was somewhat different.

Parts of the detailed map of the Arjin Mountains' foothills had been left as small white spaces. Even in these days of satellite imagery, in places where mountain gullies are obscured and dunes shift, these can still be found. These white spaces had inspired me but now, as I spat out yet another mouthful of sand, doubt set in. On past expeditions it had never occurred to me that I might not get out of a particularly tight situation. On this occasion, my pounding heart and fading strength made me think again – had my bravado been foolish?

In 1895, Sven Hedin was entertaining similarly gloomy thoughts while tackling sand dunes during his crossing of the Taklamakan desert. The Taklamakan, 'if you go in you won't come out', lies due west of Lop Nur and absorbs the Kum Tagh sand dunes which we were attempting to cross.

> Meanwhile, with my compass in one hand and my field-glass in the other, I hastened eastwards, due eastwards; for there ran the river of safety. The camp, the camels were soon lost to sight behind the summits of the sand-hills. My only companion was a solitary fly which I regarded with unusually friendly eyes. Otherwise I was alone, absolutely alone, in the midst of a death-like silence, with a sea of yellow sand dunes before me, rolling away

in fainter and fainter billows right away to the horizon. Deeper Sabbath peace never brooded over any graveyard than that which environed me. The only thing wanting to convert the simile into fact was the headstones to the graves.

I soon fancied the dunes were not as high as usual. I tried to maintain the same level as far as possible, by keeping to their crests and circling round the highest points. I knew the poor camels would have many a toilsome, many a weary step to take in my wake. A bewildering chaos of ridges, lying north-east to south-west and east to west, were flung across one another in the strangest fashion. Our position was desperate. The dunes burst up to heights of 140 to 150 feet. As I looked down from the top of one of these giant waves, the depression at my feet, on the sheltered side of the dune, looked a long way below me, at a giddy depth. We were being slowly but surely killed by these terrible ridges of sand. They impeded our advance; yet over them we must. There was no help for it, no evading them. Over them we must – a funeral procession marching to the doleful clang of the camels' bells.

The next day, Hedin continues recounting an experience similar to what we were enduring:

That day the sand-hills were the highest of any we had yet crossed – fully 200 feet high . . . It will be readily understood that, over gigantic billows of sand like this we could not advance very rapidly. We were compelled to make many a detour, involving great loss of time, in order to avoid them; in fact, we were sometimes compelled to travel for a time in the exactly opposite direction from that in which we wanted to go.

It was not just the human team that was struggling. The camels, too, sank up to their hocks in the soft sand. Our Kazakh herdsmen, just like those of Hedin, had to unstrap loads from their backs and stagger up the dunes, carrying the loads themselves. Yet even in these terrible and testing conditions, not one of the camels sat down and gave in. One by one they clambered up and over the walls of shifting sand.

As Hedin found:

The camels slid cleverly down the steep slopes. Only one of them fell, one of the two that carried the water-tanks, and had to be unloaded and reloaded. Sometimes, when our path was stopped by abrupt declivities, we were obliged to stand still whilst the men dug out and trampled a path for the animals . . . When, after some little hesitation, the camels began to slide down the loose sand, every man's utmost watchfulness was needed, for the sand poured down after them in a torrent, covering them to the knees.

'Come on, Ye Tuzi, come on,' shouted Leilei by way of encouragement.

Leilei frequently calls me Ye Tuzi – the mad hare – not without reason.

A further encouragement was the sighting of a wild Bactrian camel perched near the summit of one of the dunes in the middle distance. This meant that the dune had a firmer surface. The higher we climbed, the harder the sand became. We had reached the *ighiz kum* – high sand.

I sensed that the star of good fortune, which had shone so brightly on previous expeditions, was still twinkling overhead.

At last, the steeply rolling barrier of sand flattened out and spread to the western horizon. In front of us lay endless stretches of fine yellow sand, pock-marked like the surface of the moon. To the north-west, where the Kum Tagh stretched back towards Lop Nur, the tips of gigantic dunes peeped up one behind the other for mile after mile. This vast desert, which earlier that day had taxed our strength to the uttermost, was now extended before us in a vast spread of undulating sand. In the unbroken stillness it was a majestic, intoxicating sight.

Some of the patterns left by the wind on the sand were extraordinary and unlike anything that I had ever seen. One design in particular was made up of immaculate, parallel zigzag lines, as if a master craftsman had rhythmically wafted a light brush over the grainy surface.

'Look over there, Ye Tuzi.' Leilei tugged at my shirtsleeve and interrupted my musing. He was pointing to the centre of one of the sand craters that were dotted about in front of us. He handed me his field glasses; I raised them and immediately saw what had excited Leilei, a bull camel quietly grazing with his harem of fifteen females. Flagging spirits rose. Our domestic Bactrian camels raised their heads and sniffed the evening air.

This was compass territory. A GPS can tell you where you are, but it is the GPS's compass that tells you where to go. In a land of shifting sand it is impossible to mark dunes on a map. In three years strong winds can cause them to disappear or realign in a completely different area. So we fixed our compasses on a bearing to the east and walked accordingly, skirting where possible the base of the dunes and walking up and down steep-sided surface hollows, by now firm enough to take our weight.

That evening, the blood-red glow in the sky to the west filtered through an elongated series of darkly corrugated clouds. Just as the sun was about to set, exhausted men and beasts collapsed in a convenient hollow of firm sand, surrounded by nourishing tufts of dry vegetation for the camels.

Li Weidong lost no time in turning out an acceptable meal of noodles and tinned meat and the shoots of wild onions. Camels browsed contentedly and chopsticks click-clacked on metal bowls. When these were empty, we lay down to sleep.

For a long time I lay gazing at a rising moon and stars, which seemed to shine more brightly than I had ever seen. In the dry desert air the sky becomes a beautiful backdrop for a myriad of brilliant stars that hang clear, without the illusion of lights twinkling through holes in a curtain, as is the case in murkier climes. The Milky Way has not the whitish haze of Western skies, but is a phosphorescent shower of spots of light. As I stared up at the gigantic mass, I wondered whether we all end up as a star in the Milky Way, twinkling forever in an infinite mass of light.

Lawrence of Arabia experienced similar sensations. He wrote in *The Seven Pillars of Wisdom:* 'The brilliant stars cast about us a false light, not illumination, but rather a transparency of air, lengthening slightly the shadow below each stone and making a diffused greyness of the ground.'

The moon is more self-revealing than in northern latitudes and heavier atmospheres. It is not a mere silver cradle swinging in the void. In the desert, the moon flaunts itself, hanging in space with a particular brilliance. As the moon rises the desert embraces it. During the long hours while it travels from one side of the horizon to the other, the moon exerts her own effect on the human imagination, softening the austere outlines of the rocks and hills; saddles, water-carriers and boxes are invested with a subtle charm.

Desert travellers plan their journeys according to the phases of the moon. My Kenyan friend Jasper Evans knows instinctively the current phase of the moon and never has to check in his diary. Whether in Africa or Central Asia, we know that this most subtle of light infusions enables us to walk freely even on rough ground, swinging along behind our camels under the glittering stars.

My journal for the following day: '*I discovered a tick embedded in the hair just above the danger zone. I extracted it with tweezers and it came out with its head intact. This piece of good fortune ensured that there wasn't a post operative problem.*'

The next day, the surface of the sand reverted in places to *yaman kum*. Sometimes I reached the summit of a dune on all fours, but not Leilei. He was like a mountain goat, skipping up dunes, snapping with his camera and shouting words of encouragement when he saw me falter or flag.

There were compensations too. By the end of the day we had spotted eighty-two wild Bactrian camels since we had left Hongliugou, which out of an estimated Chinese population of 660 was high. We had only just reached the halfway point, and many more might still be found. I banished any negative thoughts. This was complete justification for the difficult route we had taken. Here were camels, precisely because the difficulty deterred travellers.

After two more days of testing dune crossing, we began our slow descent into the centre of the V. Ahead lay a series of valleys, the one furthest away appearing to have green vegetation that could signal fresh water. Although we had found water at Wutong and at Qui Shi Kan Sayi, whatever we carried we shared with our camels. When laden, a camel can travel up to thirteen days without needing to drink, but not under the harsh conditions that we had encountered. They had filled their bellies at Qui Shi Kan Sayi but after five days they were thirsty.

The next day was a rest day and Usuman and Lao Zhang set off from our camp with the camels in search of water. At midday, in need of something to do, Leilei and I decided to explore on our own. We had seen an unusual and steep-sided gully that led back into the dunes and as we tramped slowly up the slope we spotted a series of intriguing footprints.

'It's a yeti,' Leilei exclaimed excitedly, pointing at a deeply embedded footprint in the sand. It was large, uncannily human and the instep had a pronounced inward curve. There were five clearly indented toes. An inch and a half beyond each toe were five tiny pinpricks.

'I think it's a bear,' I said, pointing to the barely visible marks. 'Those were made by a bear's claws.'

Leilei, who was down on his knees measuring and photographing, nodded.

'It's strange. The mountains are miles away. A bear wouldn't normally come out this far into the desert. What could have brought it here?'

'Food or water?'

'The bear wouldn't have come here for water. It's all salt.'

'Unless there's a freshwater spring nearby that no one knows about.'

Having taken enough photographs, we started to walk up the gully in an attempt to find out where the big Tibetan brown bear was heading. If the bear could indeed lead us to a freshwater source it would be an enormous bonus.

Ten minutes later, near a bend in the gully, Leilei froze. Moving sedately down the sandy slope some fifty yards in front of us were two wild Bactrian camels.

We both stood rooted to the spot. Then high up on the left bank of the gully I spotted a stunted tamarisk bush.

'Up there, Leilei,' I whispered, 'as quietly as you can.'

We were fortunately both camouflaged in our respective tribal gear. Leilei, wore the sandy-green costume of the Chinese military. I was clothed in my habitual tweed jacket. Tailored for my teenage figure, it was cut in a very old-fashioned style with four buttons and a small lapel. The miracle was that it had survived intact and still fitted. I took it with me to the Gashun Gobi on expedition after expedition because the very heavy tweed was of a quality which, I am told, is unobtainable today. The trousers, tapered to satisfy a teenager's whim and with no turn-ups, had long since ceased to fit around my expanded waist, but the jacket, with ample pockets for pen, paper and dates, was ideal for exploring with camels in the Gobi. Topped with a stained, ragged, green African bush hat that had also accompanied me on each Gobi expedition, I felt that we had a sporting chance of observing the wild Bactrians without them noticing us.

The curve in the gully was about thirty yards in front of us and we waited for the two camels to disappear around that fortuitous bend. When they had done so, we scrambled breathlessly up behind the tiny bush. It barely gave us cover but we had a clear view down to the bottom of the gully.

The two wild camels came slowly into sight and continued to advance downhill without showing the slightest concern. The wind, which in the Gobi desert never ceases to blow, was coming from the west and straight into our faces. Our smell would not give us away.

Leilei and I stared as the two camels advanced towards us. Occasionally they stopped to sniff the air. Then, sedately bending their necks, they would turn their heads from one side to the other. Satisfied that no predator was near, they moved on, relaxed but cautious.

I had my video camera – which I had now mastered – and a conventional camera; in a situation like this it is difficult to know which to use first. As Leilei did not have a camcorder I opted for the former. Within minutes the camels were directly below us. As it was the second week of May they were moulting and we could see great tufts of hair clinging to their hindquarters. On their thighs, hair had snagged off on passing bushes, leaving huge bald patches that made the animals look as though they were suffering from mange.

The wild Bactrian camel has two much smaller and more widely spaced humps than the domestic Bactrian. As we looked down on their backs, we knew beyond doubt that these animals were not a cross between the wild and the domestic Bactrian camel. These were no hybrids; they were truly wild.

Leilei was snapping ferociously with his camera and it must have been the repetitious click that the lead camel heard. His head swivelled round towards us. At this point he could not have been more than forty feet away. For an instant he stared at us, then as his eyes filled with terror he abruptly turned and cantered full tilt back down the gully, followed by his companion.

It is difficult to describe our feelings. For years we had tracked this elusive creature in both China and Mongolia, often fruitlessly, and we had at last got almost to within touching distance. Leilei and I shook hands. We both felt certain that we would never get so close to a wild Bactrian camel again.

As for the yeti, there is a Russian scientist in Moscow who runs a society that tracks down records of sightings of wild man or Big Foot. Reports have come in from Siberia, Kazakhstan, Tibet and even North America. But, as far as I am aware, no photograph has ever been taken of the mysterious creature and the Russian's book on the subject, which is full of reports and sightings, contains not a single photo.

The Professor believes firmly in the yeti's existence, as does Lao Zhao, who claims that one ran into a camp that they had set up at 10,000 feet in the Arjin Mountains and stole a tin of food.

'Those mountains are vast,' the Professor once said to me. 'There are many valleys where no man has ever penetrated. We may even have been to one or two of them ourselves on our expeditions. One could spend a whole lifetime in the Kunlun or Arjin Mountains and still not know them properly. I've never seen wild man but I do believe that he exists. There could well be a large primate that has adapted to life in remote mountain areas. He's been seen in Tibet, North America and Siberia. Why not here? New species are still being found. One day, someone will find wild man.'

It is not difficult to speculate that some strange creature could live in this remote and fractured region. Many Tibetans acknowledge the yeti's existence and but for the bear's claws in the footprint we found, Leilei and I would be believers too.

Our herdsmen failed to find water and our supplies were getting low. Two days later I was seated on my camel Shadrak directly behind Usuman, who rocked backwards and forwards intoning a Kazakh song as he guided the caravan towards the second valley. At one point he stretched out horizontally on the rugs that were tied between his camel's humps and appeared to have fallen asleep.

Shadrak, a sure-footed and energetic camel, had been a real stalwart when we crossed the dunes. He had ploughed resolutely up and over the soft sand, never once complaining apart from emitting a grumbling groan when the going became really tough. A quiff of woolly hair spread-eagled over his nose, and between his ears he was totally bald. This strange coiffure resembled a monk's tonsure but Brother Shadrak, as I called him, was one of the most amenable camels that I have ridden.

As the valley drew nearer, Lao Zhao, who was riding behind me, attracted my attention and pointed upwards. Over twenty black vultures were circling high up in the sky ahead of us.

'Something has died or been killed,' said Lao Zhao.

Thirty minutes later we reached a rock-strewn area that bordered a gully along which snowmelt ran in the summer months. In the gully lay a disembowelled two-year-old wild Bactrian camel, recently killed by wolves.

Lao Zhao jumped off his camel and using his whip, pointed to their prints in the sand. He swiftly decoded the recent desert drama.

'There were four of them. One went for the camel's throat, one attacked its underbelly and two pulled it down from behind. It died about four hours ago.'

As our caravan moved gingerly over a lofty, narrow pass that separated the second valley from the third, a tragedy occurred. Since the first day of our trek it had become clear that one of our camels had not recovered from its ordeal when the black sandstorm blew. It had laboured stoically under its load for a week but thereafter its progress had become slower and slower. As it had started to impede our progress, we had stripped it of its loads and allowed it to wander freely behind our caravan. It joined its teammates at nightfall to be fed, watered and tied down for the night.

As the camels slowly and steadily reconnoitred the difficult, narrow downhill descent, this loose camel at the back of our caravan slipped. It fell to the ground, staggered to its feet, stood for a moment unsteadily on the very edge of the track and then fell over the side and crashed 1,500 feet to its death.

It affects me greatly whenever one of these loyal and hard-working creatures dies. They are a lifeline. On an expedition if we lose camels through death or neglect, odds start to stack heavily against us.

It had never occurred to me that an untethered, unloaded camel could fall to its death. However, these thoughts vanished when, quite unexpectedly, we entered paradise.

Down the pass and into the third valley, we noticed that not only was the vegetation green, but that it was full of wildlife. Moreover, it was wildlife that simply stood and stared at us.

Two Tibetan wild asses, normally animals that gallop away at the first sniff of man, trotted up and walked behind our caravan. The brown and white, skewbald Tibetan wild ass, even though it is a protected species, is hunted mercilessly by the Chinese, and yet here were two of them behaving like domestic donkeys.

'Look, Ye Tuzi, look!'

Leilei was pointing at a flock of sheep. This was no domestic herd. This was the wild Argali sheep normally seen, if one is lucky, as motionless, black dots on mountain tops. They were grazing as unconcernedly as a flock in an English meadow. Like *ovis poli*, the Marco Polo sheep in the Pamirs, the rams carry such large horns that it is hard to understand how they can support them. I do not carry high-powered camera lenses, yet now I didn't need them as I managed to take pictures of a ram at such close quarters that it seemed impossible to believe it was wild.

The valley's high protective hills surrounded us on three sides. As we progressed, two wild Bactrian camels stared at us from a respectable distance and slowly edged towards our caravan. This is the creature that will not stop running until it has set a mile between itself and a human intruder. It is an animal that has been hunted, slaughtered by man for food and forced into one of the harshest areas in the world: the Gashun Gobi, the bitter desert.

'Where do they drink?' I asked Lao Zhao.

'I don't know,' he replied. 'Everything looks green but I can't see a spring.'

Naturalists use the word 'naive' to classify a population of wildlife that has not had contact with man and is therefore unafraid. To discover a pocket of naive wildlife in today's world is extremely rare, even rarer than entering an area of unmapped and unexplored country. But here, deep in the centre of the Kum Tagh V, we had found exactly that.

We moved rhythmically on through the valley at a steady pace of two and a half miles an hour. After three-quarters of an hour, we were abruptly confronted with what we had been seeking. At the bottom of a vast fissure in the sand, a stream was clearly discernible. It must have been over 150 feet from the surface and both sides of the abyss were lined with black, shiny rock. It was as though the earth had ruptured under pressure from the water below.

Usuman was already looking for a path. Spotting a well-worn wild animal track, he turned and beckoned to me to follow. Handing my camel to Lao Zhang I clambered after him. It was as exciting for Usuman as it was for me. He lived in the Arjin Mountains but he had been totally unaware of this valley and its desert spring. Puffing and panting in his wake, I slithered down to the bottom of the chasm. A rocky crag projected over a section of the narrow stream ahead of us and when Usuman reached it he held up his hand and put a finger to his mouth. Crouching down he disappeared. Seconds later he was back. He waved me forward and I peered around the rock.

Just ahead of us, standing in a bed of reedy *fragmitis* grass that covered the water source, a wild Bactrian bull camel stood gulping down draught after draught of fresh spring water. He had obviously not drunk for days and his belly was extended as though he were pregnant.

We crept closer and squatted down less than thirty yards from this extraordinary spectacle. For over five minutes we gazed transfixed.

All at once, the camel raised his head. He saw us and snorting in alarm he turned to run, but such was the weight of his belly that he couldn't get his legs to function properly. With splayed feet akimbo he waddled through the water, trampling down the dry stalks of *fragmitis*. Laboriously, he clambered up the side of the crevasse, his distended tummy swinging from side to side. I could almost hear the slosh of the water inside. He paused at the top of the steep incline, took one last look, shook his head and disappeared.

Usuman and I embraced each other and laughed.

'Like a woman,' Usuman chortled. 'Like a woman carrying a baby.'

Never have I seen a wild male animal look so determinedly female. My great regret was that I had left my camera strapped to my camel on the other side of the crevasse.

There were shouts as Leilei and the rest of the team appeared around the side of the cliff face.

'Ye Tuzi,' cried Leilei, 'we will call it Kum Su – the Desert Spring.'

No wonder the spring had not previously been discovered. Tucked away below the surface of the valley it was cleverly concealed from satellites and prying human eyes.

Our own camels badly needed to drink. One by one we brought them down the steep side of the crevasse to 'Kum Su'. Each camel drank its fill and then, stomachs bloated and extended, they were returned to where Li Weidong and Lao Zhao were preparing camp. We joined them and erected our tents. As dusk fell, Leilei spotted a flock of sheep slowly moving across the valley towards the spring.

He stalked them at first, but as they were totally unconcerned, he stood up and strode towards them. One by one they disappeared down the slope with Leilei, his hair highlighted by the evening sun, shepherding them in front of him.

'Most unprofessional,' grumbled Li Weidong, whose opinion of Leilei's scientific credentials was low. 'That's not the way to observe wildlife.'

I thought to myself that neither Li Weidong nor anyone else in our party had seen wildlife react like this. Bushcraft was irrelevant. Man left them completely unperturbed.

I would like to have camped near 'Kum Su' for at least three days, to observe wildlife behaviour, but we had a problem. Our water supplies were low and although the water was 'sweet' it was partially salty and so was not ideal to drink under normal circumstances. In addition, our food was running short.

We had made contact with the Professor on the radio and discovered that he was seventy-five miles from 'Kum Su' – three days' travel by camel. That was exactly how long our water and rations would last, so, much against our will, we moved on.

As we left 'Kum Su' I vowed to return. It hadn't dawned on me that no matter how hard I tried to keep the exact location of the valleys secret, there were other members in our party who would not be able or possibly not even want to do so.

In front of us lay the sand dunes that formed the eastern arm of the V. As we travelled steadily towards them, the cohesion and spirit of the team, which so far had been excellent, evaporated. Li Weidong constantly bickered about the youth and inexperience of Leilei. Usuman fell into dispute with Lao Zhao. I had no idea what they were arguing about but a noisy slanging match ensued. It only petered out when Lao Zhao fell off his camel. Dignity severely damaged, and face completely lost, Lao Zhao was in no position to continue his harangue. Usuman thanked Allah for his judgment and continued the mournful Kazakh song, which might have been the cause of the argument in the first place.

'Camels are only suitable for eating,' Lao Zhao muttered. 'They are utterly useless creatures.'

On the night that we left the spring, Lao Zhang got drunk. Although alcohol was rationed and only drunk in any quantity at celebratory parties, he had somehow managed to conceal a bottle of Chinese *mao-tai* spirit. When he had drained it he was incoherent and embarrassing.

The spell of 'Kum Su', generated by all the discoveries and excitements of the past two days, had been broken.

The dunes forming the eastern side of the V were fortunately less harsh and not as dramatic than those further west. Nevertheless, the going was not easy and in places the sand was soft. However, this time we did not have to carry the camels' loads and after two more days of slogging through sand we finally began the downward descent. Each day we saw a substantial number of wild Bactrian camels.

My journal record: '*In the process of crossing the sand dunes we saw thirteen wild camels in four separate groups. This brings our total sightings on the trip so far to 140. This is quite amazing when you compare it with the expedition to the lake of Lop Nur when we did not see a single wild camel during the whole trip. Truly Kum Su is a very special place.*'

'Look over there. It's a vehicle. It's the Professor.'

We were halfway down the last of the dunes and Li Weidong was pointing to a tiny white speck in the desert some two to three miles away.

I raised my field glasses and saw that the jeep was stationary. The Professor had stopped to make camp and await our arrival.

'Someone's walking towards us,' exclaimed Leilei, who was also looking through field glasses. 'It's Qi Yun.'

We dismounted from our camels and, perched on a convenient rocky ledge, waited for Qi Yun to reach us.

Half an hour later we were all shaking hands and slapping backs and then we began the last camel trek, the one that would take us to our vehicles and the Professor. Qi Yun told us that they had seen twenty wild Bactrian camels on the journey from Lapeiquan.

We had arrived back just in time. Our water was finished and we had enough food for one more meal. If anything had delayed us before reaching the Professor we would have been in trouble.

Food, as ever, was what the Professor was good at preparing and he had laid out a welcoming spread to greet us. Most of the victuals came from tins, but after days in the desert, sardines, pilchards, tomatoes and assorted canned Chinese delicacies can prove very appetizing, even if they are washed down with sickly sweet Chinese wine. The Professor embraced us enthusiastically, partly because we had returned safely and partly for what we had done. After all, we had achieved something scarcely credible. We had filled in a tiny blank corner of a Chinese map.

Chinese spirit, beer and Qi Yun's flute set the stage for a highly convivial evening, but as we began to settle down to the meal a fierce wind got up. By the time we had snuggled into sleeping bags it was blowing hard and the temperature had dropped dramatically to below freezing. In the night the wind reached gale force, sending sand swirling through our tents. Next morning our makeshift camp was covered in snow.

I thought how fortunate we were. We had set out in the wake of a black sandstorm and finished our journey to be greeted by gale-force winds and snow. But during the twenty-six-day trek the weather had been perfect. Our tale would have been very different if we had had to contend with sandstorms on the dunes.

The old Nationalist road, 'the road of a thousand wash-outs', disintegrates completely in a large flood riverbed about a mile from Lapeiquan freshwater spring. The riverbed enters a sheer-sided valley and then spirals up into the rugged mountains. It was bone dry, but floodwater levels showed that in July and August it turned into a raging torrent as winter snows melt on the towering peaks. Although there was no longer a road, there were patriotic signs carved into slabs of rock by the Chinese Nationalist government road builders such as, 'Prepare a good harvest; get ready for war' and 'Our cause will triumph over evil-doers.' At the spring another rock sign proclaimed, 'The water here gives you a belly-ache.' But it didn't. We drank our fill, topped up our water containers, bathed in the freezing, clear spring and washed some of our filthy clothing. It was a beautiful spot and, fortunately, there were no encounters with bandits. After a day of rest, our hired camels set off on the return journey to Hongliugou with Usuman and Lao Zhang, following the line of the abandoned road, while we set off in our vehicles for a Kazakh town called Annanba. To get there, we had to travel 150 miles along 'the road of a thousand wash-outs'.

We wanted to go to Annanba because it is the headquarters of a nature reserve where there are about 100 wild Bactrian camels. More importantly, there was a Kazakh in Annanba, Ali Abutalerp, whom I particularly wanted to see. A thin, highly intelligent man of modest height, Ali was a key player in the fight to save and protect the wild Bactrian camel from extinction in the wild.

Annanba is in Gansu Province, which lies contiguous with the eastern border of Xinjiang. The town, high up on a plateau in the Arjin Mountains, has escaped the modernization that is sweeping through China. But not, I fear, for long. The Kazakhs are in the process of being removed by the Chinese from their mountain home to a new town in the desert called Aksai with wide roads, schools and modern amenities.

For years, the Kazakhs in Annanba have irked the Chinese authorities by refusing to abandon their nomadic way of life. The tinsel and baubles of city life rapidly seduce the younger generation. Life in the mountains tending sheep, goats and camels is hard. The winter and summer temperatures are extreme, the monetary rewards are few. Boys and girls in a gleaming new environment are all too willing to abandon the traditional life of a herdsman which, of course, is exactly what the Chinese authorities want so that they can control the Kazakhs properly.

It was very cold when we arrived in Annanba and the streets were covered in a foot of snow. The town appeared to be full of both cheeky, rosy-faced children and exceptionally fierce Tibetan mastiffs. The company of the former I much enjoyed, the latter I avoided. We were told that Ali was out of town but would return in the evening and this gave me the opportunity to attend to an urgent matter. Ever since I had been bitten by Usuman's dog I had had a nagging feeling that it would be sensible to have a series of anti-rabies jabs, late though it might be.

The Professor took me to Annanba's tiny dispensary. It was a building with few comforts. The patients sat on the uncovered springs of an iron bed and a smoky stovepipe coal fire provided the only form of heating. The small, but supremely efficient green-smocked Chinese dispenser, Miss Tan Shao Hong, bustled about briskly. Her hair was swept back severely from her unmade-up face and she was wearing thick woollen stockings and highly polished lace-up brown shoes. Such was her air of purposeful endeavour that a smile had little chance of creasing her impassive features. She was the Chinese counterpart of the old-fashioned British hospital matron, without the starch. Miss Tan laid five glass containers out on a tray, picked up one of them, unsheathed a large needle and hustled me behind a tattered, fading, brown patterned curtain. On the other side of this screen was a wooden chair and I was instructed to drop my trousers, grasp the top of the chair and bend over. The whole operation was accomplished with commendable speed and efficiency and in no time I was neatly and expertly punctured. When I emerged from behind the curtain Miss Tan handed me a box filled with the remaining glass vials holding the magic pink fluid.

'One needle every five days for the next twenty-five days,' she said. To make doubly sure that I understood her she added, 'Five by five equals twenty-five,' and looked at me quizzically over her horn-rimmed glasses. Miss Tan did not smile readily, but she did have a sense of humour.

I remarked that, 'In England they will not be able to read the Chinese label.'

'Tell them it goes into your bottom to stop you barking,' she replied.

More illuminating excursions were made later on to dispensaries in Dun Huang and Hami, large towns that we passed through on our way back to Urumqi, where the fourth injection was given. I had been surprised to learn that Chinese dispensaries, no matter how remote, always carry anti-rabies serum.

When I returned to England and went to my local dispensary clutching the one remaining dosage, the nursing sister that I encountered was no Miss Tan.

'What is this? I can't read Chinese.'

'It's anti-rabies fluid. I am on a course of injections and have had four of them. This is the last one and I need it to be put into my bottom.'

'I have never seen pink anti-rabies fluid. I don't know what I might be giving you. If I injected you, I would be acting against National Health Service regulations. I am not allowed to give you any medicine if I don't know what it is. I cannot do it.'

I stood my ground.

'I have brought this all the way from a little village in China. I have had four injections at five-day intervals. I must have the final injection. If you won't do it then please give me a needle and let me inject myself.'

'That's out of the question.'

'Then I will buy a needle and do it myself.'

She started to relent, but with a proviso.

'You must sign a declaration.'

'Saying?'

'That you indemnify us totally from our actions.'

'Willingly.'

The crucial piece of paper was typed out and signed. I was duly injected, and thankfully, whether it was on account of the hair of the dog, the pink fluid, or maybe just because Usuman's dog was not rabid, I did not start to bark.

That evening we had a meeting with Ali and his boss, Mr Mamil, the director of the Annanba Nature Reserve. Tall, slim and with an enigmatic smile, he let Ali do the talking. It emerged that the greatest threat to the wild camels in Annanba was not wolves, miners or poachers but domestic Bactrian camels. Kazakh herdsmen allow their camels to wander freely and unsupervised into the Annanba Reserve; where they wander, they invariably cross-breed with wild Bactrian stock. The result is a hybrid with an adulterated wild Bactrian camel genetic make-up. Both Kazakhs and Mongolians do not like to handle pure wild Bactrian camel calves because they are too dangerous. They frequently kill them. One two-year-old wild camel calf scalped a young Mongolian of my acquaintance; the problems are very real. A hybrid calf is a different matter. The herdsmen welcome a diluted addition of wild blood into their domestic herds. The problem has grown to such large proportions, that it has become difficult to recognize which animals in the Annanba Nature Reserve are wild and which are domestic.

Our expedition was now at an end and we set off on the long drive back to Urumqi via the towns of Dun Huang and Hami. However, this 700-mile journey was disrupted by numerous vehicle problems, from punctures to a serious fault with our truck's engine. My earlier expeditions had been dogged by similar mishaps, which had made me vow that in future I would always go into the desert mounted on a camel.

Our engine was repaired in Dun Huang, where we had had other vehicles repaired on previous expeditions. Dun Huang is a bustling, thriving town, distant in spirit and attitude from the harshness of the desert that relentlessly encroaches on its suburbs. Outside the recently reconstructed modern centre, and away from the smoke-laden patchwork of haphazard industrial development, the oasis stretches from north to south for twenty kilometres. Substantial mud-brick farmsteads stand in the centre of communal farmland, surrounded by thick, mud walls. During the Han Dynasty (206 BC to AD 220) the name Dun Huang or 'Blazing Beacon' alluded to its watch-tower and fire-beacon, which were used to signal an attack by invaders coming out of the desert to the west. Later, the name was changed to Shachow, 'City of Sands', but when the town was destroyed by fire, the new town that was rebuilt on the same site reverted to Dun Huang.

Dun Huang figures prominently in Chinese history and has had a chequered and colourful past. In AD 787 it fell to the Tibetans, who remained there until the middle of the following century. For more than a century from AD 919 it was virtually independent, although it recognized the Chinese court. In AD 1035 it fell to the Tanguts, in AD 1227 to the Mongols and in 1524 to the Mongol Khan of Turfan. In 1725 the Manchus established a military post there, and thirty-five years later it was reoccupied by the Chinese. It attracted this constant military activity because it was situated at a point where the old Silk Road from China to the West was crossed by the great north road from India through Lhasa to Mongolia and Siberia. In the 1940s it became a strategic town for Kazakhs fleeing from the Communists and who crossed the Desert of Lop on a harrowing migration from northern Xinjiang and Mongolia to India.

That evening, we walked to the crowded market-place to have a meal in a Chinese Muslim restaurant. A full moon bathed the market square in a pall of suffused light that was punctuated by a myriad of tiny coloured electric light bulbs, strung out over the bustling stalls. Having been suppressed for decades, everyday, petty commerce has returned to Dun Huang with a vengeance. The market teemed with traders and hawkers, young and old, male and female. Their wares were mostly cheap factory-produced household articles, or garishly coloured dresses, blouses, suits and jeans. Youths crowded excitedly around full-size, green beige, private enterprise snooker tables standing on massive and ornately carved wooden legs. The volatile spectators erupted into loud cheers when a player made a good shot or laughed uproariously when an easy pot was missed. Smartly dressed hostesses called out to passers-by in an attempt to persuade them to sample exotic teas. In the butchery, carcasses of pigs and sheep hung skinned and bloody, swinging gently in the wind. Apples, melons, raisins and dates dominated the fruit stalls, and bright-red tomatoes embedded in a mass of greenery were spread out on tables in front of tiny blue-suited voluble old women with creased, crumpled faces that were burnt brown by the sun. Male and female tailors and leather-workers of all ages, shapes and sizes squatted hunched over their antiquated, clattering treadle machines. I handed one old crone my battered tweed jacket and she expertly covered the frayed ends with soft, brown leather.

A wizened old man in a faded, blue serge Mao suit slowly rotated a smoke-blackened metal tube over an open fire. At frequent intervals there was a minor explosion, he opened the container and emptied freshly popped fluffy white corn on to a sheet of newspaper spread in front of him. He looked up impassively as two girls dressed in a racy modern style stooped to pick up two paper bags filled to overflowing with freshly popped corn. They were dressed identically in yellow neck scarves and delicate, turquoise-green silk blouses tucked into tightly fitting navy-blue skirts. Their heavily powdered, deathly white faces were offset by carefully applied deep-red lipstick, finely pencilled, black eyebrows and heavily lacquered, false eyelashes. They must have been twins, only a fetching dimple distinguishing one from the other. A comb of green jade was stuck into the back of carefully groomed hair that had been coiled round and round, beehive fashion, on the top of their heads. They chattered to each other like excited starlings as they walked away, their black plastic, high-heeled shoes click-clacking merrily on the grey flagstones. A group of old women squatting on tiny green-painted wooden stools turned their heads away. Their blue serge-suited husbands, huddled in the shadows behind them, stared impassively at the two girls. Were they casting their minds back to their youth when they had been at the forefront of a revolution that had caused so much terror and destruction in the backward province of Xinjiang? Were they staring after the two girls in longing, frustration, despair or was it something else? What are old people's feelings when confronted, as they are today, with everything that they had been taught, not only to abhor and despise, but to destroy?

About twelve miles to the south of Dun Huang lie the Caves of a Thousand Buddhas. These comprise hundreds of grottoes carved in a hillside and filled with Buddhist statues and paintings that were sculpted, painted or financed by religious travellers, monks and scholars over the centuries. Because Dun Huang was an important crossroads, many travellers rested there. In places where wood is scarce and the climate is harsh, a cave is an obvious repository for religious works of art. The most remarkable of the pilgrims was the seventh-century traveller and renowned Chinese scholar, Hsuan-tsang, universally know as the 'Master of the Law'. Concerned that some passages in the holy books that he had studied were irreconcilable, Hsuan-tsang conceived the bold plan of gaining accurate knowledge by undertaking a pilgrimage to India to bring back with him a library of Buddhist sacred books.

After numerous adventures and considerable hardship, he eventually reached India, where he was rewarded by an ample opportunity to study Buddhism and was able to collect a large number of books, which were eventually to lay the authoritative foundation of Buddhism in China. Fifteen years later he journeyed back to China, this time crossing the treacherous Desert of Lop.

Hsuan-tsang later retired to a monastic life where he could study undisturbed and translate into Chinese some of the 657 Buddhist books he had brought back from India, and also make use of the 157 relics that he had collected.

The fate of the manuscripts, scrolls and paintings that he had deposited in the grottoes of Ch'ien Fo-tung, the Caves of a Thousand Buddhas, remained a closely guarded secret until May 1907 and the arrival on the scene of Aurel Stein, who had journeyed west from Miran. Stein entered a chamber in one of the caves that had remained sealed for over a thousand years. Inside, he was to make the most momentous discovery in the whole of Central Asian archaeology.

The priest in charge of the caves was Abbot Wang Tao-shih. In March 1907, when Aurel Stein made his first visit to the caves, Abbot Wang was away on a begging tour but the archaeologist was able to inspect a manuscript that had been retrieved from behind a sealed chamber. Greatly excited by what he had seen, Stein returned in May and with the help of his wily secretary Chiang-Ssu-yeh, began to put pressure on Wang to open the chamber. Persuasion, diplomacy, the evocation of the name of Hsuan-tsang, who fortuitously turned out to be Abbot Wang's patron saint, and above all the jangle of money-bags finally won Wang round. Stein's secretive and underhand measures revealed that here were manuscripts in Uighur, Sogdian, Runic Turkish, Sanskrit and Tibetan and texts in the most ancient known languages of Central Asia such as Khotanese, Saka and Toacharish. There were superbly embroidered pictures and fine block-printed pictures from ninth-century China. The total number of manuscripts and rolls of printed matter amounted to no less than nine thousand. There were also specimens of silk that showed the high standard of silk-weaving long before the Han Dynasty. Wang was by now accepting 'judiciously administered doses of silver' Although Wang was at first reluctant to release the precious Chinese scrolls, Stein managed to obtain fifty of these together with many other precious texts and paintings.

Stein congratulated himself on the results of his skilful bribery but, 'my time for feeling true relief came when all the twenty-four cases, heavy with manuscript treasures rescued from the strange place of hiding, and the five more filled with paintings and other art relics from the same cave, had been deposited safely in the British Museum.'

During the next twenty years the Chinese and the Japanese were able to obtain more of the Dun Huang manuscripts, although many of these were pilfered and ended up being sold in local markets. In 1920, White Russians desecrated the caves, making fires in some of them and carving graffiti on the walls. We can only speculate on what the Red Guards would have done to the manuscripts had they still remained in the caves in the 1960s and 1970s. Mercifully, the cave paintings and sculptures were untouched during the Cultural Revolution. Under the aegis of UNESCO, the caves are well cared for and protected today. The paths worn smooth by countless pilgrims over the centuries are now trodden by the inquisitive, irreligious visitor.

There were vivid depictions of the Buddha's early life painted on the walls – the miracles of his childhood, the scenes of his youthful pleasures and the tragic encounters that called him to higher things. The paintings and sculptures are for the most part miraculously preserved by the dryness of the climate and the care and attention over the centuries of a long line of pious monks. The murals on the walls and ceilings of the caves portray scenes of religious processions, of Paradise, with contrasting scenes of evil teeming with demons and monsters. Other paintings symbolize the various forces of nature that render man helpless: sandstorms and natural disasters set against towering mountain backdrops with malevolent, dark, cloud-filled skies. Where there is no landscape or other pictorial scene, the space is filled with 'the thousand Buddha decoration', row upon row of minutely stencilled Buddhas that have given the caves their name. In one vast cave there is a huge figure of the Buddha on which, it is said,

Abbot Wang lavished some of the largesse that was given to him by Aurel Stein.

My Chinese team colleagues were not impressed when we visited the caves. Lao Zhao was clearly bored and sniggered over the life-size figures of Buddha and his companions, and Li Weidong did not bother to walk round the caves at all. They had been taught at an early age to reject such artistic, religious symbolism as completely worthless. Their regard for these ancient, religious works of art was no higher than that of a person who surveys a wall papered with posters. All they cared about was that Wang was a traitor, Stein an arch-thief and that China's honour had been impugned.

'But surely Stein and the other turn-of-the-century archaeologists saved many priceless works of art,' I asserted. 'The twentieth century hasn't exactly been peaceful in Xinjiang, Professor. Look at the destruction caused by the rebellion of General Ma, the Cultural Revolution, the Muslim abomination of painted works of art, the apathy and ignorance of farmers and insensitive irrigation projects, not to mention earthquakes. Weren't these foreigners preserving your works of art for future generations?'

I normally try to avoid discussing anything controversial, as far as politics are concerned; when in China I do not hold an opinion on anything. The Professor looked at me disdainfully. I was mouthing a time-worn argument.

'Whose generation? What generation? A Western generation? It's all a cover-up,' he said. 'You Westerners say that you stole from us to preserve these relics for the future. But just think how many priceless antiquities were destroyed when you British bombed Berlin in the Second World War and the museum received seven direct hits. What kind of preservation is that? And anyway, who are you to preserve our culture? If we wish to destroy our property, then we have an absolute right to destroy it. No, the so-called archaeologists who came here at that time were thieves. Terrible thieves. And Stein was the biggest thief of them all.'

Lao Zhao nodded vigorously in the background and drew his finger across his throat and muttered, 'Wang.'

'What about Hedin?'

The Professor paused to consider for a moment. 'Hedin was different. He put the desert on the map. He filled in the blank spaces.' He smiled. 'But even Hedin did a little stealing. He was a petty thief. We forgive Hedin.'

We wandered away from the caves through a dignified archway of desert poplar trees, *Populus diversifolia*, the ancient tree of the oases that thrives near the Caves of a Thousand Buddhas. We walked on and came upon a wild desert poplar that was covered all over in black hairless caterpillars that were rapidly denuding it of its fresh, green leaves.

The Professor turned to me with a wry smile and his eyes twinkled behind his thick-lensed spectacles. 'There,' he said, 'that's exactly what Stein did to Xinjiang. He stripped it of her beauty.'

From Dun Huang our return route led on to Hami, 660 miles to the north. The melons of Hami have long been, and still are, famous throughout China. In the past, Hami would send a yearly tribute to the old imperial court of China, which included a consignment of the famous fragrant Hami melons. They can be kept and eaten during the winter, and were so much appreciated in old Beijing that there was a popular saying which ran:

> With East Sea crabs and West Sea shrimps,
> Stand Turfan grapes and Hami melons.

On our arrival at Hami the Professor and I were invited to visit a melon farm. Mr Ma, the manager of the Government State Melon Cooperative told me that he harvests a staggering three crops a year of the unnaturally large melons. So often, fruit and vegetables in China seem to be overweight and oversized. My organic farming brain begins to question what they must have absorbed to turn them into such a perfect, unblemished state. How, I wondered, did they coax the vines into producing a crop three times in one year? I feel much safer eating, for example, an imperfectly shaped apple knowing that pesticide and chemical fertilizers have not been used. Not so these rotund and unmarked melons. They had little taste and their texture was like cotton wool.

We inspected the vines and politely praised Mr Ma for his superb managerial skills. Mr Ma was a little man, no more than five foot two. He sported enormous black-tufted eyebrows, of which he was extremely proud and which, no doubt, compensated for his lack of height. Their growth was so extreme that I idly wondered whether he applied the same fertilizers to his eyebrows as he did to his melons. Moreover, they were neatly rolled and curled at each corner so that they resembled the ears of a lynx.

As we wandered through the melons fields with Mr Ma I was distracted by the continual barking of dogs.

'Are they watch dogs?' I queried.

There was an embarrassed silence. A hand went up first to the left eyebrow, which was twirled like a roll-your-own cigarette, and then to the right, which got the same treatment. Mr Ma seemed to be fine-tuning a radio aerial to acquire a 'correct' answer. He stared at me, sizing me up.

'He's not a journalist,' the Professor said dryly.

'It's a dog farm. We farm them for food.'

Mr Ma smiled, hesitatingly at first and then when he saw that I had not reacted, his smile broadened into a grin. A grin of relief.

'Very good eating,' said the Professor. My good friend the Professor loves his food almost as much as he loves his television set.

'Can I see them?' I asked.

After a moment's hesitation I was led away to the far end of the farm, a walk of about twenty minutes. There, behind a high wire fence on a patch of land that covered almost half an acre, were at least 150 dogs. Some were in pup. Others were just about to whelp. All of them seemed reasonably well and were the same nondescript breed and colour.

'This is a sideline,' said the manager. 'My perk for running the melon farm. It does very well, we sell many dogs to the Hami people.'

I blanched as my imagination conjured up a dog steak surrounded by ornately sliced, chemically cultivated melons. I have only once been offered dog meat in China. At a banquet to celebrate the end of one of our expeditions I was told that a special dish had been prepared in my honour. It was carried in with pride on a silver platter and when the lid was taken off it was dog meat. I have eaten many odd things in the strangest surroundings. But as a dog lover this was a real test. I did not want, for diplomatic reasons, to upset my hosts. On the other hand, I certainly did not want to eat dog. I was given a Pekinese-size leg, and ate the tiniest piece while at the same time offering up prayers seeking forgiveness from all my beloved Sallys and Jaspers that have moved on. Is it because a dog is a carnivore that makes the eating of its flesh so repellent?

The oasis of Hami is referred to in Chinese history as far back as the first century of the Christian era, and was then known as I-ku. Six hundred years later it was under the domination of the Uighurs, a people whose origin is shrouded in mystery, but who left strong traces of their civilization through a wide area of Central Asia. They were great oasis makers who explored and developed the water resources of the Gobi desert, and their culture flourished in the district of Hami, or Kumul, as they themselves call it. By the sixteenth century they had been converted to Islam and were ruled by a monarch or Khan who was known as the King of the Gobi.

From time immemorial, north-western China has been a theatre of war. Various people have fought over the immense areas that later became known by the names of Dzungaria and Eastern Turkestan until united under the common name of Xinjiang (New Frontier). In 1759 the area fell to China under Emperor Chien Lung. In 1867 the renowned conqueror Yakub Beg wrested the province from China and ruled Xinjiang from Kashgar. Nine years later China reconquered the province under the energetic General Tso Tsung-tang, and Yakub Beg committed suicide. Tso Tsung-tang's achievement was a great one. He had won by conquest an area of over 1,250,000 square kilometres and his lines of communication were 2,500 kilometres long. When China became a republic in 1911, a mandarin of the old school, Yang Tseng-hsin, was appointed the governor-general of Xinjiang and violently quashed a number of rebellions in the province.

During those early years of the twentieth century the last stage of 'the great game' between Russia and British-ruled India was being played out and Xinjiang, strategically placed between Mongolia and the Himalayas, was an important buffer zone that, after the Russian Revolution, the Russians might have conquered and incorporated into the USSR. The reason they didn't was due to Yang's vigilance, shrewdness and tact. He was murdered at a banquet in 1928 and his successor Chin Shu-jen, a man from humble origins, provoked rebellion and war within Xinjiang through a mixture of misgovernment, greed and oppression. In five years he crippled the province and left it desolated. He also broke all formal links with Beijing. Throughout this time the value of money fell swiftly and the peasants were cruelly taxed and exploited by Chin's havoc-creating horde of ruffian soldiers. Discontent and lawlessness increased. Rebellion was in the air and the spark that set it off occurred in Hami. Chin abolished the ancient monarchy that had ruled the kingdom of Hami for hundreds of years and instituted an agricultural policy that confiscated the best farmlands for his followers. When a young Han Chinese tax-collector seduced an Uighur woman in Hami rebellion broke out under the banner of Islam. Chin's army suppressed the rebellion with a ferocious barbarity.

In 1931 the leaders of the Uighurs and other Muslim minority groups appealed to a young Muslim Chinese general, Ma Chung-Ying, to come to their aid. He collected about 500 men and with incredible bravery marched the great distance from Anshi in Gansu Province to

Hami in Xinjiang in the middle of a hot summer month through a waterless desert with inadequate supplies. The conflicts continued to rage throughout Xinjiang and then in January 1933 the Muslim Uighurs and the other tribal peoples who had joined them attacked Urumqi, slaughtering every Chinese person they encountered.

Gates and doors were barricaded and with the help of some White Russian émigrés who had fled from Stalin's brutalities, the forces of Ma Chung-Ying were repulsed. On 21 February, they attacked again and savage fighting took place in the western suburbs of the city. No one was spared. Uighur prisoners were not shot, they were tortured to death. Six thousand Uighur inhabitants of Urumqi were slaughtered, but the forces of Ma did not hold on to their conquest. Twenty-four hours later they were driven out of the city by reinforcements under the leadership of the White Russians and Ma Chung-Ying attacked Urumqi for a third time.

Throughout the remainder of the 1930s and through the 1940s, instability, religious and racial tension, intrigue and terror were the sad plight of Urumqi and much of Xinjiang. Then after a brief peaceful interlude under the Chinese Nationalist government there was more savage fighting until the Communists came to power and established relative stability, although the Cultural Revolution was carried through in Xinjiang with considerable severity.

From Hami we travelled on 400 miles to the village of Tikar, whose name means the 'Last Prayer' in Uighur, on the assumption that this is where you will say your last prayer before entering the Gashun Gobi. I wanted to return to Urumqi via Tikar because a check-point had been constructed there to monitor entry into the Lop Nur Wild Camel National Nature Reserve.

Tikar is situated on the very edge of a fertile area known as the Turfan depression, which lies below sea level. The setting sun, a bright-red ball suspended behind a dust haze, gave the village an insubstantial and ghostly appearance. Horse-drawn carts clip-clopped down metalled streets. The large mud houses looked prosperous and well maintained. Many sported tall, newly constructed, wooden double-entrance doors. The source of this obvious prosperity, the grape, grew everywhere. In the hazy light the fresh green leaves of the vines could be seen thriving in small irrigated plots all around the village. Through open doors they could be spotted growing in the courtyards of houses, providing welcome shade for their owners as well as a source of income. An exquisite, delicate perfume from the flowering vines hung in the dusty evening air. The contrast with the dead uniformity of the grey, shoddy blocks of flats in Hami and the polluted environment along the main road that we had recently followed could not have been sharper.

Every kind of vine flourishes in the Turfan depression, but the most prolific produce is a small, sweet, seedless variety of grape. It is also the best fruit for export, and Turfan raisins are eaten throughout the whole of north and central China. These celebrated vines are cultivated with short trunks and very long branches that stretch outward in all directions around the houses, supported by upright posts.

The fertility of the soil is due to a remarkable irrigation technique known as the *karez* system. Long lines of earthworks stretch across the wastes of Turfan as though thrown up by giant moles. The mounds are hollow in the centre and this opening leads down to an underground passage. Far below is a water-channel that conducts the melted mountain snows to the torrid fields waiting to be irrigated. The nearer to the mountains, the deeper is the *karez* and at its start the water may be fifteen metres below the surface. At its final opening it flows almost at ground level and is as cool as when it left the hills. We went to a *karez* undergoing repair: four men working under a mound, excavating spoil with a donkey hauling it out on a pulley system. The expense of caring for the *karez* system is heavy but the Turfan area produces such a phenomenal crop of fruit, grapes, raisins, grain and cotton that the time and expense appears to be justified.

Near each house in Tikar was a spacious building, the walls of which were made with sun-dried bricks laid so as to form a lattice-work that allows the wind to blow through. These are known as *chung-chi* or grape-drying halls, and are only in use for a few weeks in each year when the grapes are being dried. During that short time they are full of branched poles, hung over with thousands of bunches of the seedless grapes. The passage of the sun-heated air through the lattice-work is all that is necessary to dry the fruit. If the bunches were exposed to the direct action of the sun, both the colour and flavour would be spoilt. The dreaded scorching wind that sweeps across the depression is exactly right for the drying process and a week or ten days completes it.

During the long summer months, Tikar and the surrounding area form one of the hottest places on earth, when the temperature can register 55 °Celsius in the shade. Between May and August many of the inhabitants retire underground, even though their houses have long verandas and spacious, airy rooms. In most of their interior courtyards there is an opening that leads by a flight of steps to a deep dug-out or underground apartment. Here are comfortable rooms and a *kang*, the raised bed or sitting area constructed from mud, which can be heated from underneath by burning charcoal, wood or dried animal dung during the freezing winter months. Many people eat and sleep underground in the very hot weather and only emerge at sunset. These underground chambers are not healthy as there is little or no ventilation. The sudden chill of a dug-out on a perspiring body can result in fever.

In the 1960s, many of Tikar's present Uighur inhabitants had been moved 500 miles from a village called Sringar when it was taken over as part of the Lop Nur nuclear test site. Lao Zhao had friends in Tikar and it was possible that descendants of guides recruited in Sringar by Sven Hedin were among them. The Tikar people had in the past shot wild camels and I was keen to discover whether they had abandoned their traditional winter sport.

Lao Zhao took us to the house of his friend, Torde Ahun. A portly man of about 60, wearing a black-and-white skull cap and a traditional

Uighur cloak, he led us courteously into his palatial house. We all squatted on his large *kang* that was covered with colourful locally woven rugs.

'When I first came here they could only afford grass mats,' said Zhao with a throaty laugh. 'Just look at them now, they're all very rich.'

Giggling, clear-faced, round-eyed girls of all heights and ages wearing headscarves, long shifts and thick sagging stockings peered at us from behind an open door. They were pretty, almost European in appearance, and would have passed unremarked anywhere in Central Europe. Egging each other on, the more daring girls sidled into dark recesses in the room, their droopy stockings indicating a huge untapped market for suspenders. They stared at us and especially me, as we tucked into chicken, mutton, rice, nan bread and tomatoes. We chop-sticked our way through as much of this as we could and finally, when replete, sprawled out on the *kang* to sleep.

Next morning, to everybody's delight, we discovered that Torde Ahun's grandfather was Ordek, Sven Hedin's famous guide. He was delighted when we told him that we had met his relatives Abdu Sadik and Niazhan and that we had visited Ordek's mausoleum.

We were later introduced to Torde's relative Sadiq, a nephew of one of the boatmen on Hedin's 1934 expedition. Sadiq, a quiet, earnest Muslim, whose ambition was to make the pilgrimage to Mecca, was quite overwhelmed when I managed to show him a photocopy of a sketch made by Hedin of his uncle. The result was much mutual back-slapping, hilarity and numerous group photographs.

Sadiq, however, had another claim to fame. He had been fined 20,000 Yuan ($2000) for shooting a wild camel in the Gashun Gobi. It emerged later that Lao Zhao was treated as a local hero in Tikar because he had caught two young wild camels in 1972 in the Gashun Gobi and brought them out alive, an incredibly difficult thing to do. One of them, a male, is still alive in Beijing Zoo.

Having said farewell to the friendly Uighurs of Tikar, we skirted round the Turfan depression along an unmade road that eventually connected with the main road to Urumqi. It is claimed that the lowest part of the Turfan depression is the deepest dry area in the world. In contrast, to the north of the depression, the snow-capped peaks of Bogd Ola (Mount of God) tower to heights of over 19,000 feet and mark the highest part of the Tien Shan. In the centre of these uncompromising surroundings, Turfan city and its surrounding villages, of which Tikar is one, lie on a fertile island in a wilderness of sand, its shores lapped by grit and gravel and harassed by sandstorms of incredible ferocity. This division between arid desert and fruitful land is as defined as that between shore and ocean.

On the final day of May we eventually returned to Urumqi having successfully completed our expedition and the survey of the southern boundary of the proposed Lop Nur Reserve. In addition to the discovery of 'Kum Su', we had seen over 160 wild Bactrian camels out of a total world population of approximately 900.

Some months later, I learnt of the journey of Lao Zhang, when he had attempted to return to Ruoqian via Hongliugou with Usuman and our camels. Usuman, who roamed the Arjin Mountains with his flocks, knew the remote gullies and valleys reasonably well. But Lao Zhang, the town-dweller from Ruoqian, was not a mountain expert. They had left together but Usuman had forged ahead, leaving Lao Zhang far behind. When I next met Lao Zhang he told me what had happened.

'Usuman had gone on ahead and I was attempting to follow his camels' tracks. I stopped to rest and sat at the foot of a mound and leant my head against soft sand. I must have fallen asleep because when I opened my eyes the sun was low on the horizon. I realized with alarm that I must have been following the footprints of wild camels and not Usuman's because I was way off course.

'After the sun had set, the cold of the desert gripped me. I knew that if I was lost for more than a few days I would die of thirst. I had to keep the mountains to the north of me, but without Usuman as a guide I had no idea of the exact route that I should take. I rode on, my tethered camels following behind me, but still I could not pick up the tracks of Usuman's camels.

'As the hours went by the spirits, which walk by night in the desert, approached me. One came so close to me that it brushed my arm and I turned aside to escape it. A little later on it appeared in front of me again, so close that my hand shot out to push it away, but my hand met with no resistance.

'There were strange noises in the sand-hills but I shut my ears to them and rode on, only knowing the rough direction I should be taking.

'At last a faint gleam of grey light in the eastern sky showed me that dawn was near. Tired, I lay down to sleep. When I awoke four of my twelve camels had disappeared. For three days I continued aimlessly wandering until my water ran low. I followed a wild animal track in the hope that I would discover a spring, but the only water I could find was totally salt. On the fifth day, weak and without water, I lay down in the foothills.

'As the long hours passed, the burning sun seemed to sap the moisture through every pore of my skin until I felt thirst not only in my dry throat but throughout my whole body. A craving for water, which became more and more urgent, tormented my whole system. It cried out for the sight, the smell and the feeling of moisture. Then I lost consciousness.

'By chance, three members of a survey team were surveying a valley in the Arjin Mountains. God was with me because they found me on the point of death, gave me water and saved my life. The chances of finding anyone alive in that terrible desert are infinitesimal.'

On our arrival in Urumqi we were given another piece of disquieting news. Illegal gold miners had entered the Aqike valley in the centre of the Reserve from Dun Huang to the east. Sven Hedin had described the Aqike valley as 'the heartland of the wild Bactrian camel' and it provides the winter grazing ground for many of the wild Bactrian camels in Lop Nur.

Now, apparently, groups of miners were fighting over perceived but non-existent territorial rights. The miners were in the valley quite illegally, and had set home-made land mines near saltwater springs to blow up the wild Bactrian camel when it came out of the desert on its migratory search for water. The remains of these poor animals were collected by these largely impoverished men to serve as a source for food. I passed this information on to the provincial authorities and the State Environment Protection Agency (SEPA), China's equivalent of a Ministry of the Environment. Alas, I could do no more.

The auspices for the future of the Aqike valley were ominous. Unknown to me at the time, other more sensitive areas of the Reserve were even more at risk.

4

Take Flight and Follow

And that inverted bowl we call the sky
Whereunder, crawling cooped we live and die!

Edward Fitzgerald, *Omar Khayyam*

The presence of Kazakhs in this remote part of China is an
interesting story. Kazakh herdsmen like Usuman had been with
me on a number of expeditions and the Kazakh Ali Abutalerp from
Aksai has over the years been a great supporter of our fight to save the
wild Bactrian camel.

I knew that under Stalin and his policy of forced collectivization,
the Kazakh nomads in what is now Kazakhstan had been forcibly
settled in a most distressing way. Transferred hastily and without any
preparation for an alien way of life and method of farming, the nomadic
livestock breeders did not have the expertise to run collective farms.
This disastrous policy resulted in a 50 per cent decrease in the Kazakh
population. They declined from approximately four million to one and
three-quarter million as a result of death by starvation, mass execution
or, in the case of about a tenth of that number, by an exodus to other
countries in the region.

How did the Kazakh nomads in China fit into the human catastrophe that had afflicted Kazakh nomads further to the west? What had brought Kazakhs to the Arjin Mountains south of the Lop Nur Reserve and the forbidding Gashun Gobi, when their spiritual home was in the Altai Mountains over 2,000 miles to the north? Those magnificent mountains straddle Kazakhstan and Mongolia and many Kazakhs have lived in western Mongolia for centuries. So why should an isolated pocket of Kazakhs be living in Aksai town and Annanba village far to the south in Gansu Province in China?

By a strange coincidence I had recently received a number of letters from a correspondent who lives in Taipei. He had read my book, *The Lost Camels of Tartary*, and wrote to me to comment on a number of points that it raised. He was not a Kazakh but a Mongol of the Torgut clan, who are referred to by the Russians as Kalmuks and whose lineage extends back to Wangkidan, a rival of Genghis Khan. In the late eighteenth century, having been persecuted on religious grounds in their homeland in the Volga region of Russia and forced to accept the Orthodox faith, the Torguts sought asylum with the Manchu emperors in China, who were Buddhists and co-religionists. After a great trek they settled in the Altai area and obtained protection from the Manchu emperor. They were allowed to establish clan titles such as 'Prince', one of whom was an ancestor of my correspondent.

This man wrote:

If you have read *Seven Years in Tibet* you will recall that there is a brief mention by the author, Mr Harrer of his meeting with a family of Mongolian refugees. Here he is referring to my family. We had met him in Lhasa in Tibet in 1950 after an unbelievably hellish trek from Tsaidam [*a marshy area, 100 miles south of the Arjin Mountains on the Tibet Plateau*] where my family had been forced to flee from the Communists.

The worst memory for me was that we had to abandon a young female camel near the top of a long steep mountain pass some four days' march from Lhasa. The poor beast, having covered that terrible wasteland and many a treacherous high pass under heavy load had by now exhausted her last ounce of strength and knelt down and refused to rise. I can still hear her pathetic cries when our guide tried in vain to force her to stand up by beating her head with a stick. What right did we have to work her to collapse and leave her to die on a cruel mountain pass? This haunting memory, this feeling of guilt, will remain with me until the day I die.

When we were in Tsaidam we were told stories of an earlier Kazakh exodus across Lop Nur and that a punitive detachment was sent after them. This exacted a heavy price. Thousands of Kazakhs and their herds died, but I was so young and I am not too sure of the exact circumstances.

This prompted further investigation on my part. Especially as in another letter, my correspondent related that:

The desert town of Ta-shi [*near Aksai, where the Kazakhs live today*] is of special interest to me. After leaving the motor highway, it was the starting point, of our 1949 exodus shortly before the 'liberation' [*by the Communists*] of China. Our route took us first to the Tsaidam basin and then up and across the freezing wasteland to Tibet, all on camel back. Even to this day I still vividly recall the dear faces of the shaggy animals that carried us to safety. I feel deeply that we owe a great lot to their suffering and sacrifice. Maybe that is why I was so moved by your compassion towards the Bactrian camels. I can only hope that my shaggy companions have all been reborn to some better form of life and at least become sheltered and much-loved house pets, if not happy human beings.

So although my correspondent had indeed made the journey to Tibet when fleeing from the Communists with his family, I had still not discovered the exact reason why some Kazakhs had remained in the northern foothills of the Arjin Mountains.

After many discussions with Kazakh friends and much research into books and papers, the full story emerged. It appears that in 1948, the year before my correspondent and his family had made their epic journey, 20,000 Kazakh families with their herds of camels, sheep, horses and all their possession set out to cross Xinjiang Province, or as my correspondent prefers to call it in defiance of Chinese domination, 'Eastern Turkestan'. This is the old name for Xinjiang, still used today by Uighur and Kazakh Nationalists to rally support for an independent homeland. They set out on this tragic but unwavering exodus from their Communist-dominated homeland in the Altai Mountains and were joined by other Kazakhs living in the Tien Shan in Xinjiang.

Prior to this mass migration the Kazakhs both in Xinjiang and in the Altai had lived through turbulent times. In the 1930s they had been persecuted by the Chinese Red Beards, a terror militia under the direct instructions of the Nationalist government governor of Urumqi. These Red Beards had fled from Manchuria after the Japanese invasion in the 1930s. They had come to Xinjiang via Russia and en route had been thoroughly indoctrinated by the Communists. They were then recruited by the Nationalist government's Manchurian-born governor in Xinjiang, who was an appointee of the Nationalist government in Beijing.

One Kazakh refugee has described what these years were like to Godfrey Lias, an author who described the epic migration in 1956:

> The Red Beards stole our beasts and raped our wives and daughters before killing them. No one could understand what they said because they came from Manchuria where men speak in an uncouth dialect. They were murderers and cut-throats as well as thieves. If, when a man smiled he showed a gold tooth, they would murder him for the gold that was in it.

Because of their constant harassment by the Red Beards, who were given that name because they dyed their beards red, the Kazakhs in China switched allegiance to the Russian Soviets, who by this time had gained power in Outer Mongolia and the Kazakhstan Altai Mountain region. The Soviets had plans to conquer Xinjiang and oust the Nationalist Chinese from the province. So they gave the Kazakhs weapons and ammunition and encouraged them to rebel against the Red Beards and the Urumqi governor. However, within Nationalist China, the Chinese Communists were rapidly gaining power and overwhelming the Nationalists. When the Kazakhs saw that the Chinese Communists were winning the battle against both the Chinese Nationalists and the

Russian Soviets, they switched their allegiance to the Chinese Communists. This accord was short-lived, for the Red Beard terror militia had themselves switched allegiance to the Chinese Communists.

In this complex situation of short-term alliances, the Kazakhs realized that no side could be trusted, and that all hands were against them. From 1946 they tried desperately to defend their way of life, first against Russian attacks from the north and west, and then as Communism swept across China, from the east as well.

Their forces never numbered more than 30,000 men. For arms, they had some rifles, some machine-guns and a considerable number of hand grenades, but never enough of everything. Some fought with swords or even pieces of wood with nails in them. Their enemies of whatever political persuasion had artillery, armoured cars, tanks and aeroplanes. By 1948 their position had become untenable and the Kazakhs held a mass meeting at which it was decided to abandon their traditional homelands in both the Altai Mountains and the Tien Shan in China. The great trek south began.

In addition to continual attack and pursuit by Communist troops, the nomads, under the leadership of one Qali Beg, suffered intense hardship. Their journey took them over the Tien Shan – the snow-covered Heavenly Mountains – whose passes lie at 18,000 feet. They then dropped down to sea level and, to avoid the major city of Korla, were forced to cross the 16,000-foot Kuruk Mountains – the Dry Mountains – which form the north-western boundary of the Lop Nur Reserve. The vegetation there is sparse and patchy and there is not a drop of drinkable water.

The Kazakh migrants then entered the fearful Gashun (Bitter) Gobi, and crossed the Lop Desert, near the lake of Lop Nur. This is a hazardous undertaking as we experienced when we crossed this area on foot in 1996. On this segment of their great trek, thousands of Kazakhs and their livestock died of thirst.

A letter written by one of the survivors of the exodus spells out the plight of these nomads during the great trek from the Altai: 'At the time of our crossing we have suffered much by the waterless. We have used the urine of men and women, the blood of animals instead of water. By the waterless we have lost many of our animals except camels.'

After they had passed Lop Nur, the travel-weary, decimated band of nomads reached the Arjin Mountains. There they linked up with a fellow countryman, Hussein Tajji, who was living at Timurlik near Ghaz Kol, a lake in the Arjin Mountains that is long, straight and narrow and lies 8,000 feet above sea level.

They wintered with Hussein at Timurlik, a wide grassy area about twenty miles long with high mountains to the south and lower mountains leading to the Lop Nur depression to the north. The yurts of the Kazakhs were widely scattered along a marshy, year-round stream that flowed into the alkaline Ghaz Kol lake. Hussein generously put his possessions and livestock at the disposal of Qali Beg and his tattered survivors.

But the new arrivals could not let go of their fears just yet. They could see that Hussein Tajji was living in a virtual Shangri-la, as yet completely unaffected by the clash between Communist ideology and old China that was being played out around him. When they learnt that Communist troops had captured Dun Huang, the strategic township that lies to the east of the Desert of Lop, near the famous Caves of a Thousand Buddhas, their fears increased.

Shortly after Qali Beg and his fellow Kazakhs arrived at Ghaz Kol, two of Hussein's men returned to his encampment from Dun Huang. They told how the Communists, hearing that two Kazakhs from Ghaz Kol were in town, had sent for them and welcomed them, saying that Kazakhs had nothing to fear from a Communist regime. After entertaining them, the Communists told them to return to Ghaz Kol, carrying with them an invitation to Hussein to send delegates – the more the better – to a meeting of 'people's representatives' to be held in Lanzhou, the capital of Gansu Province in which Dun Huang is situated. The two men added that the Communists had told them it was quite safe for any Kazakh to visit Dun Huang, provided that he wore a certain badge. They had been given a quantity of these badges bearing the portrait of Mao Tse-tung. The messenger added ominously that anyone caught without the badge would be imprisoned. Any Kazakh seen carrying a weapon would be shot.

'The invitation is a trick,' Qali Beg said bluntly to Hussein Tajji, who reported it to Godfrey Lias. 'Once you send delegates to the so-called conference they will never return. They will be shot. The Chinese will then send troops here to confiscate all your livestock. We know how these people operate. We have seen it all before.' After much discussion, it was decided to send forty men to Dun Huang to make further enquiries about the true situation and return with a full report.

When the men had left, Qali Beg set guards secretly on the mountain passes between Ghaz Kol and Dun Huang to ensure that no one travelled through the mountains without their permission. After a few days, a messenger from Dun Huang reached one of these look-out posts. He said that the leader of the forty men had told him to tell Hussein Tajji that he and his men had been well received. The leader of the Communists had praised them, saying that their presence showed that the Kazakhs were beginning to understand the true nature of the Communist revolution. This messenger added that the forty had been offered lorries to take them and other delegates to a 'meeting of reconciliation' that had been organized in Lanzhou, the capital of Gansu, as it was too far for them to travel there on horseback. He added that he had been told to warn the Kazakhs gathered around Ghaz Kol that none would be admitted into the city unless they were wearing the badges that had been sent to them. He concluded by saying that the passes around Dun Huang were full of Communist troops.

This messenger was shortly followed by two more who said that they came with another message from the leader of the forty men. They began by saying that the Kazakhs should surrender all their weapons as there was now peace throughout China and that the conflict with the Chinese Nationalists was over. Qali Beg was suspicious and ordered his men to question them closely. It seemed unlikely that such a conciliatory message would have been sent from their kinsmen in Dun Huang. He was right. It became clear that the two men were Communist spies.

They were summarily shot.

The days passed and no further news came from the forty men. Anxiety mounted in Hussein's encampment. The wives and families were clamouring for Hussein to send out another party to discover what had happened to them. So two more men were sent to Dun Huang, wearing Mao badges and concealing automatic weapons under their clothes. They managed to evade the Communist soldiers guarding routes into the city and by chance arrived at Dun Huang just as the forty Kazakhs were being trucked through the city gate, bound hand and foot. When the lorries stopped, Qali Beg's two men managed to speak to one of the captured men. He warned them of Communist plans to invade the Kazakh encampment and capture Qali and Hussein.

Five unexpected visitors were over-wintering at the Timurlik encampment. One was Douglas Mackiernan, the former American vice-consul in Urumqi, who doubled as a CIA agent. He had escaped from the city on 11 September 1949, the day that the Communist army captured Urumqi, and had fled initially to the north of Hami, where he met up with Usuman Batur, the charismatic leader of the Kazakhs from whom he sought help and protection.

Mackiernan was convinced that if a Third World War were to break out, which he firmly believed would happen shortly, Usuman would be a key anti-Communist leader in this turbulent part of Central Asia. He had travelled with another American, Frank Bessac, a Fulbright scholar who had been carrying out anthropological research in north-west China. On 29 October 1949 they had both set out with three White Russians from the south of Hami to cross the Gobi on horseback. Following the camel trade road, they had skirted Dun Huang, climbed the Arjin Mountains and arrived at Timurlik on 29 November 1949. This journey of 500 miles had, according to Bessac, taken them exactly one month. Having crossed the area myself, I am surprised their horses survived so easily. There are, for the most part, only saltwater springs on the route. Neither horses nor humans could survive long on that. When I asked Bessac about this in 2007 he replied, 'Could there have been more water available fifty years ago? We did find water just about every evening. Some was brackish.' However, he did add that his report of the journey was deliberately 'fudged' in places to confuse the Chinese.

Mackiernan knew Qali well and told him that he and Bessac were attempting to cross Tibet and enter India to escape from the Communists. He asked Qali for guides and camels to carry their kit. Qali agreed to help them, but asked in return that Mackiernan would make sure that the plight of the Kazakhs in Kazakhstan and China under Communist domination became known to the outside world.

As related by Godfrey Lias, Mackiernan agreed and then reached in his pocket, pulled out a five-dollar bill and tore it in half with a flourish. 'Put your thumbprint on your half. I'll do the same on mine. When we're re-united in Delhi, we'll join the two halves together.'

Mackiernan had elicited from Qali his own decision to lead the Kazakhs over Tibet and into India. However, before they set out a dramatic incident occurred. Spring had arrived in Timurlik and Mackiernan decided it was time to attempt the Tibet crossing. He had worked out they required fifteen camels and two horses, which needed to be specially trained to eat meat when no other fodder was available. It was inevitable that there would not be enough grass and other foliage to keep the camels moving forward. Camels are not native to this area and the Tibetan nomads depend on yaks that can lick lichen off the rocks for nourishment. The Kazakhs pointed out that meat-eating camels and horses were rare and that they would ask twice the normal price for them. Mackiernan agreed to pay this price in gold, which he had strapped in a belt around his body.

When the horses and camels were delivered, Mackiernan was angered at their poor condition. He harangued the Kazakh elders and was summoned to an audience with Hussein Tajji. The Kazakh leader berated the two Americans for gross ingratitude. Had they not been the guests of the Kazakhs for almost four months? How dared Mackiernan abuse the tribal 'white beards'? Mackiernan had thrown his weight about when in effect he should have patiently bargained for stock of a higher quality. Hussein relented and did in the end provide them with animals in a tougher condition – after he had been given forty-five ounces of gold.

On 20 March 1950 Mackiernan and Bessac set off with fifteen fresh meat-eating camels, two meat-eating horses, the three White Russians and two Kazakh guides. It is related in Frank and Susanne Bessac's book, *Death on the Chang Tang* how meat was fed to their camels on the journey:

> A big bull yak planted himself in our path, challenging our way. He was over six feet tall at the shoulders with long sharp horns. Tibetan nomads hold wild, old bulls in great awe and believe that they are protected as special property of the Gods. Without much thought Doug [*Mackiernan*] fired at the magnificent beast. It was so large we could not turn him over. We cut off some slabs of meat, then left the rest for the vultures that had already spotted the kill. They hovered close with piercing, gimlet eyes. Early in spring after a hard winter the bull had not an ounce of fat on him. The meat was too tough to cook at that altitude. We fed the meat to our camels. To see a camel, with wild frenzied eyes devour a chunk of bloody flesh is a horrible sight. A cold wind whipped by. I felt uneasy. Had we broken some powerful taboo? To kill so magnificent an animal for shoe leather was wasteful, desperate act. We were so small, so insignificant in this vast landscape. Would our animals survive with the inadequate fodder?

A film produced in 1942 by Ernst Schaefer called *Geheimnis Tibet* (Secret or Mysterious Tibet) shows Tibetan Post Service ponies being fed on blood and meal to give them plenty of strength. So both Kazakhs and Tibetans trained camels and horses to eat meat.

A week later the two guides returned, telling Qali Beg that they had been dismissed as soon as they reached the Tibet pre-invasion border. If the story is true, it was a disastrous decision on Mackiernan's part.

The two guides knew a route across the frontier where no guards were stationed. The route the two Americans followed led straight to a border post where there were Tibetan guards on the look-out for brigands. Lhasa had been notified by the CIA that two Americans were attempting to cross Tibet and that they should be allowed entry. However, this message did not reach the border post in time. Mackiernan and two of the White Russians were shot dead. Bessac escaped unharmed and with the wounded Vasili Zvansov, the third White Russian, reached Lhasa. Both of them were eventually repatriated to the United States from India. Bessac subsequently published an article in *Life* magazine, which told his version of the Tibetan crossing, although the route taken and the dates of their journey were deliberately falsified. *(See Appendix 1)*

Back at Timurlik, the Kazakhs migrants had been joined by Usuman Batur, who had been the driving force behind the initial Kazakh uprising against the Communists in the Altai. Outnumbered and outgunned, he had repeatedly taken the fight to the enemy on horseback, but when the Communists were able to call up Russian-manned aircraft that strafed and bombed his horsemen from the air, he could do so no longer. He was forced to flee following the same hazardous route that Qali Beg had taken across the Kuruk Mountains, the Gashun Gobi and the Lop Desert.

On his arrival, he took command of the 3,000 men, women and children who lived with their flocks at the camp. There was no dispute. Usuman's reputation was such that any Kazakh in Central Asia would have followed him to the uttermost ends of the earth.

On 1 February 1951 a disaster occurred. Communist forces carried out a surprise attack with armoured vehicles on the Kazakhs camped at Timurlik around Ghaz Kol lake. The nomads fled with their flocks into the surrounding mountains where the Communist vehicles were immobilized. Although many families and their flocks escaped, the Communists captured two of their leaders.

Usuman Batur rode over the mountains firing an automatic weapon from the hip in an attempt to recapture his daughter who had been taken prisoner. Despite this courageous effort, he, too, was captured. This was a huge prize for the Communists. For years he had been the most feared resistance leader and there was a high price on his head. After six months of sustained torture and humiliation in Urumqi, during which he was periodically paraded through the streets with a placard round his neck that proclaimed, 'He boasted that he would deliver Turkestan from the Chinese, but he has not done so.' Usuman Batur was executed in public in August 1951. The people of Urumqi, including school children, were forced to witness the event.

The British consul in Urumqi at the time wrote:

> I watched with pain as Usuman Batur was led through the streets and lanes to be shot. His hair, beard and moustache were matted and his clothes were in a terrible condition. It was quite apparent that he had been tortured. He had bare feet and his hands were tied behind his back but in spite of this, his head was held high. On his face there was no sign of fear. He had not lost either his innate nobility or his courage and his behaviour and walk showed this quite clearly. In spite of his appearance, he did not seem to be going to his death. He looked like a young man, going to a wedding ceremony.

Usuman was not the only Kazakh leader who suffered this fate. Jamin Khan, a former finance minister of Xinjiang, was also captured at Ghaz Kol. He had been a popular minister with the Kazakhs. After his public execution, supporters set fire to trees on the hills that surrounded the Xinjiang capital. Many thousands of acres of timber were destroyed and the city was wreathed in a funerary pall of smoke for many days until the fires eventually burnt themselves out.

After the tragedy at Ghaz Kol, the surviving Kazakhs divided into groups around leaders of their choice. With Qali Beg, Hussein Tajji and others who had escaped death or capture, they broke camp and set out on the long march south over the formidable Tibet Plateau to an unknown land and a precarious future. Half of the men, women and children who set out on the formidable journey died. Nearly all of their already decimated flocks were lost. The survivors eventually reached India six and a half months later.

Hussein Tajji was quoted as saying before he departed that, 'It is better to die than to live like an animal. An animal looks to man as though he were God. It is not right that a man should look to other men in the same fashion.'

Not all the Kazakhs left Ghaz Kol. A small group decided to stay behind with their camels and their flocks in the Arjin Mountains near the Altai and Annanba villages. They were determined to try to make a life under the new Communist regime. Their descendants include Ali Abutalerp, Mr Mamil, Usuman, his delightful wife who gave me 'the hair of the dog', and the other camel herdsmen who followed me on my expeditions in the foothills of the Arjin Mountains.

5

Hie to the Deserts Wild

We were dreamers dreaming greatly in the man-stifled town,
We yearned beyond the sky-line where the strange roads go down.

Sir Hanns Vischer

Bilgee tossed back his head, pointed his camera up at the branch of an acacia tree festooned with brightly coloured, weaver birds' nests, and clicked the shutter.

'Got him,' he exclaimed with huge delight. 'I've got him.'

'And I think he's got you,' said Jasper Evans drolly as a jabbering Sykes monkey neatly deposited a sloppy faecal dollop cleanly onto Bilgee's head. It slithered slowly down his tee-shirt and then his trousers. The monkey had known exactly what it was doing. Its aim was precise and accurate.

'This must be a first,' I mused. 'Quite a headline, "Kenyan monkey plasters Mongol cameraman".'

Bilgee, who had been standing beside Jasper's picturesque tree-lined dam, home to birds and wildlife of all descriptions, recoiled in utter disgust. Leilei creased with laughter.

'Don't you laugh too soon, Leilei,' shouted Bilgee. 'It'll be your turn next.'

Jasper Evans' 30,000-acre ranch on Laikipia in northern Kenya provided a perfect setting for training both Chinese and Mongolians in nature reserve management skills. In particular, they were working together on completely neutral territory. Normally the Chinese are somewhat disdainful of the Mongols and the Mongols distrustful of the Chinese, but in Kenya both Chinese and Mongolians were faced with both a totally novel environment and different cultural problems. They rapidly came together as a team and friendships were forged.

Our charity, the Wild Camel Protection Foundation (WCPF) had, with the backing of the Zoological Society of London (ZSL), set up the two-week training programme. Jasper Evans, a WCPF co-trustee, had made available training facilities and accommodation on his ranch and Kate Rae, one of the managing trustees of the WCPF, and I had flown to Kenya to organize and participate in the course. ZSL had seconded an excellent instructor – the admirable and highly professional Tim Wacher, an expert in endangered species survival programmes who had worked for a number of years to save the rare oryx and gazelle in the Middle East and north Africa. In addition, the immensely affable Tim was a first-rate ornithologist, having written a book on east African birds, and he enlivened the course with his encyclopedic knowledge of Kenyan birds. On Jasper's ranch alone he identified 130 species.

The course proved a resounding success. Tim was primarily concerned with showing the trainees how to track and monitor wildlife, collate the information and store it on a computer's database using a GPS. The Chinese and Mongolians had been plucked out of a winter of -30 °Celsius and dropped into an African dry season, which hovered in the 35-plus range. So it was a climatic as well as a cultural shock for all of them. It also provided an opportunity for each participant to see what field methods were being used and how the monitoring of wildlife was recorded in the each country's nature reserve.

However, Mijjidorj (Mijji), director of the Great Gobi Specially Protected Area (SPA) Reserve 'A' (Gobi 'A'), our project director Bilgee and Mongolian Nature Ministry official Tserenbataa Tuya quickly picked up the basics. Phlegmatic, rosy-faced Mijji spoke more English than he let on. A shy, highly intelligent man of few words, his ever-sparkling eyes betrayed his agile and astute mind. During course sessions he would sit quietly and alert but saying very little. When question time arrived, he invariably asked the most pertinent question of the day.

In contrast, the pretty, vivacious Tuya, released from the bureaucratic corset of her ministerial responsibilities, blossomed under the African sun in an extraordinary fashion; frequently coquettish and cheeky, she displayed a wholly new side to her character that she had successfully concealed as a professional scientist. These three Mongol participants frequently succumbed when Jasper appeared at six o'clock with the sundowner bottle.

'Now come on, Mijji, you've had a hard day putting up with all these *wazungus* [white men]. It's time we relaxed together with a little drop of "whisk".'

Jasper's blandishments are not easy to resist, and a relaxation session invariably ensued. After drinks, supper and maybe a Mongolian song, the trio would retire to the tent that they shared. The late evening was frequently punctuated with shrieks of ribald Mongolian laughter.

Leilei and Deputy Zhang, who was the vice-director of the Lop Nur Reserve were the Chinese participants. They, too, mastered Tim's technical brief and much to their surprise discovered that the Mongolian scientists were more knowledgeable than they were on field surveys and recording wildlife data.

The course aimed to teach wildlife tracking and recording skills. Game abounded on Jasper's ranch and provided an opportunity to record giraffe, zebra, gazelles and impala. Each team member had a GPS on which he or she planned a route and then recorded their findings. These records could then be fed into a computer and valuable data stored that could identify trends and movements of the wild Bactrian camel at different times of year. Another prime aim of the workshop was to encourage the exchange of data between the two Reserve Headquarters.

Deputy Zhang was the maverick. A bespectacled, short, bland-faced city man, he was more used to pushing a pen than observing wildlife. His English was poor and he relied on Leilei for contact with the Mongolians and us. In the heat of the African sun he sported a belted raincoat and a peaked cap. This made him look as though he was on a short walk through Urumqi city streets rather than undergoing training in the African bush. A rolled umbrella would have completed the picture. For some reason, Zhang fascinated the wildlife. They homed in on this strange city-dweller with remarkable regularity. In spite of frequent warnings, Deputy Zhang had a perverse penchant for solitary expeditions into the bush. One moment he was with the group, the next he had vanished, all the time dressed in his strange apparel. No wonder by the end of the course, he had been chased by an elephant, dangerously alerted a snorting buffalo and was stopped by Tim in the very act of placing his foot on a lethal puff adder that was basking peacefully in the afternoon sun. Somehow he survived intact, never realizing just how narrowly he had been tempting fate.

The course carried forward the resolutions on joint country cooperation agreed at a Beijing conference five years earlier and ended with further Chinese and Mongolian statements of cooperative intent. In particular, each country issued invitations to the other to join wild Bactrian camel and wildlife surveys in their respective reserves.

As a final statement of international goodwill, the Mongolians and the Chinese volunteered to cook a farewell dinner. Deputy Zhang excelled as a dumpling cook and Mijji masterminded the mutton. With Jasper and sundry Kenyans providing the liquor, the evening ended appropriately with national sing-songs. This time it was Tuya who topped the trillers. She warbled like a songbird, with Mijji and Bilgee singing the appropriate male sections. To listen to traditional

Mongolian songs is to be transported to the vast steppe. The songs echo the chirrups and calls of the wonderful Mongolian bird-life. They are full of wistful longing, and Tuya's singing conjured up a hauntingly beautiful atmosphere that many of us will never forget.

We arranged for an expedition in Gobi 'A' to take place in March, shortly after the Mongolians had returned from Kenya. The Chinese were duly invited and I was to join them. At my express wish, the expedition was to be undertaken by domestic camel. At the very last minute the Chinese withdrew without explanation, so I was left to set off with the Mongolians towards and then over the remote Atis Mountains in the south-west corner of Gobi 'A' — along a route that was considered impassable for a four-wheel-drive vehicle.

Although the terrain was rugged and the mountains remote, there were no white spaces on the map. The Russians who were in control in Mongolia prior to the collapse of the Soviet Union were assiduous in their mapping, and highly trained and competent scientists visited the Gobi on an annual basis. My first visit to Gobi 'A' had been with Russian scientists in 1993 and I found their work and attention to detail impressive. Even so, the Atis Mountains had not been nearly so intensively surveyed for wildlife as other sectors of the Reserve and it was still possible that by travelling with camels we might discover a water point that had not been previously discovered. However, the area is not devoid of fresh water and unlike the Desert of Lop in China the wild camel does not have to rely on saltwater slush for survival.

Tsoijin, a retired ranger who was a legend in Mongolia for his exploits in the Gobi over a period of forty years, was to be our guide. This was wonderful news. The expedition could not have set out under more knowledgeable leadership.

Also in the team was Adiya, from the Institute of Biology in Ulan Bator, a chunky, tough, hard-working and immensely likeable young Mongolian scientist. Consistently cheerful and full of spirit, Adiya was the ideal companion. He had acquired a reputation for resolute endurance, having walked ninety kilometres on his own without food or water out of the Gobi 'A' to seek help when his vehicle had broken down. Without water the desert is nothing but a grave. Adiya ran out of water and survived the ordeal by drinking his own urine on the long trek. He arrived at the Reserve Headquarters having displayed all the remarkable virtues and strength of character of the traditional Mongol nomad. His contemporaries saw Adiya as a worthy successor to Tsoijin. They called him 'little Tsoijin'.

On my arrival Adiya enquired about what kit I needed.

'It's going to be cold,' Adiya said to me. 'You'll definitely need fur-lined boots. The best place to find them is in the Black Market.'

I grimaced, I knew the Black Market well.

A few years before, I had visited the market myself and I hadn't been prepared to find 10,000-plus Mongolians, possibly a third of Ulan Bator's population, packed into the tiny market square. One narrow hole in the wall doubled as both entrance and exit and to get in and out of the market during rush hour was a major undertaking. Unwittingly, I arrived at peak time. Having established with four black leather-jacketed Mongolian townies that I was attempting to move forwards and not backwards, I hooked onto two of them and allowed myself to be propelled through the wall.

Once inside the market, the only available option was to rotate clockwise around the square with the human flow. A few fortunates had found space to spread cheap trinkets on the ground near the wall, but towards the centre of the square, vendors were forced to stand their ground waving their goods above their heads. I was swept helplessly past knife-sellers, hat-sellers, boot-sellers, pot-sellers, sellers of gazelle skins, dog skins and even the skins of the highly endangered snow leopard. The joys of the free market economy had clearly broken out all over. A man holding out a round, grey rock tried to pass it off as a dinosaur egg. There were no market rules and not an official in sight. It was a pick-pockets' paradise, but as the average Mongolian's standard of living is not high there must have been meagre pickings in the pockets.

The human coil spiralled on and it was impossible to move in any other direction. When a circuit of the square was completed, the battle to escape began. But if that struggle against the surge of new arrivals was lost, another circuit had to be made. I just managed to escape by locking arms with two old men wearing brightly coloured *dels* (cloaks) and pork-pie hats. Dressed in my old tweed jacket we must have made an unusual threesome but respect for the 'old cloth', Mongolian and British, opened a path up before us. This market was definitely not a place for anyone prone to claustrophobia. As a permanent reminder of the experience I later discovered that the inside of my jacket pocket had been neatly slit with a sharp knife.

However, Adiya told me that the market had now been shifted to a new site that was spacious and open. It operated every day and not just on Sunday. So we drove out to the eastern side of the rapidly expanding city and soon I was at the boot market sellers' stalls. Adiya was right. No longer were items for sale waved overhead. Men and women were not now left to battle on their own. The market had metal stalls that were primly aligned in neat rows. No more did one fight and shove nor allow oneself to be swept around the tight little square. There was ample space.

After much deliberation I settled for a pair of felt boots. Although my feet are not large, Mongolian feet are much smaller and the felt boots were the only pair that I could wear in reasonable comfort.

At midday on 21 March Bilgee, Adiya and I left Ulan Bator on the 1,200-mile drive along roads of varying quality to Bayan Toroi, the headquarters of the Gobi 'A' from where the expedition into the Reserve was to take place. The previous evening we had loaded up with food in a remarkably well-stocked local supermarket. Much had changed in the ten years since I last prepared to set out on an expedition from Ulan Bator; at that time only one 'foreigners' store sold imported food. Now the shops were overflowing with goods and food from China, Korea and Japan.

Bilgee had arranged for a United Nations Development Programme (UNDP) vehicle to take the three of us to Bayan Toroi. Unfortunately, our driver completely lost his way on the dirt tracks three times and we eventually reached a wildlife ranger's *ger* at a place called Bayan Teg long after sunset. We only managed to wake the poor ranger's wife with prolonged and persistent blasts on the jeep's horn.

Mongol hospitality insisted that we were fed and watered despite the late hour. Mutton was cooked and Mongolian milk tea and fermented mares' milk passed round. Another hour had passed before we wriggled down in our sleeping bags like sardines in a tin, head to foot, toe to head, onto the wooden floor of the *ger*.

The other occupants of the *ger* consisted of the ranger, his wife and daughter, two young boys who lay sprawled asleep on a wooden bed and a very elderly man who was desperately thin. This poor soul was obviously dying and he lay on his back staring up at the wooden wheel that is the centre point of the *ger*'s roof. He inhaled heavily and gurgled and wheezed as his breath was expelled. Opposite him, seated on another bed, an old lady who I assumed to be his wife was sitting patiently staring at him. She neither ate nor uttered a word and seemed to be waiting for the moment when his last tortured breath left his body.

No sooner had we settled down on the floor, than the old man's throat emitted the most alarming rattle. This did not deter my Mongolian colleagues for a moment and soon they were fast asleep. On one side of me, Adiya began to snore loudly and lustily. On the other, the old man rattled away. It took a long time for sleep to carry me off.

When I woke, the canvas exterior flap, covering the interior wooden wheel of the *ger*, had been partly withdrawn and a shaft of brilliant dust-laden sunlight shone directly onto the face of the old man. His eyes were shut and his throat no longer rattled. Bathed in sunlight, his breathing had returned to normal.

Next day we drove on, moving down the steppes towards the Gobi desert and at dusk arrived at the *sum* (local government) headquarters of Bayan Toroi, where the head office of the Gobi 'A' was situated. Mijji and his intelligent, jolly, rosy-faced wife were there to greet us, as was young Dovchin, another member of the expedition.

That evening, Mijji and his wife invited us into their simple and sparsely furnished wooden home. Oiled with Johnny Walker Black Label, which I had brought with me from England, we plotted the route, intently studied the maps and made plans for the next day. Once again, the maps that we were poring over were Russian.

'They are the most reliable,' said Mijji softly when I questioned him on their origin.

This interested me because I always carried Russian maps with me when I went into the Gobi in China. This had not only annoyed the Professor in the past, but had amazed my other Chinese travelling companions. Procured from an unlikely source in Lithuania, they were far more accurate and detailed than the latest Chinese maps.

'How did the Russians know that this spring was here,' Professor Yuan Guoying would exclaim in astonishment, 'when our map shows absolutely nothing at all?'

I love maps, but for some people a map will never be more than a bland representation on paper of a section of the earth's surface, an inconsequential squiggle of lines that momentarily enlivens a boring geography lesson or in later life is produced to show where an aeroplane might be landing in a few hours' time. That modern technological marvel, the satellite navigation system, can never, for me, replace a really good and detailed map. For a person who travels on foot or at the natural pace of a camel, donkey or horse, it ceases to be merely a map. All of its detailed markings take on a vital significance. The technical lines by which mountains, lakes, rivers or roads are indicated become mental pictures that reveal the layout of a particular area in its entirety. A map throws up questions as well as answering them. The explorer is drawn towards the question marks and constantly seeks to find answers, a tiny island in a lake that is merely a dot on a patch of blue. Another speck marks a village; tightly knit contours indicate the steepness of the terrain ahead, and a stippled surface marks off a desert. The very few remaining blank spaces on maps, usually left in white, have always exerted an irresistible hold on any explorer's imagination. I am drawn towards these white areas as if pulled by a magnet. For me, a map has a hypnotic power.

Across the map of Central Asia the Great Gobi Desert covers the enormous space of six million square miles. This huge area never touches a seacoast, and presents a physical phenomenon without parallel on the face of the earth. Its northern reaches mark the exact spot on the globe that is farthest removed from any sea or ocean. This remoteness from any seaboard, combined with certain characteristics of the land surface, reduces the amount of rainfall to a minimum and accounts for the extremes of temperature during the winter and summer months. Such variance of temperature produces fierce winds, which sweep across the desert with a terrible force, blotting out the sun and carrying huge quantities of fine sand from one locality to another.

On other occasions there is the constant low moan of the all-prevailing wind. Then there is a total silence, a silence that is not disturbed by the sound of a single living thing. To be enveloped by total silence in an arena of lost horizons is a humbling experience. Light only from the sun, the moon and the stars, no sound except for the wind or the creak of a camel's loads as its bearer strides across limitless desert. What an immense privilege it is to have such an experience in our modern world of constant sound and artificial light.

In March, the month of our expedition, the silence of the desert and the low murmur of the wind can be turned within minutes into a blistering explosion of flying dust and sand; an incident that I was on another occasion to experience in the even more harsh and remote deserts of north-west China. Although the Gobi is not without rivers and lakes, they present one peculiarity in that they have no outlet to the sea so that watercourses that torrent during mountain-top snowmelts are gradually caught in the sand and forced to merge into salt marshes, where they disappear.

Climatic conditions of such extreme sterility have resulted in a very sparse population. There are vast areas that can sustain no human life at all, in which the traveller's track leading from one waterhole to another marks the only line on which man can exist. As the years go by, the effects of evaporation, the increasing depth of saline deposit in the saltwater-points and the slow choking of lake and riverbed with drifting sand and the accumulation of desiccated matter cause a ceaseless encroachment of the desert. In recent years, the activities of man, in particular deforestation, have caused the pace of desert advance to quicken. Beijing suffers from the effect of sandstorms to a far greater extent than it did fifty or even twenty years ago.

Side by side with vast expanses blighted by desiccation are wide areas covered with stones varying in size from those that form the dark smooth surface of what is referred to as Black Gobi to loose coarse grit or rounded pebbles. Other parts lie buried under salty clay or break out into saline crystals, the spongy treacherous surface of which affords no means of existence even to the least exacting forms of animal life.

In some areas of the Gobi that still sustain life, an assortment of small animals such as gerbils, jerboas and insects emerge from their hiding places as soon as night falls. All through the hours of heat, they sleep in a tunnelled world underground, the openings frequently to be found on the sheltered side of many a tiny sand-mound, blown up round the foot of a tuft of low bush or scrub. During the night, these creatures move ceaselessly, silently and invisibly over the sand. After sunrise, the sand is patterned with all kinds of tracks left by these rodents, and other insects, which scuttle underground as the sun rises. But this occurs in increasingly fewer areas because, as winds become stronger, the Gobi becomes drier and even the smallest lifeforms are forced to retreat. All this combines to make parts of the Gobi the most desolate wilderness on earth.

Yet even though the Gobi Desert forms one of the bleakest areas on the face of our planet, it is also one of the most varied in character, for it is traversed by ranges crowned with perpetual snow, by barren volcanic hills, and is dotted over with jagged rocks of every shape, size and colour. The surface mainly consists of wide expanses of sand, dunes or stone-littered plains, but a wealth of detailed variety is hidden under a superficial cloak of uniformity, and to a close observer each day's trek by camel has a definitive stamp of individuality.

By reason of their vivid and varied colourings these stones are one of the glories of the Gobi and sometimes a traveller's trek leads through a litter of small multicoloured pebbles that are rose-pink, green, peach, lilac, white, red and black, burnished in turn by sand, sun and wind. The whole forms a matchless mosaic that changes colour imperceptibly during the rising and setting of the sun. Often I have stood at sunset watching in wonder as landscape shades refined and subtly changed minute by minute in front of me.

On one occasion in the Gashun Gobi near Lop Nur, after snow had fallen all night, the snowmelt the following day on the sides of hills and mountains intensified the multicoloured diversity of the rock to an extraordinary degree. It was as though scales had fallen from my eyes.

One of the loveliest tints is red rust, warm and glowing; and there are jagged peaks of green shale, so soft that from a distance they appear to be covered in lichen although there is not the slightest trace of vegetation on them. Other hills are cone shaped and covered with chips of white stone, as though a miraculous snowstorm had dusted them with flakes. This landscape of immense variety and interest is entirely made of rock.

A few years ago, when I was shown a satellite map of Mars portraying the most unforgiving, harsh yet curiously compelling landscape, I was moved to comment with total conviction, 'I have been there.' Every time I look at a map of the Gobi that sets out an area that I have not yet explored, my spirits lift. The Gobi has captivated me. When I meet up with my camels knowing that they will take me into this utterly barren wilderness, my heart sings.

So as we pored over the map on which lay the objectives of our expedition into the Mongolian Gobi, my finger traced the tightly knit contours of the Atis Mountains with nervous excitement. These mountains lie near the Chinese border in the south-west corner of the Great Gobi SPA Reserve 'A'. Their slopes are rugged, steep and riven with gullies. I did not think it was possible for a four-wheel-drive vehicle to cross over them.

'Only camels can take us over the Atis Mountains,' said Adiya, abruptly articulating my unspoken thoughts. 'I haven't climbed them before and none of us know an exact route. We'll get over by trial and error. Tsoijin will find a way.'

'We should find wild camels to the north, south and east of the Atis,' interjected Mijji. 'The Atis Mountains lie in the heart of wild camel country.'

'Excellent.' I said.

If Adiya had never crossed the mountains and Tsoijin did not know an exact route, we were about to enter relatively unexplored terrain. Not for us the aggravating problems of noisy and unreliable vehicles. Travelling by camel would increase our chances of seeing their wild cousins.

The following day, we travelled to the place where Mijji had arranged for our twenty domestic camels to be waiting. They were gathered together in a fold of the Endrigen Nuru hills which form the northern boundary of the Great Gobi SPA Reserve 'A', about ten miles from the Reserve headquarters. From this expedition base the Gobi Desert rolled out before us and disappeared into a dust-laden distance.

Mijji had selected well. The camels were fit and in good condition. Not having been on a camel expedition since we completed our 1,500-mile crossing of the Sahara in February 2002, it was a wonderful to be once again loading up a camel caravan. I delighted in the grunt of protest as ropes were tightened and the guttural snarl as an indignant camel swung his head round to confront a careless handler. Some camels are always petulant, others exude endless patience and utter no protest, as heavy boxes, sacks and sundry loads and kit are carefully positioned on either side of their humps. Other camels are unknown quantities, sometimes biddable and docile, at others unbelievably grumpy, depending on their prevailing mood.

It's a timeless scene that has been acted out in deserts the world over for at least three millennia. At the commencement of loading, a rope has to be positioned under the chest of a squatting camel whose front and sometimes back legs have been hobbled. At times the rope is placed on the ground so that the camel squats down on top of it before hobbles are tied. At other times it is poked under the squatting, hobbled camel with a stick. If there are two handlers loading one camel, the rope is frequently pushed through by hand from one to the other.

Whichever technique is used, the method of securing the rope under the camel is unchanging, as are the knots, the looping of the ropes over the pommel, the methods of tightening and tying. All these skills have been passed down from one generation to another, whether by the Tuareg in the Sahara, the Somali and Rendille in Kenya or the Kazahks and Mongols in Central Asia. To be a part of this scene is to step back in time.

Adam, a descendant of a Tuareg slave, said to me that his ability to tie a good knot ensured that he would find a pretty and worthwhile wife.

'Good girls won't look at you unless you can tie your knots,' he said.

It takes about two hours for four handlers to load twenty camels, especially on the first occasion, when unfamiliar loads are weighed and balanced against a correspondingly equal weight on the other side of the camel's body. Equitable balance is important, otherwise loads slip and galls and sores are unwittingly inflicted.

Frequently a fractious camel will abruptly rise to its feet in spite of its hobbles, before its loads have been tied onto its back. Then the camel will run or hop off, depending of the efficiency of the hobble, with ropes flying and half-tied loads spilling onto the ground. The herdsmen will run about waving sticks and coaxing the animal back onto its knees with shouts and clicks of the tongue. The other camels in the caravan pay scant regard. Craning round their long necks to see exactly what is going on, these camels seem to be saying: 'Now what on earth is the matter with him? Why is he behaving in such an extraordinary fashion?'

I have a decorative wall-hanging of a print of an ink painting by the famous Chinese artist, Wu Zuoren (1909–97), who specialized in painting camels and pandas. Two Bactrian camels are depicted with heads turned. They are looking enquiringly and with total disdain at another camel, which is trotting away in fright. It captures camel behaviour perfectly.

One of the herdsmen who chased after the errant camel on this occasion was Tsog Erdene, the herdsman who looks after the captive wild camels at Zakhyn Us. He was with us on a sabbatical – a break from his full-time job. Tsog Erdene is reliable, calm and has a deep knowledge of working with camels, of their varied moods and their characteristics. He is a camel man through and through. It was good that he was with us as he never complains or makes a fuss.

Two hours later we were ready. We shook hands with Mijji, who wished us God speed, we jumped onto our riding camels and set off at a pace of two and a half miles an hour into the desert. It was sunny but cool. I was elated to be on the back of a camel once again.

Tsoijin took the lead, sitting bolt upright on his lead camel, staring towards the far horizon. His upturned mouth, twinkling, narrowed eyes and the tufted grey side-burns that lined a weather-beaten face gave him a natural authority. It was a continual irritant that I could only communicate with Tsoijin through a third party. He knew a vast amount of Mongolian traditional folklore and my inability to talk to him easily was frustrating. Occasionally Tsoijin would reach for the field glasses that dangled around his neck to check on something that had caught his attention. Although nearly 70, he had, like most Mongolians, phenomenal eyesight.

Some years ago, a Mongolian friend said to me, 'If you steal a Mongolian's personal possessions you'll be in big trouble. Mongolians have eyes like hawks. You'll be tracked all the way back to England!'

I remembered those words when another Mongolian friend once visited my house. On my kitchen wall I had hung a photograph of a Mongolian *ger*, taken against the background of a thundery sky and a double rainbow. Outside the *ger*, the tiny figure of a man wearing a bright red cloak or *del* could just be seen. On entering the room and seeing the picture for the first time my friend burst into laughter.

'What's the joke?' I asked.

'Can't you see?' he said, shaking all over with laughter. 'That man came out of his *ger* to have a pee. Look at him glowering angrily over his shoulder at the photographer who has caught him in such an undignified situation.'

I took a magnifying glass and peered at the minute figure to confirm that my friend was absolutely right.

We headed for the low-lying Tsenkcher Mountains and after five hours' travelling stopped just short of the foothills and pitched camp. At five o'clock the temperature dropped dramatically. That night it fell to -15 °Celsius and I was disconcerted to find that my newly acquired 'arctic' sleeping bag was not as resistent to cold as I had been led to believe.

For three days we travelled south-west, covering an average of twenty miles a day. The trek was enlivened by sightings of the black-tailed or goitered gazelle, the *kulan* or wild ass and the sighting of our first three wild camels, a male with two females. On the fourth day the Atis Mountains were in sight. My journal for that day records:

Break camp about 9.30 a.m. and head for the Atis Mountains. We cross a large open plain and then enter a steep-sided, black, shale-strewn valley. Just before we entered the valley we discovered the footprints of the extremely rare Gobi Bear (ursus gobiensis) [there are presumed to be approximately only thirty-two in the world and there is continuing debate among scientists over whether they are a true species or a sub-species].

Moved out of the shale towards another low-lying range where we stopped for lunch and our camels cantered off to eat snow that was lying near the hills. They love to gobble up snow when fresh water is short and they fight to get their muzzles into the deepest drifts. As we had found snow, we moved quickly past Baru Toroi freshwater spring where there is supposed to be a tiny colony of four Gobi bears.

The Reserve authorities have plans to capture four Gobi bears and to start a captive bear breeding programme. With such a tiny numbers of bears in existence, is this wise?

Tsoijin asserted that in general the wildlife was far wilder and more timid than it had been years ago.

'Too much harassment by vehicles,' he commented.

In three weeks' time Dovchin is going to give a dissertation on wild camel herd structure. He takes himself very seriously when explaining this to me and Bilgee and Adiya pull his leg unmercifully.

The next day, Easter Monday, was an extraordinary day. We had entered and begun to climb the shale-strewn, 12,000-foot Atis Mountains. We had hardly been climbing for an hour before we saw the Ibex antelope, many wild asses, wild Argali sheep and the spoor and tracks of the snow leopard.

Yet, crossing the mountains had not been easy. There was no specific track to follow, other than those made by wandering wildlife, and we had made five attempts to find a way to cross them. Dead ends or steep drops had negated these attempts. After the fifth thwarted effort, Adiya and Dovchin had scurried up two neighbouring peaks to try to identify a passable route. Thirty minutes later, Adiya discovered one and with shouts and hand signals, pointed it out to us from on high. We had just begun a successful downward descent when we noticed that Dovchin had not joined us.

'Don't worry,' said Bilgee. 'He'll find us, he's clever.'

But by the time we had pitched camp in a gully a thousand feet above the desert surface, Dovchin had still not appeared. The sun was sinking fast and it would soon be dark. I suggested that we light fires on lesser peaks as a signal to Dovchin to indicate the route we had taken and where we had camped. If we could establish blazing beacons before complete darkness set in, he would have time to descend and find our campsite. The fires were lit and blazed merrily away, but there was still no sign of Dovchin. The temperature dropped to well below freezing. Two wolves set up a mournful howl.

At seven o'clock Tsoijin was to be found blowing hard on his cupped right hand, bent forward and studying intently twenty-one pebbles, neatly arranged in four separated piles in front of him. The stones had been positioned on a chopping board, balanced on his lap and he huddled over them, perched on a pink plastic stool. His leathery features creased in concentration as he took three stones out of one pile and placed them carefully against a pile of six. He closed his eyes and swayed slowly back and forth. Once again he blew on his cupped hand and after a brief pause moved two stones into another pile. He stopped swaying and looked up at us.

'He's all right,' Tsoijin said in Mongolian. 'He'll return tomorrow.'

Tsoijin then tipped all the stones onto the ground and abruptly stood up. He had consulted the twenty-one stones and seen into the future. Dovchin would be all right.

Tsoijin later explained to me that stones may be picked up at random but that they should be reasonably small. It is their number that is significant.

'There must be twenty-one stones for an accurate assessment to be made.'

I had read of another traditional Mongolian method of forecasting the future using a discarded mutton bone. The bone is thrown into the ashes of a fire, which is hot enough to make it crack. The cracks are then examined and the diviner can, from their formation, foretell the future.

This is an age-old method of divination. A thirteenth-century traveller had written that a Mongol servant 'does nothing in the world without consulting the bones'. In 1921, Baron Ungern-Sternberg used the same mutton-bone method for forward planning when he launched an attack on a Chinese warlord ensconced in the Bogd Ula Mountains near Ulan Bator. The baron had seized power in a political vacuum that had been caused by the retreat of the White Russians. The Chinese warlord had taken the Bogd Khan, the traditional ruler of Mongolia, prisoner. Following the mutton-bone diagnosis, the baron sent a small force of 300 men up the thickly wooded mountain slopes, burst into the khan's palace and released the blind old man. They then hoisted him onto a horse and galloped away with him as fast as they could. The rest of the baron's men then engaged the Chinese on three fronts. Before long, the battle had become a massacre and the soldiers of the warlord were completely routed. Ungern-Sternberg's mutton-bone plan of action resulted in an overwhelming victory that convinced the Mongolians that the Mad Baron was a reincarnation of the God of War, sent from heaven to lead them. But a few months later the bones did not save him from the Communists' advance.

Now I had witnessed at first hand another Mongolian method of divining the future. As I crawled into my tent, with the wolves howling higher up in the mountains, I knew that poor Dovchin must be having a miserable night. We all slept fitfully. Next morning, with no sign of him, we ate our breakfast in silence. We were all now seriously worried for his safety.

The sun had risen and the huge shadows thrown up by the lowering mountains on either side of the steep-sided gully were gradually diminishing. Should we send a search party up into the mountains? We all agreed that this was the only thing we could do. Tsoijin once again asked for twenty-one stones. The small pebbles were gathered up and we all huddled round him as he repeated the intricate formalities; blowing on his cupped hand, moving stones from one pile to another. All at once, Tsoijin stood up and swept the stones off his lap and into the sand.

'He's coming,' he muttered, 'he'll be here in ten minutes.'

Exactly ten minutes later, an exhausted Dovchin walked slowly into the camp.

Bilgee is a modern Mongolian. He is a wizard on a computer and is perfectly at home with a GPS. He has travelled overseas and seen many countries in the modern world. But he was moved to say, 'I always thought that the stones were superstitious rubbish. Now I am not so sure.'

We all praised Tsoijin's efforts. As for Dovchin, he had spent an extremely uncomfortable night high up on a mountain ledge, unable to sleep because of the cold and not attempting to do so because of the wolves. He had seen our beacons, but wisely resisted the temptation to attempt a descent down a very steep slope in failing light. He told me how he had hopped from one foot to the other all night to keep himself warm and alert. Later, Adiya confided in me that he was going to ask Tsoijin to teach him the secret of the stones.

With a bitterly cold north wind blowing hard, bringing with it flurries of snow, we turned due east towards a spring called Bogt Sagaan. I discovered that high up on a camel is not the best place to be in falling temperatures.

We had left the Chinese boundary to the south and with heads down, muffled up as best we could against the wind and snow, we walked slowly through the foothills of the Atis Mountains. Dovchin was understandably subdued. The poor fellow was exhausted. On reaching a campsite after trekking for twenty-two miles we pitched our camp in a blizzard. By this time I had realized that the 'arctic' sleeping bag was a misnomer. I was cold when the temperature plummeted to almost -25 °Celsius and for two nights rather alarmingly lost all feeling in my feet.

When I needed urgently to pee in the middle of the night it was quite a struggle to wriggle out of the arctic bag and unzip the tent flap. It seemed to me to be nearly as 'arctic' inside the sleeping bag as out. Mistrustful of my feet, I crawled out of my tent on all fours. The ground outside was littered with pebbles. It must have been the coldest hour of the night. Later, my addled brain made the highly unoriginal discovery that an empty whisky bottle served the purpose. Johnny Walker served me well in the middle of the night on several subsequent occasions.

The next day, we passed a solitary hill whose top was sprinkled with white shale. It was shaped exactly like a miniature Kilimanjaro. After nine hours' travelling, we arrived at Bogt Sagaan spring. Fortunately the spring water was drinkable by both man and beast. This was timely as the melted snow water that we had been drinking was nearly exhausted.

Near the spring, the Mongolian Reserve authorities had constructed a *ger*. Built in stone to the same dimensions as a traditional felt and skin *ger,* the wooden roof was crafted with the traditional wheel through which poked the chimney of the stove. The roof was plastered with mud so that from a short distance it was remarkably well concealed. There was plenty of wood inside; the fire soon heated the *ger* and I was greatly relieved when my feet at last came back to life. Crudely crafted wooden beds were placed head to toe around the *ger*. My choice of a sleeper was poor: my bed had one of its three legs shorter than the others. But this did not matter in the slightest. I was warm.

Our camels' feet had suffered during the three-day crossing of the Atis Mountains. A camel's foot is large, round and spongy and understandably they dislike crossing rocks and slippery shale as it damages their protective footpads. The mountains had thoroughly tested the camels. After we had set up camp at Bogt Sagaan spring we discovered that six camels, including my riding camel, needed veterinary treatment. They were not lame, but their pads were either slit by sharp rocks or punctured by slivers of shale. Unless their wounds were dressed the camels would not be able to continue.

The first step was to tie up the legs of a camel to stop it kicking out while being treated. A camel's kick is powerful and comes without warning. Tsog Erdene and the other herdsmen had woven soft, flexible yet very strong rope out of camel hair. This is superior to coloured nylon rope, which stiffens in rain and its cheap blue or green dye tends to rub off, staining camel and handler alike. Once soundly trussed, an injured camel is rolled onto its side. Mutton fat is heated over a fire until it turns to liquid and then poured into the crack in its pad where it then cools and solidifies. When the fat is fixed, the camel is untied and released. Most camels stoically endure this painful ordeal.

A puncture wound is treated differently. If a thorn or splinter has entered the pad then this has to be extracted with pliers or in extreme cases with teeth. If the wound is not too large, it is treated in the same way as a bicycle inner tube – with glue and a rubber patch. Once the patch has been applied and allowed to dry, the camel is released. If the puncture is very deep, then the hot mutton-fat treatment is applied and when the fat has cooled the rubber patch is positioned with glue on top of the fat. Interestingly, I have seen the same mutton fat treatment used by the camel-owning Turkana nomads in northern Kenya.

The tough, wild Turkana tribe, whom the present Kenyan government – like the British before them – cannot fully control, have a custom that I have never seen performed anywhere else either in Africa or Central Asia. Northern Kenya is frequently confronted with cycles of prolonged drought. These droughts bring hunger and can cause heavy loss of life among both the Turkana and their livestock. Faced with near-famine conditions, a Turkana will slice open the top of a camel's hump and scoop fat into a tin or glass jar for food. When he has extracted enough of this fat, he will carefully replace the flap of skin and apply an antiseptic paste made from local herbs. The wound heals, the camel lives and the Turkana survive another drought.

The next day, we headed north, with a cold, northerly headwind blowing hard in our faces. We startled fourteen black-tailed gazelles and then as my journal describes:

In the near distance, about 400 yards to the north, Tsoijin pointed to a group of four wild Bactrian camels grazing contentedly on a few miserable tufts of dry grass. Fortunately, they were not able to pick up our scent as the prevailing wind was blowing hard from the north. Tsoijin motioned to us to dismount. We did so and bending low, stalked towards them using our domestic camels as cover.

The four wild Bactrian camels stood still, staring at our camels as they walked slowly towards them. We managed to get within fifty yards of them before one of the wild camels abruptly raised his head.

He took three strides towards us and then, fearful, turned abruptly and ran off to
the north, closely followed by his three companions.

In 2003, Tsoijin had discovered a large spring of unmapped fresh
water to the north of the Atis Mountains. In his honour it had been
named Tsoi Spring. This was our destination. The plan was to spend at
least two nights at the spring in the hope that while we were there, the
spring water would attract wild camels and other wildlife.

We arrived at Tsoi at about 4 p.m. and were encouraged when we
saw numerous footprints of wild camels around the sandy edge of the
spring. After we had unloaded our domestic camels and set up camp,
we allowed them to wander down to the spring in the hope that wild
camels would join them

It was easy to understand why Tsoi Spring had not been discovered
earlier. To the south it is bounded by a rocky outcrop, whose northern
slopes are covered with wind-driven sand. These rocky hillocks curve
in a half moon around the southern boundary of the spring and act as
a barrier to wildlife attempting an approach from the south. They also
provide a welcome barrier against the prying eyes of man. To the east
and west, sand dunes covered with ancient tamarisk bushes provide
further cover and to the north another rocky projection provides
additional camouflage for this precious water source. So well concealed
is the spring by these natural features, that it was only discovered in
2003 when Tsoijin was part of an aerial survey team.

'If we are lucky, wild camels will come to drink early next morning,'
said Tsoijin that evening.

We talked in whispers and tried not to clatter our tin plates and
mugs when we squatted down to a meal of mutton broth and dumplings
before settling down for an early night. The wind dropped but it was
still very cold. About 5.30 a.m. my right foot, which was gradually
losing any connection with the rest of my body, was grasped and shaken
vigorously. My mind raced back to an early morning incident in the
Sahara when a camel had got to its feet and stepped first on Jasper

Evans and then on me. Then as now, I thought that we were under some form of attack. My racing heart relaxed when Tsog Erdene thrust his weather-beaten face through the frosted flap of my tent. He grinned and raised a finger to his lips. Gesticulating excitedly, he indicated that I was to get up and follow him outside.

Numbed, stiff fingers struggled with the laces of my boots. Tsog Erdene shook his head vigorously from side to side.

'*Havtagai* [wild camel]. Many *havtagai*. No time for shoe. Come, come.'

I pulled a jacket over my three thick sweaters and with laces flapping followed Tsog Erdene out of the tent and round the base of a dune.

Further to the west, I could make out the figures of Adiya and Bilgee, crouching low on top of a sand dune that overlooked the spring. They were well concealed by a stunted and wind-blasted tamarisk bush.

I heard a scuffle behind me.

'Hello, Dovchin,' I spluttered, gasping for breath in the freezing cold.

I spotted Tsoijin crouching behind another tamarisk and looking intently towards the spring through field glasses.

Dovchin and I scrambled after Tsog Erdene and after a hectic ten minutes, which left me puffing and wheezing, we came to the base of a steep dune. A tamarisk was growing on top, its roots entwined around a dome of hard sand. This was superb cover. The three of us clambered up the dune and wriggled into the cold sand. Then we slowly raised our heads and peered down at the water below us.

The rising sun was on our backs and shafts of steadily expanding light lit up one side of the spring. The sun's reflection on the clear spring water caused it to glitter and sparkle with a myriad of dancing stars. Beyond this water dazzle was deep shadow. I squinted into this contrasting panorama of light, striving to see what had attracted the attention of my teammates. Gradually, I began to determine the famil-iar shape of camels – many camels: large, bull camels, medium-sized camels and young three-month-old calves. They were moving slowly along the water's edge, out of the shadows, into the glittering sunlight and back into shadow again. My fingers grasped my field glasses and I methodically attempted to count their numbers. After twenty minutes of intense concentration, with cold and discomfort totally forgotten, I had arrived at a total of thirty-nine wild Bactrian camels, the largest number in one group that I had ever seen. There were four bulls, eleven two-year-olds, seven three-year-olds and seventeen females.

In China in 1995, deep in a fold of the Kum Tagh sand dunes, we had, quite by chance, come across a wild Bactrian female camel that had just given birth. We managed to obtain a unique photographic record of a wild camel calf that was under twenty-four hours old. I felt that what I was witnessing at Tsoi Spring in Mongolia was a sighting in the same rare category.

For over two hours, we watched as the wild Bactrian camels drank, wandered away from the spring to graze on the surrounding vegetation and then return. Young virile bulls fought, another chased three females. Mothers trotted fretfully after errant and wayward calves. It was a slow-moving and totally engrossing tapestry of wild Bactrian camel behaviour. This was my sixth wild camel expedition but I had never seen anything like it.

Having had no time to pee when Tsog Erdene woke me, two hours and twenty minutes later I was fit to burst. Observing Dovchin's rapidly increasing shift of position, it appeared that he was having the same problem. If I sat up, the camels would see me. My fingers were cold and stiff and in no state to fiddle with a zip or buttons in a sitting position.

Something had to be done, quickly, and I attempted to slide down the side of the dune. As I did so, a block of hardened sand, which had solidified around a root of the tamarisk bush, broke loose and rolled down towards and into the spring. Dovchin, seeing my movements and confronted with a similar problem, abruptly stood up.

Wild camel heads peered up at the dune. Having a highly developed detection mechanism as far as man is concerned, they immediately spotted us. With heads held aloft, all thirty-nine of them broke into a

1. The author standing next to the second-century Buddhist shrine at Miran.

2. Our injured camel on the road between Hongliugou and Miran, after the black sandstorm.

3. Travelling east in the foothills of the Arjin Mountains with Tibet in the background.

4. Descending from the Kum Tagh sand dunes with our camels.

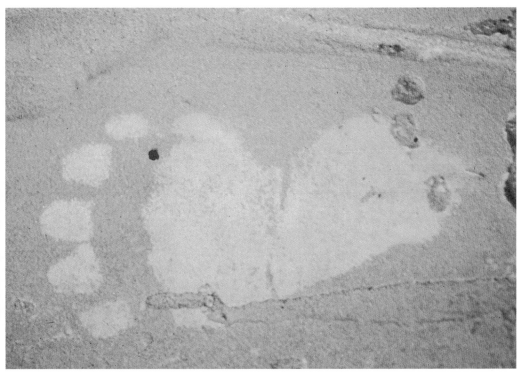

5. The footprint of a Tibetan bear, mistaken at first by Leilei as the footprint of a 'yeti'.

6. One of two wild Bactrian camels encountered in the Kum Tagh.

7. Usuman leads us towards the two unmapped valleys.

8. A wild Argali ram at the Kum Su spring.

9. One of our Kazakh herdsmen.

10. The 'Professor', Yuan Guoying.

11. The skull of an Argali ram, shot by miners, at Kum Su.

剧毒品

6

12. One of the many drums of potassium cyanide found at Kum Su.
It reads 'Deadly Poison'.

13. Mr Mamil with some of the potassium cyanide drums at Kum Su.

14. The late Tsoijin, a legendary ranger in the Mongolian camel reserve.

15. Tsoijin using twenty-one stones to divine the whereabouts of Dovchin.

16. Wild Bactrian camels at Tsoi Spring.

trot and then a canter. In no time they had fled from the spring and into the desert.

Adiya called out to us. He was furious.

'You shouldn't have let the camels see you. They'll be frightened of coming back here again. We could have stayed here for at least another three hours.'

We trudged back to camp with Adiya muttering in Mongolian to Bilgee. Having had over two hours of intensive observation I could not grasp why he was so upset.

Over a bowl of instant noodles and a cup of tea, I talked to Adiya and his anger gradually subsided.

'We've been very lucky. That was a very rare sight. But, you shouldn't have rolled down the dune and disturbed the camels.'

Tsoijin's face was a picture of delight. He had done his job. The expedition had achieved real success. The sighting at Tsoi Spring, his own spring, would be remembered for a very long time.

Later that day in the middle of the afternoon, as our camels plodded across a large featureless plain under a sun that was warm enough to raise the temperature, we spotted four three-year-old bull camels. When they spotted us, instead of turning and running away, they started to walk steadily towards us. We were in no position to dismount, so we bent down behind our camels' humps, intrigued to find out just how close we could get to them.

They must have covered at least half a mile before one of the wild camels spotted something odd. He turned and ran off but the other two camels stood their ground. After advancing another twenty yards, they too wheeled about and fled.

My journal again: '*This sighting justifies the long-term view that I have held that it is much better and easier to see a wild camel from a domestic camel's back rather than from a jeep. In addition, wheel tracks are not left behind. A vehicle track in the desert takes years before it is obliterated.*'

We were now heading for home, but before we reached Zakhyn Us we made another discovery. Twenty miles north of Tsoi Spring is a range of hills called Burrin Hayar. As we approached the outlying foothills we noticed that there were numerous wild animal tracks leading up to a jagged cleft, set in the side of a wall of rock.

'There could be a spring there,' remarked Tsoijin – and he was right.

We clambered up to the cleft and on entering the wide gash in the rock we were confronted with a pool of salty water, too brackish for humans but drinkable for wildlife and our camels. Further up the crevasse there was another pool and then another.

In all we found six salt pools and it was clear that many species of wildlife visited this spot. Then something else was found.

'Look,' said Adiya coming down a rocky slope with the newly shot skull of an Argali sheep in his arms. 'Poachers have been here.'

He opened his hand and showed me a spent cartridge. So although Mijji and the Reserve authorities were unaware of this spring there were others who knew of its existence only too well.

'Is there much poaching in the Reserve?'

'Not much,' replied Adiya. 'But there are other problems. Last month a vehicle belonging to an ex-minister was spotted near here. He wasn't poaching. He was looking for gold.'

When former environmental ministers resort to mineral exploration in a protected area, there is clearly cause for concern, which outweighs the worry of an occasional poacher.

Next day was a hard slog, as my journal relates:

Pushed north all day with heads down against the wind. We covered 30 miles today which is good going in the desert. Vast plains of shale are dissected by ranges of hills running from east to west. Excellent vegetation for wildlife but no wildlife seen. Our water is almost finished and we are on half rations, but we are not yet reduced to eating snow like the camels!

It is amazing how the weather in the Gobi can vary so rapidly. As the Mongolians say, you can experience all four seasons in one day. When we set off in the morning we were buffeted by a strong yet warm wind blowing from the west. By midday it had

swung back to the north and it had become bitterly cold. The temperature must have
dropped fifteen degrees in an hour.

We stopped for lunch and had some fun with Tsoijin's rifle, taking pot shots at a
piece of dry camel dung placed on the top of a spiked stick which had been stuck in
the ground thirty yards away. To the Mongols' utter amazement, and my own, I hit
it with my first shot.

On the last day our water ran out. The temperature dropped to well below freezing and the thirty-five miles that we covered on our camels seemed unending. During the last fifteen miles, gusting snow blew into our faces. Our camels, our loads and ourselves were covered in freezing sleet.

The camels plodded on, hour after hour, step after rhythmic step, without the slightest complaint. As the sun sank in the east and the temperature dropped even lower, the ropes securing the loads stiffened, causing each bound bundle to produce its own individual groan or squeak. I hummed in unison to my loads' creaking lullaby in an effort to stop my eyes closing. I knew that if I fell asleep I could easily fall from the camel with disastrous consequences. Brains numbed, chatter fell away. When we reached Zakhyn Us just after dusk, there was general relief.

The expedition had proved a huge success. We had seen 117 wild Bactrian camels, seventy-six wild asses, forty-three wild Argali sheep and eighty-six black-tailed or goitered gazelles.

All these wildlife sightings had been recorded on a GPS carried by each team member. They had all put into practice the lessons that had been taught in Kenya. In addition, we had discovered an unmapped spring, something of huge significance in the waterless wasteland of the Gobi Desert. And for me, the travelling by camel rather than jeep had been vindicated.

That night, as I lay snuggled in my sleeping bag close to a roaring fire in the centre of the *ger*, a great wind got up. It howled furiously around the circular felt tent. As driving hail, sleet and snow followed the wind,

I realized how lucky we had been not to be caught in the desert in the middle of this particular storm. My little tent would have been blown to Lop Nur in China.

Before the wind started to blow, the evening had been enlivened by the arrival of Dorgotov, Mijji's number two at the Reserve headquarters. Dorgotov is in his mid-thirties and has an interesting face. His skin is fair, his hair is wavy and his eyes are green. A tight ironic smile constantly played around his mouth, as though his private thoughts positioned him ahead of everyone else in life's game. I wasn't surprised to learn that he was a champion chess player.

That night, after welcoming us back effusively and passing round a bottle of Wild Camel vodka in great style, he showed his hand, sweeping my fellow travellers out of the *ger* like a shepherd with his sheep. His destination was a broken-down truck that had ended its working life behind Tsog Erdene's *ger*.

As he stepped out into the storm followed by my grinning teammates Dorgotov waved cheerily to me. Money jingled in one pocket and a pack of cards poked out of the other. Dorgotov had come to gamble with the boys from the bush and everyone, apart from Tsog Erdene, Tsoijin and myself, sat down with him in the truck. The vodka must have kept them warm because the truck had no heating.

The game of blackjack masterminded by Dorgotov lasted all night long through the driving wind and swirling snow. From time to time I woke to angry shouts and raucous laughter echoing through the howling wind. It was as though desert demons dancing around the *ger* had acquired powers of speech. As I drifted in and out of a disturbed sleep my imagination raced. I remembered how Hsuan-tsang had described the Gobi as the 'haunt of poisonous imps and fiends'. As Dorgotov played his cards, the poisonous imps made merry.

Next morning in freezing temperatures and with a high wind still blowing, our disconsolate team returned bleary-eyed to breakfast off fermented mares' milk and mutton. Dorgotov, looking as wily and as fresh as ever, had cleaned them all out.

The following day we returned to Bayan Toroi, the Reserve headquarters, in the WCPF jeeps and reported to Mijji. He was naturally delighted to learn of our success at Tsoi Spring and the discovery of a new source of water for wildlife within the protected area. Following Mongolian custom, I had bought bottles of vodka for Tsoijin, Tsog Erdene and Mijji. Having given each his individual bottle, I thought no more of it, unaware that the Mongol convention ordained that I myself would receive a bottle on the understanding that I drink it with the donor. Three visits and three bottles of vodka later I was in no state whatsoever to accede to Bilgee's request to come to the Bayan Toroi bar. Everyone had gathered there and they wanted to drink toasts to a successful expedition. With the Mongolian landscape starting to slowly revolve, I steadied myself and much against better judgement walked with Bilgee towards the bar.

The bar in Bayan Toroi, which was about a hundred yards from the Reserve *ger* where I was staying, couldn't have measured more than twelve feet square. It only sold beer, and the scrum inside was like the earlier version of Ulan Bator's Black Market. Once inside there was no way out. You were given beer, one brand only, and it was passed to you over the heads of the swaying massed ranks of sweating, cheerful topers.

The wonderful thing about Mongolian men, who are hardened drinkers, is that nothing whatsoever is mentioned after a night's shenanigans. Next morning is a new dawn. It is as if nothing had ever happened.

6

Death's Shadow at the Door

> The hungry sheep look up, and are not fed,
> But, swoln with wind and the rank mist they draw
> Rot inwardly and foul contagion spread.
>
> John Milton, 'Lycidas'

Six months later I was back in China and this time the planned expedition included my two Mongolian friends, Adiya and Dovchin. Ever since the discovery of Kum Su spring, I had wanted to return to the valleys that held the naive population of wildlife. I put it to the Lop Nur Reserve headquarters that we make an attempt to approach the freshwater spring from the east and not from the west as we had done earlier.

Deputy Zhang agreed to this proposal and with funding from the Grocers' Livery Company in London, whose logo is the Bactrian camel, and from Arysta Life Science, a commercial agricultural company with strong links to China, the expedition was planned for mid-October. None of my previous expeditions in China had been undertaken in the autumn so travelling conditions at that time were unknown to me.

The addition of the Mongolians was a breakthrough. Lop Nur, a former nuclear test site, is a highly restricted area to both foreigners and Beijing-based journalists. Five years earlier, the Chinese would not have considered allowing Mongolian scientists to enter this sensitive area. But attitudes had changed, perhaps as a result of the successful Kenyan training programme, and invitations were extended by the Chinese to both Dovchin and Adiya.

For the two young Mongolian scientists this was a great opportunity and when we met up at Beijing airport to fly to Urumqi they were understandably very excited. We were once again planning to travel into the Gobi with domestic Bactrian camels; our success in Mongolia the previous spring had provided me with an excellent argument for this. The expedition began, as is routine in China, with a banquet hosted by the Lop Nur Reserve headquarters. No expense had been spared and though I have attended many such ritual feasts I had never before seen a whole cooked lamb wheeled into the banqueting hall on a specially prepared trolley. It had been propped up into a kneeling position and every section of its skinned body was cooked to perfection but wholly intact. If this had been done to impress the Mongolians it certainly succeeded. Adiya was speechless.

Dish followed exotic dish. Beautifully presented whole de-boned fish smothered in colourful sauces, artistically arranged vegetables, fungi and every conceivable type of fowl. There was beef and pork in addition to the kneeling lamb.

As is common in China, everyone involved in the expedition attended the banquet, including the drivers who would take us the 1,400 miles to our waiting domestic camels. Director Zhang, the head of the Reserve, was there, as was the vice-director, Deputy Zhang, who had been part of the Chinese delegation in Kenya.

I sensed that one of the drivers, Zhang Ying, could be a problem. He was short and vocal. His tummy protruded and as Chinese spirits were knocked back he puffed himself up. To my utter astonishment, having stuffed himself to the limit, he proceeded to pull up his shirt, expose his rotund belly and pat it vigorously. At the same time he invited a startled Adiya to do likewise. In the interests of Sino-Mongolian friendship Adiya did so, much to the amusement of Director Zhang, who later made a slightly incomprehensible speech in praise of valiant Mongolian scientists, Genghis Khan and nomadic culture before setting about his bottle in earnest.

Next morning, the planning meeting that I had sought took place. I was surprised to learn that we were to be a team of fourteen but that only fourteen camels were available. The Chinese domestic Bactrian camels are usually not in the same condition as the ones that we use in Mongolia. If a camel goes sick or injured then we would be in difficulty.

'The journalist and the TV team will walk.'

'The journalist, TV team, who are they?'

The Chinese knew I had an aversion to TV cameramen coming on an expedition.

'We feel that they will generate good publicity for the Reserve and for the wild Bactrian camel.'

The new tarmac road from Urumqi to Hami built with World Bank funds has cut travelling time on the 600-mile journey by three hours. Whereas before, we were frequently stuck on winding roads behind heavily laden lorries for mile after seemingly unending mile, the new road was straight and true.

Thirty miles outside Urumqi alongside the main road is the largest wind turbine site in Asia. I had seen it develop in the last ten years from empty desert to a five-mile stretch of hundreds of whirling blades. Although the wind was keen, when we passed them on this occasion all the turbines had stopped working.

I was delighted that the Professor and Leilei were coming with us once again. Sadly our guide, Lao Zhao, who like the Professor and his son had been with me on five previous expeditions, was not a team member. He had died two years previously in the Kunlun Mountains bordering Tibet, when his driver had lost control of the jeep he was driving. Lao Zhao had been a highly competent and knowledgeable guide and in the Desert of Lop and the Gashun Gobi he had been the best in China.

It emerged that our jeep driver, Zhang Ying, was an incurable sniffer. He sniffed with a precise frequency (once every forty seconds), which at first became an irritant and then became a problem. Three hundred miles into our 1,500-mile drive my head was reeling and my frustration levels were rising. Zhang Ying was also very loud. He had been inordinately noisy at the farewell banquet when he had exposed his tummy and embraced Adiya. As a non-Chinese speaker who only knows how to ask for my noodles and give my name, I could to some extent switch off to Zhang Ying's chatter, but over 1,500 miles it wasn't easy

Mercifully, one hour after dark, we reached Dun Huang, our designated stop on the long jeep journey that was to take us from Hami to New Aksai, where we were due to meet with the Kazakh herdsmen who were to accompany us to Kum Su.

Our overnight stay at a small hotel in Dung Huang was a setting for the Professor to demonstrate his mysterious art of table-turning. I had experienced this phenomenon in the Professor's apartment in Urumqi and in a hotel in Hami, but I had never before seen the Professor pull back a multi-stained, threadbare, blue hotel bedroom carpet with such gusto. I watched in amazement as he ripped the carpet from the concrete. Satisfied with his work, he stood up.

'It never works on a carpet,' he said, 'on the ground or on concrete but not on a carpet.' He bustled over to the bathroom. I heard the sound of running water.

'This should do,' he said as he placed a coloured metal bowl on the concrete floor. 'Remember, you mustn't fill the bowl more than three-quarters full and it must be metal. Plastic will not work. Now, please help me with the table.'

Having cleared everything away from the top of a large wooden table that stood between our two iron beds at the end of the room,

we positioned it carefully upside down on top of the metal bowl. The
Professor bent down, made one or two adjustments, nodded his head
up and down and said, 'Good.' Then he bustled out of the bedroom,
returning moments later with Leilei and Zhang Ying.

'Now then,' he explained, 'follow me very carefully. Stand at each
corner of the table and place the third finger of your right hand on the
top of the upturned leg. It must be the correct finger.'

The four of us did so.

'Now empty your minds, please, and stare at the fingernail that is
touching the table leg. Don't push the table; just touch it very lightly. If
it starts to move, walk with it.'

We stared at our fingernails, attempted to empty our minds and
waited for the Professor's magic to work. After a few minutes, the
table wobbled.

'It's working,' the Professor said quietly.

The table floated up above the metal bowl. Then, it started to rotate
clockwise, slowly at first and then with increasing speed.

'Walk with it, don't lose finger contact,' the Professor called out.

The speed increased until suddenly we were all running to keep up
with the revolving table. Inevitably, finger contact was broken. When
we lifted the table off the metal bowl, the water was still whirling
around inside. There was a wet patch on the tabletop that matched the
size of the bowl.

'Chinese magic,' said the Professor with a laugh. 'You have very good
power. Come, let's try it with the two of us.'

The Professor and I went through the mind-emptying, finger-
touching procedure on our own. The table revolved at a breathtaking
speed and we both collapsed on our beds laughing and panting when
we were eventually forced to break contact.

It hadn't seemed magical or supernatural. It was as though the
Professor and I were a conduit for a force of energy that, when it
combined with wood, metal and water, made the table rotate. I've since
performed the Professor's Chinese table-turning with Africans on the

shores of Lake Turkana in Kenya, in the Bayan Gol Hotel in Mongolia, in the Hua Du Hotel in Beijing and in various people's houses in England. But it doesn't always work and I asked the Professor why that was.

'Some people have negative thoughts,' he replied enigmatically.

On our arrival at New Aksai, Ali Abutalerp was there to meet us. I had not seen him for five years and he still looked exactly the same. Ali told me that the holy month of Ramadan was about to start.

'So sorry, Mr John, I'm afraid that I'll not be coming with you to Kum Su, but my boss Mr Mamil, who doesn't worry about Ramadan, will come in my place.'

Mamil was in charge of the expedition herdsmen. From his manner when dealing with the Chinese, it was clear that he had made his peace with Communism and China a long time ago. He had also worked out his own salvation as far as religious observance was concerned. Mr Mamil held no scruples over drinking or eating food out of hours during Ramadan. If the drink was enlivened with alcohol, so much the better.

That evening Ali took me to see the New Aksai mosque and introduced me to the alert nonagenarian father of Mamil. This old man was one of the survivors of the Kazakh exodus across Lop Nur. His memory of that terrible crossing was clear and he was able to give me fascinating first-hand information. There were other men there with equally long memories and clear heads and I spent a long time talking to them about many aspects of Kazakh life and behaviour. I liked and respected these elderly Kazakhs, many of whom had endured such great hardship and trauma when they were young. Now in their very old age their days were spent in or near their mosque. They exuded a sense of being utterly at peace with the world.

This story related by Godfrey Lias shows how the Kazakhs like to think of themselves:

For the devout Muslim, Paradise is of course the most perfect abode, but the Prophet Mohammed was aware of murmuring in Paradise, to the effect that, though perfect in nearly every way, it lacked some of the delights of life on earth. It was suggested to Mohammed that if some of these delights could be added, Paradise would truly be a place of the most utter perfection.

The Prophet dutifully reported these complaints to Allah who listened very carefully. Allah replied that Paradise should be incomparably better than anything that could be found on earth, so if He could add to the delights of Paradise then He would be delighted to do so.

After much thought Allah decided to go to earth and find out how He could improve conditions in Paradise by asking the people who lived there himself. He decided to go to Xinjiang in northwestern China, and first visited the Uighurs in order to discover what they liked to do best. The Muslim Uighurs in Xinjiang represented the majority of the souls of the blessed.

Allah put on a turban, mounted a small donkey so that His feet almost dragged in the oasis dust as is fitting for a man of status, and set out to find a group of Uighurs. He had not travelled far when He noticed a group of men squatting close together, animatedly throwing small pieces of bone into the dust. He pushed His way into their circle and asked,

'Is this what you like to do best?'

The Uighurs answered, 'Of course, gambling with sheep's knuckles is the best of all pastimes.'

But gambling is forbidden in Paradise and so Allah left them and rode on to find another ethnic group.

Allah decided that perhaps he should talk to a group who sent the fewest souls to Paradise, Mongolians who had converted to Islam. Allah dressed in a Mongolian *del* and went to a *ger* where He met a Mongolian Muslim whom He asked,

'How do you Mongolian Muslims enjoy yourselves?'

The Mongolian took Him to a Muslim friend's *ger* where a lively party was in full swing.

'What is the occasion for all this merriment?' Allah asked.

'We are having a party and drinking lots of vodka. Drinking is the greatest of our pleasures,' the Mongolian Muslim replied.

Allah left very quickly. Alcohol is forbidden in Paradise.

Allah then decided to seek out a more educated group. He put on a white skullcap and went to a shop that was owned by Chinese Muslims or Hui Hui.

'What is your most blissful of pastimes?' Allah asked.

The Hui Hui beckoned, led him to the back entrance of his shop. Inside lay five men on a rug on the floor, all smoking cigarettes.

Smoking is not permitted in Paradise.

Finally, Allah decided to seek out the least educated, simplest, wildest and the most natural people in Xinjiang. Perhaps, Allah thought, they might be the most honest. Maybe their simple, natural pleasures could enhance the pleasures of Paradise.

Allah put on a Kazakh hat, a *tomak*, with a bunch of owl feathers at the top to show that He was true hero. He leapt onto a fine stallion and galloped towards a Kazakh encampment. Allah reached the *yurt* of the leader of the Kazakhs who rushed out to invite this imposing visitor inside. After exchanging the necessary phrases of polite introduction, Allah got down to business.

'What is the greatest pleasure for a Kazakh?' Allah asked.

His host was surprised by this question.

'Why, sheep stealing of course. There is no greater pleasure for us.'

Allah sadly excused Himself and returned to Paradise. Next time the Prophet Mohammad told Him that the souls in Paradise were complaining He lent back wearily and said,

'Tell them they can take Paradise the way it is or join Satan in Hell.'

Ali, who acted as my interpreter during our conversation with Mamil's father, explained that there was a current boycott of Japanese-manufactured goods in Aksai. I was aware that there was a great deal of anti-Japanese feeling in China at this time because of a Japanese refusal to acknowledge and apologize for the brutalities of the 1930s Nanjing massacre, when 300,000 people are alleged to have been slaughtered by invading Japanese soldiers. The Chinese were particularly incensed because the Japanese had made no mention of Nanjing in a new history curriculum that had been introduced into Japanese schools in 2004.

This Nanjing massacre, commonly known as the 'Rape of Nanjing', is an infamous war crime committed by Japanese troops in and around Nanjing (then known in English as Nanking), China, after it fell to the Imperial Japanese Army on 13 December 1937. The duration of the massacre is not clearly defined, although the period of carnage lasted for well over six weeks until early February 1938.

During the occupation of Nanjing, the Japanese army committed numerous atrocities: rape, looting, arson and the execution of prisoners of war and civilians. Although the executions began under the pretext of eliminating Chinese soldiers disguised as civilians, a large number of innocent men were identified as enemy combatants and killed, or simply slaughtered regardless as the massacre gathered momentum. A large number of women and children were also killed, as rape and murder became more widespread. The extent of the atrocities is hotly debated between China and Japan, with numbers ranging from some Japanese claims of several hundred, to the Chinese claim of a non-combatant death toll of 300,000.

The Professor, who is virulently anti-Japanese, greatly enjoys watching old Chinese propaganda films where Japanese militarists are soundly trounced by Chinese soldiery. It is one of his favourite methods of relaxation. I have watched him whoop in delight or leap to his feet and shake a clenched fist at the black-and-white images flickering on the box in front of him.

On my return from the mosque, I asked the Professor about the current problem with Japan. He made no secret of his feelings.

'The Japanese are a very bad and dangerous people,' he said when I remarked how surprised I was to find Japanese goods being boycotted in Aksai. 'They cannot be trusted.'

'How do the people here know about the Chinese boycott of Japanese goods? This place is so remote.'

'Television tells us all,' replied the Professor. 'Ninety per cent of all Chinese and minority peoples watch television. You know, John,' he continued, switching the conversation to another topic, 'the minority people in China are not clever. In 1951, after Mao had seized power, there were Buddhists living in southern Gansu who, in spite of many representations from the central government, refused to accept Communist rule.'

The Professor looked up at me and smiled.

'So a decision was taken to bomb one of their ancient Buddhist temples in order to persuade them. This was done and the temple was completely destroyed. There were no more problems. When the people saw what had happened they immediately accepted Communism and the rule of Chairman Mao. You see, minorities are very simple people.'

I looked at the Professor and said nothing. I recalled a defining moment on our camel journey across the Sahara: after a particularly difficult day, he had explained the tremendous hardships that he had endured during his time as a student in Lanzhou. It was in the early 1960s, during Mao's 'Great Leap Forward', the agricultural catastrophe that caused famine and mass starvation throughout rural China. Countless peasants died. The Professor told me how hunger had driven him to gather grass to eat to stay alive. His brother-in-law had done the same but had died of starvation. The Professor had watched him die.

In the middle of the Sahara desert miles from any other people apart from our camel team, the Professor had opened his heart to me as he had never done before. I had glimpsed, albeit briefly, the real man who had been forced by circumstance to shelter behind a protective shield for over forty years. As a foreigner, I felt honoured to have been given an insight into the Professor's past.

Yet three years later he could tell me what he considered to be a 'humorous' story about the sufferings of a Chinese minority people, seemingly oblivious of his own personal suffering under the same regime. Among people of a certain age and generation in modern China there lie many unanswerable enigmas.

Our domestic camels were tethered in a remote area of the Kum Tagh, waiting our arrival — near the spot where in 1995 we had seen a wild Bactrian camel just after it had given birth. The Kum Tagh can be stunningly beautiful. In early morning or evening light the sun highlights intricate shades of white, black and grey sand. These sand dunes can sometimes reach 7,000 feet and in places the sand partially covers jagged outcrops of black rock. We passed a lone conical-shaped hillock whose pointed top was evenly sprinkled with the very purest white sand.

A truck carrying our provisions had left an hour ahead of us. I was riding in one of the two jeeps following its tracks and after travelling about 150 miles, with the Kum Tagh Mountains stretching out endlessly to the north of us, it dawned on us that our truck was lost. Judging by its tracks, which at one point crossed over each other, it appeared to have been aimlessly driven in huge circles.

At 7 p.m. we found it, bogged down in soft sand. Moments later we too sank into a treacherous drift. As the light was fading rapidly, we decided to set up camp. Next morning, shovels and planks, push and shove freed the truck. After six futile attempts we managed to move the jeep with one great heave. When we arrived at the rendezvous site we found that the Kazakhs had already erected a large *ger*.

That evening Deputy Zhang, the expedition leader, gave us a pep talk. It consisted of two stipulations. No one was to wander off on his own and no one was to stand behind a camel in case he was kicked. That was all. Deputy Zhang is a very likeable man but I wondered at the time whether he really had it in him to lead an expedition on camels to the remote Kum Su desert spring.

My journal: '*At night the temperature drops to -12 °Celsius but I am as warm as toast in the new sleeping bag that the Mongolians had brought me from*

Ulan Bator. I pee during the night into an empty tin. In the morning I note that it has frozen solid.'

Zhao Honglin and Liu Dong were the two team members from Central China Television (CCTV). Zhao, the boss, was soon nicknamed CC and his cameraman Liu, TV. My initial misgivings were completely unfounded: they proved to be a delightful duo, pitching in to help in all sorts of ways and constantly at pains to be unobtrusive. They were as alike as peas in a pod, short and round-faced with cheerful smiles and sparkling eyes. They always went around together whether on or off duty and occasionally one would finish a sentence that the other had started.

Journalist Chen Zhirven was very different. Although he, too, came with a cheerful smile that creased his large flat face, he was assertive, sometimes truculent and prone to moody silences. He had a hefty frame and I thought that if he ever flared up, we could be in for trouble.

For the next four days we averaged twenty-five miles a day, trekking to the west between the Kum Tagh and the Arjin Mountains. The wind was moderate, the temperature relatively benign.

On the fifth day we headed south towards the Arjin Mountains. The herdsmen knew the whereabouts of a spring where we could water our camels. My journal takes up the story:

> *At twelve o'clock we pass Hartabar valley where the Professor met us at the end of the first expedition to Kum Su. So far we have seen very little wildlife, foxes, hares and a few goitered gazelles but no wild Bactrian camels. This is a disappointment but no doubt when we reach Kum Su we'll get our reward.*
>
> *At 3.30 p.m. we set up camp at the head of a dry riverbed in a valley called Kum Kulak. Mamil tells us that a freshwater spring can be found in the mountains three miles to the south. He suggests that we take the camels there to water them and expedition leader Zhang agrees. Our camels are tired and have not been watered for six days. One has been carrying sixteen gallons of water as well as substantial kit.*

I set off on a camel with Leilei, CC, TV and the Kazakh herdsmen to take the camels to be watered. We travelled for just over an hour and then Mamil said that we should turn east and enter a narrow gully. At the end of it, he said, we would find the spring.

Leilei was riding in front of us, singing happily to himself. He broke off from his reverie, turned to us and called out,

'I think that the spring is further down the valley. You're turning too early. I'm sure you're wrong. I'll ride on and if I don't find it I'll join you later.'

I seemed strange to me that Leilei should want to travel solo. I knew that he'd never been here before. Why was he so sure that we were wrong?

'See you soon,' he called out to me, broke into a Chinese army song and trotted off down the riverbed.

Twenty minutes later we found the spring. It was well camouflaged and unless you knew exactly what you were looking for you could easily miss it. Two hours later, the camels had been watered and fed. Our herdsmen hollered and called, but there was no answering shout. Leilei had disappeared and the sun had set.

It was a dark, moonless night as we headed back up the riverbed towards our camp. At about nine o'clock, having ridden for an hour, we noticed that there were fires and lights flickering and flashing in front of us.

'What's going on?' I asked Mamil.

'It looks as though they're making sure that we know where the camp is. I can't understand why, it's not difficult to find.'

Then we heard the unmistakable sound of a camel, trotting towards us at high speed. Seated on its back was a wide-eyed, breathless Leilei.

'Thank goodness I've found you. I thought that you were lost. I called and shouted but when no one answered I rode back to camp and told them that you had vanished. They lit beacons to guide you back.'

'But, Leilei, you were the one who vanished, not us. We've watered the camels and we're returning back to the camp as planned.'

The next day we rested. Kum Su was a day's journey away. To reach it we had to cross over some substantial sand dunes, so the camels needed to be rested before they made the arduous crossing.

Leilei celebrated his thirty-fifth birthday that evening. Unfortunately at a rather early stage he unwisely mixed vodka with some whisky that I had been saving for him. We sang songs and toasted Leilei, but the Professor's only son was blissfully unaware of our salutations. For most of the evening he lay curled up in total oblivion beside the campfire.

The next day was the day that I had been waiting for. This was the day when after long years of waiting, we would at last return to Kum Su. The plan was to spend at least three nights there, observing and photographing the wildlife, trying to assess their numbers and in particular the ages and sex of the wild Bactrian camels.

After much deliberation, Deputy Zhang decided that the Professor, Leilei, Adiya, CC, TV, Mamil and I would go to Kum Su. We would take basic food and kit to last us for three days. We were to set off at 3.30 p.m., having packed only bare essentials. When we reached the spring, we would attempt to set up an observation point. The rest of the team would remain at a base camp at the head of Hartabar valley to await our return.

At midday a huge commotion erupted. CC and TV, normally the most agreeable of companions who had until this point behaved with total decorum, suddenly started to quarrel and shout. I had no idea what caused this major dispute. The quiet of the desert was shattered by hostile verbal onslaughts that at one point looked as though they might descend to the physical. My own and others' attempts to intervene were hopeless. Totally oblivious to every entreaty, CC and TV continued to argue ferociously. Then, as abruptly as it had started, the ruction died away. Hands were shaken, smiles appeared like the sun emerging after a particularly fierce sandstorm, friendship was reaffirmed. It was all quite extraordinary. On no other occasion on the expedition was a cross word exchanged between the pair.

The sand dunes to the east of Kum Su were higher than I remembered and although we laboured, the surface of the sand was firm. There was no need to shed boots or carry camel loads. By 5.30 p.m. we could see rocks in the distance that surrounded the beautiful sheer-sided valley that concealed the hidden spring. My spirits rose as each stride of my camel took me nearer to this magical spot. Kum Su was so meaningful that to revisit it after a long separation brought on an overwhelming sense of expectation.

We were about forty-five minutes' ride away when high spirits began to sink and expectations started to shatter. The first unwelcome discovery was the skull of a dead wild Bactrian camel. I told myself it must have died of old age, but for a nine-year-old camel this seemed odd. Then Mamil spotted the skull of an Argali ram with magnificent horns. I dismounted and walked over to look at it more closely. This was certainly not a casualty of old age. The Argali had been shot.

As we approached the hidden valley, I noticed a large section of plastic sheeting, snagged on a tamarisk shrub and flapping in the wind. I tried to convince myself that it must have been blown for miles by a fierce wind. When I saw the rusty lid of a forty-four-gallon metal drum, I knew that something was very wrong.

When we had arrived previously Kum Su was pristine and unmapped. What had happened? We descended slowly with our camels into the vast crevasse that shielded the spring. The sides of the gorge were lined with long strips of tattered blue-and-white plastic sheeting. I saw two more empty, rusting drums. Our chatter died away and we fell silent.

On the east bank, perched on a ledge abutting the spring, we came to a primitive miners' camp. It had been recently abandoned but had clearly been occupied for a long time, maybe for as much as two years. One solitary rectangular building built of mud adobe had two partitions that divided the sleeping quarters from a crude cooking area. At one end was a store. There were empty, rusty, blue metal drums littering both this storeroom and the site. Sixteen discarded drums had been used to prop up a crudely erected galvanized-iron roof on which were placed small boulders to prevent the metal sheeting being blown away in the wind. There were discarded rubber boots, some of them of children's sizes. It had appeared that a number of families had made the mud dwelling their permanent home.

The forty-four-gallon drums had contained potassium cyanide that had been used to separate gold from rock. On the outside of each drum a skull and crossbones had been painted. Underneath this macabre logo were Chinese characters stating 'Deadly Poison'. There were other Chinese characters near the bottom of each drum that indicated that the cyanide had been made in China. Using potassium cyanide to extract gold from rock is a primitive and totally destructive practice that not only pollutes fresh water, but also poisons the surrounding vegetation.

I remembered how in 1995, south of the Mongolian border in the northern reaches of Gansu Province, we had found an upright slab of rock on which was written two Chinese characters that proclaimed, 'Don't graze your livestock here, the vegetation has been poisoned.'

Now we were seeing the effects of the same form of pollution with our own eyes. Potassium cyanide is a crystal. Once that crystal comes into contact with water, it dissolves, becoming a danger to all living organisms. For example, in Romania, on 31 January 2000, cyanide from a gold smelting plant, Aurul SA, leaked into the Hungarian river Tisza. The effects were immediate. Hundreds of dead fish were found floating in the river, a tributary of the Danube. More fish were discovered in the Danube, drifting towards Belgrade. Cyanide starves all living organisms of oxygen, killing them almost instantaneously. The cyanide spillage from the Romanian-based Aurul SA is considered the worst ecological disaster in the region since Chernobyl in 1986.

And in Kum Su, where were the Tibetan asses that had trotted behind our domestic camels? Where were the flocks of Argali sheep that we wandered through as though we were meandering among domestic sheep? Where were the wild camels that stood and stared at us, but did not run away?

It would appear that all of them had died, shot for miners' food.

I dismounted from my camel and wandered aimlessly among the debris and squalor of the miners' campsite. I was devastated. I could not even speak to my colleagues. What was the point? There was absolutely nothing to say.

CC pointed his microphone in front of me. 'Speak,' he gestured, 'say what you feel.' I started to make a comment but it was too emotional. I had not had time to collect my thoughts.

'Later,' I murmured, 'later CC, not now.'

For some time now both CC and TV had been wondering whether the trip would provide them with a worthy environmental story. They wanted a tale that would captivate viewers. They had hoped to film amazing scenes of unspoiled wildlife. Now they had their story, but it certainly wasn't the one that they had anticipated. I watched grimly as the Professor talked to the TV camera. He, like me, was clearly very upset. It was a small consolation that CC and TV were with us. It ensured that the tragedy of Kum Su would reach a wider world.

Mamil brought me back to my senses. He had counted the empty potassium cyanide containers. There were seventy-four. More importantly, there were seven of the forty-four-gallon drums that were full and unopened. These drums contained more than enough cyanide to poison the whole of a major city's water supply. What a bonanza for a potential terrorist.

The people who had worked with the potassium cyanide were poor peasants from Gansu. This was clear from the detritus that we found at their campsite. It seemed that the men behind the whole mining enterprise were wealthy Chinese, employing cheap labour on a large scale. The earth was covered with donkey tracks and it appeared that the miners had arranged for donkeys to bring the gold embedded in rock down from the Arjin Mountains. They had financed the washing of the rock in the freshwater spring, had paid for the plastic sheeting roll, for the equipment and for the potassium cyanide. It was an extremely well-run enterprise.

Where and who was the boss of this operation? Were he and his colleagues known to the provincial authorities? Were the authorities in league with him? There is a great deal of corruption at provincial level in China. Even the army is not immune. In 1995 on a wild camel expedition, we had come across a Chinese army gold mine operating in northern Gansu. It was highly organized and efficiently run on army lines. The sites that they were exploiting were guarded by soldiers with guns. Once again, potassium cyanide was being used. I am certain it wasn't legal, but who would or could stop the army?

The Arjin Mountains are not idly named the 'gold' mountains. There is gold in the hills and this has been known for centuries. Sven Hedin had encountered gold miners, and Przhevalsky had had a conflict with them in the same mountainous area that formed the backdrop to Kum Su spring. The camp also had an electric generator. Cabling was festooned around the source of the spring and a crude wooden hoist had been constructed to house electric lighting. Like the construction workers who are rapidly erecting the buildings of the new China, the miners had worked both by day and by night.

It was late afternoon and the setting sun was throwing lengthening shadows across the narrow gorge. We changed our plans without dissent. No one wanted to spend a night in this poisoned place – let alone three nights. It reeked of destruction. The Garden of Eden had been turned into a Valley of Death in six short years.

I had done my very best to keep secret the exact location of Kum Su. It had been too precious a discovery to broadcast its exact whereabouts. Even in articles that I had written, no detailed map had been printed. I believe my Chinese colleagues had behaved in similar fashion. But what of the herdsmen who had been with us? They could have talked and the news would have spread everywhere. Two unmapped valleys full of wildlife. A freshwater spring in a saltwater desert. What a story.

I can only conclude that it reached the ears of miners and the ears of someone who had the power and the money to recruit poor peasants to carry out gold mining on their behalf.

I returned to the place on the riverbed where I had left my camel. He had not attempted to move but was sitting upright, head erect and quivering all over. I put out a hand to calm him but he jerked his head away from me. He was agitated and fearful.

Camels, like many other animals, have heightened sensory powers. I had seen similar agitation when travelling across the Sahara from Lake Chad to Tripoli when we came to an oasis called Mestuta. It was an unoccupied small oasis and in the centre were the ruins of an old fort that dated from Roman times. This fort was surrounded by a graveyard. Our camels had had a long, hot and tiring day and we were thankful that at Mestuta there was ample vegetation, including nutritious acacia shrubs and trees. We unloaded the camels, hobbled their two front feet and let them free to feed.

Incredibly they did not do so. They all huddled together quivering with fear. Then with a rush they made for one of the acacia bushes, normally such a welcoming source of food. Moments later, clearly very agitated and distressed, they all rushed towards another bush. They continued to repeat this extraordinary behaviour at least twenty times without once snatching a mouthful of food. It was with great difficulty that we persuaded them to settle for the night.

I turned to one of our Tuareg herdsmen.

'What's the matter with them? Why are they behaving like this? I have never seen anything like it before.'

Argali, the herdsman, looked at me.

'Jinns [evil spirits of the desert] are trying to ride them,' he said. 'They will not settle until they leave this place.'

In order to mount my usually docile camel, I started to swing my leg over his rear hump. I had done this many times on the journey and normally he would squat quite contentedly until I was settled in the saddle. Not this time. As my right leg was positioned exactly over the apex of his rear hump, his back legs rose abruptly. This is the classic reaction of a fractious camel. As he rose, the top of the hump caught my leg and I was tossed into the air. For a few seconds I was airborne, and then I landed with a bump on some rocks in the riverbed.

Adiya was the only one who saw the incident. As I stumbled to my feet he grabbed my camel's rope and made him squat.

'Damn, damn, damn,' he said. 'Are you OK, John?'

'Yes,' I replied. My rear end was stiffening, but nothing seemed to be broken. Adiya held on to the camel's nose rope so that his head was tight on the ground. I cautiously mounted. My camel rose, still shaking, to its feet.

Strangely, my back and behind felt much more comfortable when I was swaying back and forth in time with the movement of my camel. I recalled how, when one of our team had fallen off his camel in the Sahara, the Tuaregs had dug a large hole in the sand and in it had lit a fire. When the wood had burnt they then scraped the ash away. The unfortunate had been asked to strip off his clothes and lie in the hot sand. This he did with great difficulty. That treatment had worked and his stiffening limbs were eased. It was not a treatment known to the inhabitants of the Gobi.

Everyone had been affected by the catastrophe at Kum Su. We were all preoccupied with dire thoughts. As we rode quickly away from the polluted spot, two of our herdsmen cantered up sharply behind the Professor. His mind must have been elsewhere because he abruptly lost his balance and fell with a great thump to the ground. I was just behind him and managed to persuade my camel to kneel. I clambered stiffly off his back and went over to the Professor, who was lying prone and still on the ground. Leilei was at his father's side.

It had been a heavy fall and I was concerned that the Professor might have a serious injury. However, he was only slightly concussed and in a few moments he rose shakily to his feet and clambered back onto his camel. It seemed as though the jinns of the Gobi that haunted Kum Su were now pursuing us.

7

Over the Unknown Pass

The pass was steep and rugged,
The wolves they howled and whined;
But he ran like a whirlwind up the pass,
And he left the wolves behind.

Thomas Babbington Macaulay, 'Marriage of Tirzah and Ahirad'

It all started with strident shouting. Then cooking pots were banged and tins thumped. In a few moments, the whole camp erupted in a cacophony of sound that echoed backwards and forwards through the foothills of the Arjin Mountains. If a wild Bactrian camel was lurking in the vicinity it would have fled for the safety of the Kum Tagh. The Professor was the most vociferous. His shouts easily outdid other members of our team, all of whom were wailing like people possessed.

What caused the slumbering campsite to erupt in such discord was the chilling wail of five wolves. Snug in my luxurious Mongolian sleeping bag, I had been listening to their mournful lament for the previous thirty minutes. Emboldened by the dying embers of our campfire, the wolves had crept nearer to our domestic camels that were squatting some thirty yards from my tent.

With the dramatic explosion of noise from our camp, the wolves retreated and the howling abruptly ceased. One by one everyone crawled back into sleeping bags. The camp fell silent. The wolves fell silent, too, until three in the morning when once again the howling began. They were further away, perched, so it seemed, on a ledge in the mountains. This time the nerves of our camels could take no more. As one body, they rose and fled towards the Arjin Mountains up a valley called Kum Bulak. The wolves continued to howl until the first flaming flicker of the rising sun drove them back to their lair, no doubt hungry and dissatisfied

'They killed a man last year,' the lugubrious Mamil told me the next morning. 'He was a miner, looking for gold in the mountains. They killed him at night and ate him.'

We were camped at Kum Bulak, having spent the previous day clambering over the dunes that surround Kum Su. These dunes had been tougher than I had anticipated. I was horrendously stiff after my fall. When we had to dismount and walk because of the softness of the sand, my stiffness forced me to cling onto a rope that secured one of our camels' loads. By grasping it and holding on tight, I was pulled relentlessly forward and consequently did not get left behind.

I had given up trying to persuade the Chinese to hobble our camels at night. I had had the same problem in 1997 when camped on the shore of Lop Nur. Then, the camels had fled in a virulent sandstorm, leaving us stranded near the dried-up lake and we were faced with a 350-kilometre walk to our vehicles if the camels were not recaptured. Fortunately, they were, but even after this experience the Chinese could still not be persuaded to tie up their camels. It is a complete mystery to me why they are so reluctant to perform this simple task. In Mongolia it is a standard procedure.

Jasper Evans had begun a chapter in a book that he had written on practical camel management by saying that if you wanted to return from the desert alive, then you should always ensure that your camels are securely tied up at night. This is nothing more than common sense and on trek in northern Kenya, surrounded by lions, leopards, hyenas and other camel predators, one would never have left them to stay unsecured through a night in the African bush.

The wildlife predators in this part of the Gobi were wolves and they were well-documented camel killers. It took four hours for the Kazakhs to recover the camels. They were unharmed, but after their chilling experience at Kum Su and unnerving night at Kum Bulak, the poor creatures seemed anxious and wild-eyed. My stiffness had forced me reluctantly to decide not to go with the Kazakhs on this occasion.

The next two days were spent dodging rocky outcrops and boulders as we wound west towards the spring of Lapeiquan, where a Lop Nur Reserve check-point had been established. Our campsites were cold and wet as we camped out in riverbeds where ice was beginning to thaw. There was an acute shortage of firewood and our meals were very rudimentary, relying mainly on the cold tinned fish and bully beef or the occasional Chinese sausage made from goodness knows what and wrapped in red plastic.

However, the damp conditions made for a wet surface where prints of wandering wildlife could readily be seen. There certainly seemed to be many more Kiang, the wild Tibetan ass, than when I was last in this area. In Hong Gu valley, we made the exciting discovery of snow leopard tracks. The snow leopard tends to see the traveller, but it is very rare for the traveller to spot the snow leopard.

Leilei, who penetrated deeper into the valley than the rest of us, found a place where a snow leopard had recently killed a gazelle. Disquietingly, he also found the remains of a hunter's hide.

On the third day, Leilei indicated to me that there was a route over the mountains that led directly to Lapeiquan.

'Instead of following the foothills, we can take this route,' he said flourishing a map under my nose.

'There doesn't seem to be much of a track, Leilei.'

'No, John, but look at the contours here and here,' he pointed discerningly to the brown wavy lines with his finger. 'They do not seem to be so steep. We should be able to cross without too much difficulty. I shouldn't think that the route has been followed before and it could save us two days' travel.' I thought Leilei's route looked interesting and he informed Deputy Zhang, who also appeared to acquiesce. Only the Professor seemed to have doubts, but as he was officially in retirement he felt that it would be unwise to assert his authority.

It did not take long for Leilei to discover that deciphering a route on a map is one thing, travelling over it is quite another. Once we had completed a laborious climb up a steep track into the mountains, the trail became fainter and then completely disappeared. We looked down on to a fascinating and beautiful panorama of fractured mountains and deep-set valleys that spread in front of us as far as we could see. Wild animal tracks wound around some of the mountains and it was these that we attempted to follow. There was no set route and each rider took his own line or followed another who appeared to be making steady progress.

Meanwhile, Leilei kept stopping, staring at his GPS and trying to relate the satellite reading to the map that he was following. It soon became obvious that he was having the greatest difficulty in relating to either. Either the map was inaccurate or the GPS was faulty.

When we approached one particularly dangerous mountain peak, I decided to take a route that seemed to be not so steep. The herdsman that I was travelling with opted for a much steeper yet ostensibly quicker route. On arrival at the summit a narrow plateau was arrayed before me and it was not long before I linked up with the herdsman who had taken the steeper option. As the remainder of the caravan was still behind us the herdsman and I decided to wait for them to catch us up.

Twenty minutes later we heard shouts coming from the other side of the summit. Then all was quiet. We opted to stay put on our narrow ridge and we waited for two hours before eventually, and to our great relief, we saw camels emerging over the summit and wending their way towards us. Apparently, two loaded camels had slipped down the side of the mountain, taking their loads with them and – for part of the way – the Professor. Incredibly, both the Professor and the camels were unharmed although a number of food items had been scattered or smashed. It was a situation where we could easily have lost the two camels and indeed the Professor. Fortunately, he had managed to disentangle himself from his fallen camel at an early stage on its downward slide.

Leilei emerged looking pale and anxious; so did Deputy Zhang. This was an area where we should have been using the sure-footed yak. The yak is vastly superior to a camel in its ability to reconnoitre narrow mountain paths.

My journal:

The remainder of the journey after the camels' mishap was both exhilarating and extremely testing and quite the most dangerous journey that I have ever undertaken with domestic camels. It evolved into a seemingly unending slog up and over sheer-sided mountains. Coming down was by far the most dangerous part of the exercise because the mountain surface was frequently covered in loose black shale, which gave when stepped on by a camel. A camel had to be ridden downhill at a slow and carefully controlled pace to prevent it slipping. In addition, one needed carefully to position oneself between the camel's humps. If you leant too far forwards or too far backwards this could easily upset your camel's balance and could send both of you tumbling to either injury or death.

Before I had set out on this expedition one of our backers had asked me to fill out a 'risk assessment form'. I had considered this for quite a long time, not knowing quite what to write. As I knew to some extent the area that we were attempting to cross, I had eventually written: 'The risks are so high that they are impossible to assess.'

There was huge relief felt by all the team when we finally emerged at Lapeiquan at four o'clock in the afternoon. Fortunately all the camels and their riders were unscathed.

There was no doubt that the Lop Nur Reserve's Lapeiquan check-point had been sited in the wrong place. Staff who work at remote check-points must have access to a village. Women and children cannot be expected to join their husbands who have to live in such isolated situations. In the case of Lapeiquan, although it was strategically sited near a freshwater spring and a major mountain river valley, the only humans in the vicinity were nomadic Kazakh herdsmen. The fact that they were nomads meant that human contact was minimal. The nearest village of any substance is Annanba, over 300 miles west and its inhabitants are being moved to New Aksai which lies another 150 miles further to the west. Annanba will soon be totally deserted.

Lapeiquan highlights the difficulties of adequately patrolling and protecting a vast nature reserve whose southern boundary comprises towering mountains 400 miles long, riven with crevasses and gullies, many still unexplored. It explains how the disaster at Kum Su occurred. With limited finances and a headquarters over 1,000 miles away in Urumqi, it is not possible to police such a huge area unless there is access to bottomless financial resources. In addition, because part of the area is still under military control, aerial surveys of the wild Bactrian camel are not permitted. Some years ago, when Sir Richard Branson was attempting to circumnavigate the world in a hot-air balloon, he was directed to fly south over Tibet by the Chinese. They did not want him flying over the Desert of Lop.

All the foregoing reinforces the need for more Reserve check-points, more rangers and above all more money to police this vast inhospitable area.

Lapeiquan was in a sorry state. The check-point had not been newly built but adapted from abandoned coal miners' quarters. We found it covered in crude graffiti that Kazakhs and others had scrawled over the recently painted interior. Newspapers, old tins and sundry detritus lay everywhere. All this was inevitable. The site was far too isolated to expect anyone to spend a winter there when temperatures in January plummet to -40 °Celsius.

We camped in a cold and draughty depression near Lapeiquan check-point. CC and TV attempted to put together an informative documentary on the Kum Su disaster and the Professor and I both tried to express our feelings into their voluminous microphone.

The next morning our truck and two jeeps arrived to pick us up, having been informed of our whereabouts by radio. We moved thirty kilometres away from the riverbed and pitched camp in a more benign spot with the objective of driving towards the Kum Tagh to see if we could see any wild camels. We were nearly at the end of our expedition and so far we had not seen one, although Kiang had been numerous and we had seen over forty. Our domestic camels were taken back to Annanba by the herdsmen, except for Mamil who remained with us. They had been excellent camels, biddable, quiet and easy to load and unload and they had put up a remarkable performance during the mountain crossing.

The following morning we set off in jeeps, leaving the truck at our base camp. Zhang Ying was back with his jeep and his sniffing still occurred with the same monotonous frequency.

We headed to the Kum Tagh and came to a most remarkable crack in a large rock that formed part of the sand mountains. In the bright early morning light it appeared in a stunningly beautiful setting. Through the fissure could be seen outlying boulders leading to a desert beyond that stretched thirty miles towards the southern shore of Lop Nur. The sand on the surrounding dunes was a brilliant blue sprinkled with grey and white. The light was perfect and the sand sparkled and shone in a riot of colour that appeared to change by the minute in the rays of the rising sun.

We walked through the narrow gap and were delighted to see that we were not the first living creatures to do so. Hair from wild Bactrian camels had snagged on both sides of the divide and the footprints of a herd of at least ten showed that this was an important migration route through the dunes for wild camels.

We clambered over enormous boulders admiring the desert view, breakfasted and then returned to our two jeeps. We made preparations to undertake the wild camel expedition by driving along the southern side of the sand mountains. The Professor thought that the reason we had seen no wild camels so far was because they had already migrated to the north from the Arjin Mountains and over the Kum Tagh sand mountains. This is a normal seasonal migration pattern for wild Bactrian camels in this area. In the spring they return to the foothills of the mountains where, after the snow and ice melts, the new vegetation starts to grow. He felt that we might catch up with some stragglers that had not yet crossed the dunes on their journey north.

The Professor was right. After forty minutes' drive east we spotted eight camels to the south of our vehicle — four females, one bull and three two-year-olds.

At this moment, Zhang Ying went mad. In spite of our urgent remonstrations, he drove straight towards the wild Bactrian camel herd as fast as he could. The surface was reasonably firm but it was strewn with rocks and criss-crossed with narrow gullies, causing us to bounce wildly up and down. Zhang paid no heed. His eyes had glazed over and for twenty minutes he indulged in the highly dangerous escapade of camel chasing in a jeep travelling at fifty miles an hour.

The terrified camels saw us coming and promptly scattered, the two-year-olds and the female running in one direction, the bull in another.

'Stop, you fool, stop,' cried the Professor.

Zhang Ying was deaf to everyone. As I was in the front seat, I considered making a dive for the jeep's key so that I could switch off the engine. However, Zhang's belly overlapped the bottom of the steering wheel and obscured my view of the key. I was not going to attempt an unsighted grab, for if I had done so Zhang Ying might have unwittingly turned the jeep over. We careered on, steadily gaining on the bull camel, which naturally was flagging. He was a fine specimen, big and strong but the poor terrified creature was frothing at the mouth and his nostrils were flared.

'Photo, photo, photo,' shouted the exultant Zhang as he drove straight towards the bull.

Then disaster occurred. As Zhang Ying attempted to whip the steering wheel to the left, he hit the camel with the jeep's bumper on its right hind leg. Enough was enough. I grabbed the steering wheel forcing Zhang to lurch to the left. I spotted the key and turned off the engine.

Zhang Ying looked at me furiously and shouted something in Chinese to Leilei, who was seated behind him. Leilei grabbed him by both shoulders as he lunged towards me. Meanwhile, the exhausted bull camel moved off towards the Kum Tagh at a fast trot. Mercifully he seemed unhurt and did not appear to be limping.

'Say something to him, Leilei,' I cried. 'What he has done is terrible. Please tell him. You must never take this man on an expedition again.'

It was late afternoon when we returned. The director of the Reserve, Dr Zhang, joined us at our campsite and I told him how we had hit a wild bull camel. He listened attentively but whether he appreciated the gravity of what had happened I have no idea. Fortunately, the Professor did appreciate it and remonstrated at great length with the driver.

That evening an end-of-expedition banquet had been prepared. Director Zhang had brought with him numerous tins filled with such delicacies as tuna in brine, bamboo stalks, bullocks' testicles in syrup, chickens' feet and other Chinese delights. Deputy Zhang had spent the whole afternoon making noodles and the Professor had prepared delicious minced-mutton dumplings. There were also the inevitable bottles of Chinese beer, *mao-tai* spirit and sweet Chinese wines and – to make the Mongolians feel at home – six bottles of vodka.

The evening started well. Zhang Ying was sitting quietly on his own in the background. During the singing interlude, I managed to teach both English and non-English speakers how to sing, 'Old Macdonald Had a Farm'. The Kazakhs imitated cows, the Mongols imitated ducks and the Chinese prepared themselves for the Year of the Pig by joining in with the 'oink' of the porker.

More national songs were sung until Director Zhang called everyone to order for the toasts. The director made the first toast and handed the next one to me. The sequence moved around the circle of squatting celebrants with each member of the team standing and paying suitable compliments to the others before inviting everyone to join him in a toast.

Director Zhang at this point was sitting cross-legged like an amiable Buddha, beaming at everyone in turn and raising his glass rhythmically to his lips in time with the latest flow of honeyed words. Then it was the turn of journalist Chen. He had, up until this time, played a low-key role during the expedition. He had not offended or upset anyone and his relationship with the two Mongolian scientists seemed to be good.

However, it transpired that during the expedition he had asked Adiya to teach him English, and one of the words that Adiya had taught him was 'bastard'. Chen, eager to show off his newfound skill and thinking that the word 'bastard' was a term of endearment duly raised his can of beer. A great smile spread across his face, he held his beer can aloft, stared at Director Zhang and proclaimed in English,

'I drink to you bastards.'

Director Zhang, eyes half-closed, nodded sagely at the beaming journalist. Director Zhang understood not a word of English but those of us who did burst into spontaneous laughter and started to applaud. Chen was bemused.

'Why are you laughing at me?' he queried.

When Leilei explained to him in Chinese the meaning of what he had said, his whole demeanour changed. Chen flew into a tremendous rage.

'You Mongolian trickster,' he bellowed shaking a fist in the direction of Adiya. A large vein stood out on his forehead and his eyes bulged. He stared at Adiya as though he was preparing to commit a murder.

'You are a bastard,' he roared. 'You are a Mongolian bastard.'

Placing his beer can on the ground, he crushed it with his right foot. Then, still staring hard at Adiya with a frightening intensity, he picked up another can, downed it in one gulp and once again smashed it to pulp. Three more beers followed and the cans were dispatched in a similar fashion. Eventually, five flattened metal containers littered the ground in front of him. He indicated that he heartily wished that they were the flattened torso of the thoroughly nervous young Mongolian scientist who was sitting next to me. With each thundering stamp of his foot, he bellowed, 'bastard' and glared even more menacingly at Adiya.

'I didn't teach him to say that,' Adiya whispered to me. 'He's got it wrong. It's not what I taught him. He's muddled it up with something else.'

Adiya, though strong, was half the size of the chunky Chen. He looked, not unnaturally, exceptionally nervous and confided, 'Goodnight, I am going to my tent.'

By this time all the Chinese were beseeching Chen to calm down, explaining that Adiya had only been playing a harmless joke, and that Chen did not understand what he was saying. For a moment, I thought Chen was going to leap on Adiya and that a serious incident was about to take place. I glanced at Director Zhang, he was rocking gently backwards and forwards muttering softly to himself. Then Chen gave a little shudder, looked round at us all and said one word.

'Sorry.'

As abruptly as this bizarre incident had flared up, it had just as quickly died away.

'Shake hands,' the Professor said to Chen in Chinese. 'Shake hands with our Mongolian guest.'

The Professor had been instrumental in calming Chen down. The journalist gave another little shudder, stood up, walked over to Adiya and grasped him by the hand. Adiya offered him a drink. They stared into each other's eyes and downed a vodka.

'Chen has a very violent temper,' Leilei explained to me when we were quietly discussing what had occurred the previous evening. 'He is also very sensitive and hates to lose face. A combination of violence and extreme sensitivity is a very dangerous mixture. Luckily, nothing happened during the expedition to excite him and it was only at the end that his temper got the better of him.'

Leilei, Director Zhang, the Professor and I had made plans to travel back to Urumqi via Lanzhou, the capital of Gansu Province. There we were to meet Ma Chongyu, the director of the Gansu Forestry Bureau and his team who were in charge of wildlife protection in Gansu. Tuya and Mijji were coming from Mongolia to join the meeting. They had concerns about wild camels that crossed the international border and wandered from Mongolia into China.

Director Ma Chongyu had a pair of truly magnificent eyebrows, quite the bushiest that I have ever seen. My eye was instinctively drawn towards them and they enhanced his appearance as team leader. He had high, prominent cheekbones defining a swarthy face dominated by black eyebrows that met in the middle and then bushed out spectacularly on either side of his brow. The eyebrows sported by the Mr Ma whom I had met at the Hami melon and dog farm paled into insignificance beside those of the director.

It was Director Ma Chongyu whom I had met two years previously during an earlier visit to Lanzhou. We were seated around a circular table and after initial introductions, Ma Chongyu, speaking through an interpreter, said to me, 'I enjoyed your book.'

I knew that Ma Chongyu spoke not a word of English and that he could not possibly have understood a word of my book.

'Thank you very much,' I said. 'Did someone translate it for you?'

'Oh no,' he replied, 'I bought it here in Lanzhou. I have a copy in my briefcase.'

I looked on incredulously as Director Ma pulled from his bag a copy of a Chinese edition of my book that I had never seen before. The production was of a high quality and the photos were well produced. I should, I suppose, feel flattered that there was enough interest in the book to make it worthwhile for someone to pirate it.

'First of all let me begin by saying', Ma Chongyu began after he had welcomed us effusively to the meeting in the Friendship Hotel, 'that we have no problems in our Nature Reserves at all. All the wildlife and the wild Bactrian camels are well protected and under no threat.'

He continued in this vein for twenty minutes. At the end of his oration, Director Ma asked for questions. None of our Chinese team dared to offend him or cause loss of face, by informing him of the disaster our recent expedition had uncovered. It was left to me as the foreigner to inform him about the illegal Kum Su gold mine, the potassium cyanide and our view that this was the work of miners from Gansu.

'Ah, interesting,' said Ma Chongyu, 'very interesting.'

'So everything is not quite perfect?'

'No, I suppose not,' he concurred. 'However, I am sure that this a very rare occurrence.'

The meeting ended inconclusively, but one revealing fact did emerge. The Chinese were apparently constructing, at considerable expense, a six-foot-high fence along the international border with Mongolia, with the result that they were cutting across the migrating route of the wild Bactrian camel and preventing it from entering China. Maybe this is a good thing, because once in China the wild camels are immediately under threat from miners and others as a source of food.

Adiya and Dovchin had gone on ahead of us to Urumqi and had not come to the meeting in Lanzhou. After we had arrived back in Urumqi, Adiya unfortunately became involved in a bizarre incident. We were lodged in an old hotel that had recently been refurbished with a glass sliding door at the entrance. Director Zhang had hosted yet another valedictory dinner and once again the drink flowed. Speeches and bonhomie abounded, although fortunately Zhang Ying was subdued. Adiya, just 27 years old and the senior Mongolian at the banquet, had the responsibility of his country on his shoulders. He manfully made speech after speech extolling Chinese virtues and undying friendship between their two countries. At the end of each speech he toasted the guests in turn. In between each speech he fortified himself with vodka in preparation for further bursts of eloquence. By the end of the evening Adiya had acquitted himself very well and nothing untoward had occurred.

Dovchin and I were staying in the refurbished hotel with Adiya and when we were later dropped outside its door Adiya was in an ebullient mood. Dovchin and I were behind him as he sprang out of the car and up the steps of the hotel. Without waiting for the sliding door to open, Adiya walked straight through the plate glass.

My subconscious image of someone who walks through a glass door is no doubt culled from cartoons that I watched as a boy, where the outline of the man's body is left in the glass. However, in reality, this does not happen. What does happen is that if it is knocked hard enough and Adiya has a tough, robust body, both sliding doors detach from their sliding frame and crash to the ground. And what a crash it was. Glass shattered and flew everywhere. An appalled receptionist sprang from behind her desk, holding a dainty right hand up to her face to cover her mouth. Then she retreated to the safety of her long wooden desk, where she cowered in fright, waiting to see what this crazy Mongolian would do next. Completely unharmed and without a single scratch, Adiya walked through, on and over the shattered glass and twisted metal of the chaos he had unwittingly created. Then he stopped, turned round, viewed the mayhem and burst out laughing.

'I have never seen a door like that,' he said. 'What an extraordinary thing.'

By this time, the receptionist had recovered a few of her wits and was frantically phoning for the hotel manager, whom she fervently hoped was somewhere in the building. He appeared moments later, at a run, accompanied by two uniformed security men. Some late-night guests crowded round Adiya, who continued to laugh and then, controlling himself, he offered to clear up the mess. Meanwhile, the receptionist, who looked as though she would swoon with fright at any moment, breathlessly recounted to her manager exactly what had occurred.

Two Chinese cleaners appeared with brooms and metal shovels. It was cold, well below freezing, and the air from outside was doing battle with the hotel's central heating system and clearly winning. The receptionist, clad in a flimsy dark-blue dress with a large white bow tied in front, began to shiver.

'What can we do?' she wailed, expressively thrusting her upturned hands out in front of her.

It was by now well after midnight and there was nothing that could be done until the morning. Adiya, who had ceased smiling and who had by now realized the enormity of what he had done, apologized profusely to the manager. To the latter's credit, he appeared to accept the apology, although his face betrayed what he really thought of Mongolian late-night behaviour. Eventually, we all retired to our bedrooms leaving the hotel security to the icy job of guarding the exposed front entrance of the hotel. I don't know whether the receptionist stuck it out in the freezing cold; somehow I imagine that she didn't.

Next morning we found workmen repairing the doors with brand-new glass. Later, Director Zhang and the director of the Xinjiang Environmental Protection Bureau came on a site visit. As the Bureau would have to foot the bill, they were clearly not amused.

Historically the Chinese in Urumqi are no strangers to drink-related drama. It was in 1916 that the governor of Urumqi, General Yang Tseng-hsin invited to a banquet all those whom he suspected of plotting to overthrow him. When they were full of drink, he left the hall for a moment and returned, followed by a soldier. While the band played on outside, lulling the senses of the guests, he ordered the soldier to behead them one by one, which he did.

Twelve years later the Chinese proverb 'He who murders at a feast shall have his own blood shed at a feast,' was fulfilled. In 1928, the general was shot dead by his minister of foreign affairs, Fan Yao-nan, while proposing a toast to a Soviet official at a banquet held after the Russian Language School's graduation ceremony.

In this context Adiya's misdemeanour was insignificant.

On my return to England, I made representations to the Chinese embassy in London about the disaster at Kum Su and fortunately managed to place an article in the London *Times* and in magazines including the *National Geographic*. I outlined the problem on BBC radio, and the vice-director of the Chinese State Environment Protection Agency (SEPA) in Beijing, who was an old friend, was also informed.

All this varied activity had an effect, because we learnt from Leilei that the Environmental Protection Bureau in Urumqi received urgent orders from SEPA to clean up Kum Su. The pressure put on the bureau was apparently so great that three clean-up expeditions were undertaken. They cleared up all the used and unused drums of potassium cyanide, the many sundry items of miners' kit and belongings and the yards of plastic sheeting that were strewn along either side of the valley that led to the spring.

Leilei went with the Bureau officials on all three clean-up expeditions and told me that on the last one he had seen twelve wild Bactrian camels and a number of Kiang near Kum Su. But the Argali wild sheep that had so entranced me previously were nowhere to be seen.

8

The Desert's Dusty Face

There is a silence where hath been no sound,
There is a silence where no sound may be,
In the cold grave – under the deep deep sea,
Or in wide desert where no life is found.

Thomas Hood, 'Silence'

What are the two great deserts – the Gashun Gobi and the Desert of Lop – that surround the ear-shaped dried-up lake of Lop Nur really like? From 1953 until 1979 they formed the nuclear test site of China and underground tests are still being carried out to this day. There are very few Westerners who can provide an authentic answer to the question, as since 1953 it has been almost impossible for a foreigner to enter the area. Today, the two deserts have become a magnet for fortune seekers and miners, both legal and illegal, spurred on by the Chinese government's exhortation to 'Develop the West.'

The Gashun (Bitter) Gobi stretching to the south and east of the Kuruk Mountains south of Turfan, and the Desert of Lop stretching to the south and west of Lop Nur form one of the most hostile and forbidding regions on earth. Freezing cold in winter, where temperatures plummet to -40 °Celsius, and overwhelmingly hot in summer when they rise to a stifling +55 °Celsius. In the spring and autumn these deserts are blasted by ferocious sandstorms. The 18,000-foot mountain ranges of the Tibet Plateau bound the deserts to the south. To the north, the beautiful Tien Shan form part of their northern border. In addition, some areas in the north-west lie below sea level.

There is no fresh water in both deserts, only salt springs. No human being, not even the hardy nomad, can live permanently in this utterly barren wilderness of over 2,000 square kilometres. The only mammal that has the ability to survive in these vast deserts is the wild Bactrian camel; far removed from contact with domestic Bactrians, the wild camels migrate from one saltwater spring to another, some of which are over 100 miles apart.

The Gashun Gobi and the Desert of Lop are natural deserts. Yet every year their boundaries widen and the habitable desert fringe is turned into true desert. This is caused by the relentless increase in man's activities: excess water extraction for irrigation, the cutting of trees and the building of new settlements. On the eastern side of the road from Korla to Ruoqian this desertification is starkly illustrated by the slow death of countless age-old wild poplars.

An aerial view of these two deserts would show a burning arid waste of dunes and multicoloured rocky outcrops, interspersed with monotonous rolling expanses of gravel and crossed by occasional ridges of high mountains whose foothills dwindle to low rocky mounds. The whole of this stone desert is shadeless and exposed to scorching heat under a merciless sun. At night it is quite otherwise, and as darkness falls, the scorching heat gives way to a sudden chill that rises from the ground and strikes with a cold impact, leaving a warm upper stratum of air. Soon, this layer, too, is permeated by the penetrating chill.

Sometimes, on the horizon, a slender spiral of sand will rise, circle, glide along the ground and then vanish into the sky. Then all at once the desert floor becomes alive with these 'dust devils' sending sand

and stone spiralling upwards. These whirling columns of sand give the impression of an invisible being wrapping a layer of dust around its unseen form. Some choose to whirl to the left and others to the right. In Central Asia, as in Africa, many people still consider dust devils to be the home of lost souls, eternally restless spirits who agitate the desert in a desperate search for rest and peace of mind.

'That one is the male and that one is the female,' explained Leilei to me one day with a laugh, pointing to two dust devils that appeared to be dancing with each other, spinning round and round in opposite directions. 'We call them *kwei* and you can always distinguish which is which by the way they fold their dust cloak around them, right to left or left to right.' This particular 'couple' moved towards us but fortunately turned aside before they were too close.

The remains of rocketry have been scattered around this wilderness of unimaginable bleakness. A kingdom of death reigns; not a beast, not a track, not even the skull of some old wild camel that had dragged itself here to die in solitude. Occasionally, on one of our expeditions into the area, we saw a dried-up tussock in a gully. Jet-black shale littered the surrounding hills. The shale was loose and sharp and we slithered and slipped and tore our hands and clothing in an attempt to climb some of the highest peaks. The wind would suddenly freshen, forcing us to cling with one hand to a sharp rock as we gripped binoculars or spotter-scopes with the other. Far, far below, a forgotten, disordered world tinged with a pale blue colourwash sprawled around us like a gigantic maze. There were no vehicle tracks to show that others had penetrated this area. Here and there a broken shard of debris from outer space glittered in the sun, a sun that seemed to be constantly positioned directly above us. There was no shade and no shadow. In one place we found old camel droppings scattered on the ground; dry, hard and bleached a dirty grey by the burning desert sun. What had driven wild camels to enter such a region, where there is no water for many kilometres? The answer is man, the only wild Bactrian camel predator of any significance.

Fortunately for us on that particular occasion, the gates of Hell had opened on a quiet day. When the fearsome, howling desert winds stoked up the furnaces and hurled the sand, shale and shingle through those gullies and around those hillocks to create a seemingly unending inferno then nothing, not even the mysterious wild camel could survive. Sandstorms are not to be trifled with, as this description by the early twentieth-century German archaeologist Albert von Le Coq shows:

> Quite suddenly the sky grows dark, the sun becomes a dark-red ball of fire seen through the fast-thickening veil of dust, a muffled howl is followed by a piercing whistle, and a moment after, the storm bursts with appalling violence upon the caravan. Enormous masses of sand, mixed with pebbles, are forcibly lifted up, whirled round and dashed down on man and beast; the darkness increases and strange, clashing noises mingle with the roar and howl of the storm, caused by the violent contact of great stones as they are whirled up through the air. The whole happening is like Hell let loose, and the Chinese tell of the scream of the spirit eagle so confusing men, that they rush madly into the desert wilds and there meet a terrible death far from frequented paths.
>
> Any traveller overwhelmed by such a storm must, in spite of heat, entirely envelop himself in felts to escape injury from the stones dashing round him with such mad force; man and horse must lie down and endure the rage of the hurricane, which often lasts for hours together. And woe to the rider who does not keep a firm hold on his horse's bridle, for the beasts, too, lose their reason from terror of the sandstorm and rush off to a lingering death in the desert solitudes . . .

As related earlier, our camels rushed off in terror when they scattered in all directions during a black sandstorm that burst on the encampment at Hongliugou.

Many people have entered these deserts and totally vanished. Seven centuries ago, while travelling along the Southern Silk Road south of the Kum Tagh in the Desert of Lop, Marco Polo noted that:

> When a man is riding by night through the desert and something happens to make him loiter and lose touch with his companions he hears spirits talking

in such a way that they seem to be his colleagues. Sometimes, indeed, they even hail him by name. Often these voices make him stray from the path, so that he never finds it again. And in this way many travellers in the great desert of Lop have been lost and have perished.

In July 1990, five miners looking illegally for crystal disappeared with their vehicle. Neither they nor their vehicle have ever been found. In June 1996, a Chinese explorer from Shanghai attempted to follow our tracks to the ancient city of Lou Lan. He was discovered lying dead in the sand, totally naked. He had died of heat exhaustion.

The most celebrated of the people who have recently disappeared is Professor Peng Jiamu, who vanished without trace in June 1980. In 1979, Peng Jiamu had been appointed the vice-president of the Xinjiang branch of the Chinese Academy of Sciences and in the summer of 1980 he led a team of chemists, geologists, biologists and archaeologists into the Gashun Gobi. Wang Wanxuan, Peng's driver, recalled that the road was very difficult and water supplies were short. Some people in the team began to complain and asked that the research be terminated so that they could return. Peng gathered together all his team members and said firmly, 'The study of science is to walk along a road not travelled by other people.'

His confidence helped to raise the spirits of the team and the agitation to head back home died away.

'I will never forget the encouraging words and the decisive attitude of Peng,' said driver Wang.

Five days after this speech, Peng walked out of the scientists' camp, having left a note saying that he was going out to look for water. Like Captain Robert Scott's colleague, Lawrence Oates, who said to Scott on his fatal 1912 Antarctic expedition, 'I am just going outside, and I may be some time,' Peng Jiamu was never seen again.

The news of Peng's disappearance reached Beijing and upset the top Chinese leaders, including Deng Xiaoping. The central government ordered the military to dispatch more than ten planes, helicopters and hundreds of soldiers to search for him. Six police officers from Shanghai and the provinces of Shandong and Jiangsu were called in to search with their police dogs. In total, the military and local government organized three large-scale rescue operations. In November 1980, another search team drove into the area for a final attempt to find Peng's remains.

'In each search, we examined every inch of land around the old campsite,' said Xia Xuncheng, a former deputy to Peng, 'but nothing was found.'

Meanwhile, Peng's disappearance made headlines in newspapers nationwide. He was portrayed as a martyr ready to sacrifice himself for science. Xia, who led the search and subsequent scientific desert explorations, summarized two possibilities for Peng's fate. One was that Peng was buried in a sandstorm because between 16 and 17 June there was a huge wind that created a violent storm.

'Three days after that storm we lost a camel. The next day we found its body. It had almost been covered up completely. Only the lower part of one leg was sticking out above the sand,' wrote Xia.

Another possibility is that Peng was buried by a sand dune. Travellers and explorers often use sand dunes for protection against a strong wind. A powerful wind, such as the one which occurred on 16 and 17 June, could cause a dune to collapse, instantly burying those who were taking shelter underneath. Many years later, this article was published in *The People's Daily*, an English-language Chinese newspaper:

A Chinese expedition has found a mummy on the brink of Lop Nur, where a well-known scientist went mysteriously missing nearly 26 years ago. Another expedition is now prepared to ascertain the identity of the mummy, which was found near the place where Professor Peng Jiamu, a recognized bio-chemist who led a scientific investigation across Lop Nur, was reported missing. Xia Xuncheng, a former colleague of Peng, said in an exclusive telephone interview, 'We're not sure about the identity of the mummified figure, but it's very near the place we lost Jiamu. If we are able to find any conclusive evidence,' Xia continued, 'we would need to undertake DNA matching between the sample we will take from the mummy and others taken from Peng's relatives.'

The mummified body has recently been retrieved and is undergoing DNA tests in Dun Huang.

Near the spot where Professor Peng Jiamu had disappeared, we were on a wild camel survey and came across a memorial that had been erected by one of the teams who had searched for his remains. Our expedition guide, the late Lao Zhao, had worked with Jiamu as had Professor Yuan Guoying and they were both greatly attached to his memory. Lao Zhao had brought with him a small tin of pillar-box red paint to touch up the faded Chinese characters that were inscribed on one side of the obelisk.

Having carefully repainted the faded inscription, Lao Zhao burnt newspaper to let Professor Peng Jiamu know that we had arrived, poured a bottle of beer around the wooden railings surrounding the memorial to cheer him up and left some food for him to enjoy after we'd left. Then he sat and meditated for a full hour, staring as if transfixed at the characters on the memorial plinth. It was an eerie and somewhat awesome sight to see Lao Zhao so deeply affected by the memorial to his dead colleague.

Lop Nur lake, long famed in Chinese history, was dubbed by Hedin 'The Wandering Lake'. Two feeder rivers from the mighty river Tarim had over the centuries carried melted snow water from the west and north-west into the lake. The snowmelt comes from the towering mountains, the Pamirs and the Tien Shan, which surround the deserts of Lop, the Gashun Gobi, and the Taklamakan to the west and to the north.

When Sven Hedin first entered the Desert of Lop in 1893, he canoed down the Konche Dariya, the name of one of the tributaries. He reached a junction where the river and its water turned south.

However, another tributary, the Kuruk Dariya, headed due east. This river was totally dry and Hedin was determined to follow the eastern route. Abandoning his boats he set out on foot along the dry riverbed.

It was during the course of this walk that Ordek, the Uighur expedition guide whose grave we visited, was sent by Hedin back into the desert to recover the lost spade and came across ancient wild poplar timbers sticking out of the ground: not the stumps of dead trees but the remains of timber-framed buildings. As already mentioned, they proved to be the remains of the ancient city of Lou Lan, which had been abandoned in about AD 400. The reason for the flight from the city was now clear to Hedin. Lou Lan had been left high and dry. The inhabitants had left their prosperous city because the snowmelt had diverted from the Kuruk Dariya into the Konche Dariya, causing the Kuruk Dariya to dry up. A new lake had formed 150 miles to the south of Lou Lan.

After the discovery of Lou Lan by Ordek, Sven Hedin excavated some of the houses and found many Chinese manuscripts from the third century AD. Stein made his further archaeological excavations in 1906 and 1914, investigating the packed earth-and-straw wall that surrounded the city. It was over 1,000 feet high and twenty feet thick at the base. Stein also recovered a wool-pile carpet fragment, some yellow silk and Gandharan architectural wood carvings.

The primary aim of Stein's 1914 expedition was to undertake further excavations at Lou Lan. Setting off from India with a small party, he travelled over the Pamir knot (the meeting point of the Pamir, Karakoram and Hindu Kush mountain ranges) to Kashgar where Chiang-Ssu-yeh, a young Chinese interpreter, was taken onto the payroll. Before setting out for Lou Lan, Stein reinforced his small party with two local guides, fifty labourers and eighteen camels to supplement their seven baggage camels. Eleven days out of Ruoqian the caravan reached the ancient city and started excavations. Working in howling gales and keeping themselves from dying of exposure by burning the trunks of long dead trees, Stein and his men excavated the sand-filled buildings for the next eleven days. They left Lou Lan with a rich haul of Chinese documents detailing life in this distant outpost and a quantity of tablets in Kharoshthi (an ancient Indian script). The Kharoshthi tablets refer to the city as Kroraina and show that the Chinese military authorities allowed the indigenous administration to continue in the hands of the local ruling families.

Stein left to replenish his supplies and then returned to Lou Lan by a different route, where they found rows of fallen dead trees lining the dry Kuruk Dariya. Excavations in this area revealed abundant Neolithic arrowheads and jade, showing that the area must have been fertile and productive for a long time span.

Stein had unearthed manuscripts and letters written on paper and wooden staves, which accurately dated the abandonment of the city. They show that Lou Lan had an inn, a hospital, a post office building and a temple. Most of the letters dealt with routine administrative matters but one translated into a very human and heartfelt sentiment. Written upon receiving sad news, Tsi Ch'eng writes: 'Miss Yin having been without any previous illness, the misfortune that so suddenly befell her was quite beyond expectation. I received the sad news and so much greater is, therefore, my deep-felt sympathy and regret. But a deep wound cannot be endured. What then can help?'

After further excavations at Lou Lan, Stein's expedition left in a north-easterly direction, excavating along a line of forts and cemeteries that lined the Middle Silk Road all the way to Dun Huang. One fort that he missed was Tu-ying, which our expedition found lying close to the northern shore of Lop Nur. About twenty-five miles from Lou Lan, it must have been a strategic look-out post for inhabitants of the city as it overlooked both the lake and the Silk Road. Lao Zhao our guide assured me at the time that none of the early explorers had discovered Tu-ying. A Chinese archaeologist came across it by chance in the 1930s, and Hedin learnt about when he returned to Lop Nur in 1934. 'No one has been here since. You're the very first foreigner to reach Tu-ying in recorded history.'

Later research revealed that unfortunately this was not wholly true. Although Stein and others had certainly not been to Tu-ying, the incredible Hedin had, if only for an hour. Hedin had written of his 1934 expedition:

> There was a minimum temperature of 42.4 degrees on the night of May 8–9, strangely cold for so late in the year! The scouts had been out, and when we got up in the morning they reported that they had not been able to find an arm of the river with any current, but that they had found the ruins of a fair-size house on the mainland to the north-west. Chen [*Hedin's Chinese expedition scientist*] suspected at once that this was the fort T'u-ken, discovered by the archaeologist Hwang Wen-pi in 1930. Just on nine we got into a double canoe and rowed to a place over open water free of reeds. It took scarcely half an hour to reach the place.
>
> The posts of the house rose from a low mound situated on a peninsular, which had water on three sides – west, south and east. Chen had been there in the early spring of 1931 during Horner's expedition to Lop-nor, and recognized the place at once.
>
> Some of our boatmen had dug a hole in the middle of the house without finding anything . . . We stayed for about an hour, which I needed to make a sketch of the place with all its details. Chen took some photographs and measurements.

I suspect that our 'find' of Tu-ying was Hedin's T'u-ken.

Later we became the first expedition to reach Lou Lan from the east as Hedin, Stein and the other archaeologists and explorers had all reached the city from the west. When our expedition truck was bogged down in sand, our journey involved a forty-four-mile round trip on foot, which we completed in sixteen hours. Our arrival at the Buddhist temple on the outskirts of Lou Lan, after trudging through the very worst scenery that nature could devise, gave us all a sense of uplift. We hugged each other and took an endless succession of posed photographs. Then we sat down on some massive timbers and ate our meagre rations. Lao Zhao was very happy. As our guide, compass bearer and map interpreter, he had, after all, borne the greatest responsibility.

After half an hour's rest we set off for the ancient city itself. Although the route was difficult, there was an added spring in our step and it took us just over an hour. We headed for the awesome central tower. This watch-tower, standing plumb in the middle of the city, is surrounded by the remains of houses to the east, south and west and an open square to the north. The flagstaff erected on the tower's summit by two members of Hedin's team, Chen and Horner, in 1931, still remains in place and, although the steps that wind to the top have mostly worn away, the tower is still climbable. The view from the top is breathtaking. Grey desolation and decay spread out in all directions and I gasped aloud when I saw the jigsaw puzzle of hummocks and gullies that we had managed to cross.

The dimensions of a number of the ancient houses can still be identified by the woven tamarisk and reed building material that once formed the base of their external walls. Many of the buildings could also be accurately plotted by the distance between their upright support poles. A large building near a market square had been the city's municipal centre or *yamen* and within it, individual rooms could quite clearly be seen. One building had a door lintel, firmly positioned between two upright posts, and another large construction had a massive end wall that had splayed out on either side to form a huge V. Man-made square notches could also be seen in a number of collapsed cross-pieces.

Our team searched hard among the ruins for gems, earrings, coins, spoons, tweezers, hairpins and Roman and Syrian glass, trinkets and necessities that earlier explorers had unearthed. But apart from numerous pieces of pottery, most of which were too cumbersome to carry, we only found a fragment of a bronze mirror and a coin.

The extent of the city and the quality of preservation are remarkable. Only in the desperately dry air of the Gobi, where measurable rainfall may occur once in a decade, can this phenomenon occur. Nevertheless, I was surprised that 1,600 years of violent sandstorms had left so much for us to explore. It was not at all difficult to imagine that this was a very important centre on the longest caravan route on earth, that great highway – the Silk Road – which linked east to west. And from the top of the tower, one could almost hear the tinkling caravan bells and see the endless processions of camels, winding across the desert and through the city gates. Are those flickering shadows in the square below us crowds of walkers, riders, donkeys, camels and carts? Are those people off-loading bales of silk from squatting camels on the far side of the square, traders from the East. And those over there, spreading their wares out before them on woven blankets of camel hair, are they merchants from the West? Surely those are the shouts of camel drovers, the cries of hawkers and traders, the laughter of girls and the guffaws of ribald men? Or is it only the ever-present wind, moaning around the cracks and crevices of the tower and making fools of us all?

On this occasion, we stayed in Lou Lan for as long as we dared. Without provisions or water it was dangerous not to return to our truck that night, especially as Lao Zhao had grossly underestimated the distance. If a sand storm sprung up and we were marooned in Lou Lan we could find ourselves in considerable difficulty. It is as dangerous to lose one's way in the maze of *yardangs* surrounding Lou Lan as in the subterranean passages of the Roman catacombs. All of us felt a growing sense of unease as the watery sun, half-hidden by dust, started to dip towards the horizon. None of us wanted to remain in the ancient city after dark.

We set off to reach our truck into a setting sun, which provided a spectacular backdrop for this ghostly city. We headed directly for the riverbed, avoiding the Buddhist tower. The sun disappeared and, as we reached the river, our torches lit up the footprints left by our outward journey. Fortunately, as our batteries faded, a weak moon rose. If there had been no moon and if the wind had not changed direction to blow from behind us, it would have been much more difficult. It was too cold to rest. When we tried to do so, we stiffened up with cold. We left the riverbed as our torches died and to our great relief saw a 'star in the east', the light from a bulb placed on a pole on the top of our truck and powered by a generator. As we walked towards it, the moonlight faded away. The going became increasingly difficult and we stumbled around *yardangs* and through crumbling shale for over three hours. Suddenly, our 'star' disappeared!

At this point our situation was serious. We were looking for a needle in a haystack with nothing to guide us. The moon had completely vanished and a second party, who was following our footsteps, was a long way behind. If we missed the truck and carried on into the featureless wasteland, we could easily disappear for good like so many Gobi travellers before us.

'I suggest that we spread out in a line as far apart as possible,' I said. 'We can't be too far away from the truck because we left the riverbed three hours ago. Whatever we do, we mustn't lose contact with each other.'

We spread out as far as we dared and in the total darkness called out constantly to each other. The Professor was in the centre, Lao Zhao on his right and myself on his left. The shadows ahead of us played constant tricks. What appeared to be a truck turned out to be yet another hummock of twisted wood. We stopped constantly to call out, hoping that our truck driver would hear us. There was no response. Apart from the howling wind, it was as silent as the tomb. And then unexpectedly, just as our hearts were sinking into the sand, Lao Zhao gave a great shout. He had spotted the truck. We were safe. It was 1.30 a.m. on Easter Sunday and we had risen indeed!

Our thoughts were for the party behind us. Professor Yuan roused the truck driver from his slumbers in his cab and gave him a dressing down. The driver had thought that we would not be returning that night and so had switched off the generator. I was nearly asleep on my feet. After two steaming bowls of porridge oats, I stumbled into my tent and collapsed in an insensible heap. I was woken at 7.30 a.m. by stirring shouts announcing the arrival of the rest of our team. They had walked much more slowly than we had as one of them had a swollen knee. Fortunately, they had seen the light on the truck when it was switched back on. But, uncertain of the distance to the camp, they had decided to light a fire, get some sleep and continue their trek at daybreak. To their utter astonishment they woke to find that they had camped only 500 yards away.

A Chinese architectural team recently made further discoveries at Lou Lan. They found a man-made canal, fifteen feet deep and fifty-five feet wide, running through the city from north-west to south-east. They also collected 797 objects from the area, including vessels of wood, bronze objects, jewellery and coins, and Mesolithic stone tools.

In 2003 other reported finds included mummies and ancient burial grounds, ephedra sticks, a string bracelet that holds a hollowed jade stone, a leather pouch, a woollen loincloth, a wooden mask painted red and with large nose and teeth, boat-shaped coffins, a bow with arrows and a straw basket.

The area surrounding Lou Lan lies just above sea level and is very flat. The difference in height between Lou Lan and the northern shore line of the dried-up lake is six feet. The Lop Desert as a whole is as horizontal and as even as the sea. Wide areas of old lake bottom consist of *shorr*, or salt-bearing clay, stiffened into slabs and ridges as hard as brick. Hedin worked out that over a period of time the tributary carrying water had silted up. When this happens, the mountain snowmelt diverts into the other riverbed.

He concluded that this is why Lou Lan had been abandoned. Hedin likened this process to the pendulum of a clock that swung every 1,600 years or thereabouts. This was the time it took for one tributary or the other to silt up and for the flow of water to divert into the other.

Imagine his incredulity, when in 1921 it did just that. It swung back into the Kuruk Dariya and the northern lakebed that flowed past the now-deserted Lou Lan filled again with water after a 1,600-year interval. Hedin was thunderstruck. It meant not only that the theories that he had put forward twenty-eight years earlier were right, but his prophecy that the lake would return to its former site had also come true.

In 1933, Hedin canoed down the very stretch of river where as a young man he had walked. He caught sizeable freshwater fish in Lop Nur and prophesied that the fertility of the area would return and that in time it would become a great agricultural breadbasket. He wrote:

I had occupied myself with the geographical problems of Lop Nur since 1896. The old Middle Silk Road had run along its northern bank and along the Kuruk Dariya. Lou Lan was its chief place in the region. When the river and lake moved south around AD 330, the Silk Road had been cut, Lou Loan abandoned and forgotten. Now the water had come back into old beds, and new prospects of historic significance were unrolled before our eyes. Drought, the silence of death and oblivion had enveloped this region for sixteen centuries, but now it had suddenly come to life again, and it was reserved for our expedition to fasten together the links in the chain. Behind lay 2,000 years in which Lop Nur had been known to the Chinese, and before – we grew dizzy at the thought of the countless shadowy years to come in which new arteries of communication – motor roads, railways, strategic roads – would be created in the heart of Asia, and new posts and towns would grow up in a desert region which for 1,600 years had been so poor that it could not provide a home even for scorpions and lizards. Only the wild camels had now and then wandered into it from their salt springs in the Kuruk Mountains – but now, when the water had returned and men would see with consternation the frontiers of their ancient sanctuary curtailed and withdrawn.

How hard and tiring those marches along the bed of the Kuruk Dariya had been, twenty-eight years ago! I recalled in memory the aspect of the river-bed, broad, deep and winding but dried up, with the dead timber on the banks. There stood the trees like tombstones in a cemetery, grey, split, dead for 1,600 years, and as brittle as though made of clay. No life, not a drop of water in that bed, where a mighty river once ran and the desert wind murmured in the summits of leafy poplars.

Yes, so it was in 1900. In 1921 the river had returned to its old bed and in 1928 I received the first news that my prediction had come true.

What Hedin could not foretell was the development of the nuclear bomb and China's choice of Lop Nur as its site for tests. He could not foresee that much further to the west on the mighty Tarim River, a dam would be constructed to divert the river's waters into channels to irrigate farmland.

When I first visited Lop Nur, I had no idea what I would find – a lake full of water or a lake totally dry. In the event we found the lake to be as dry as it was in 1893 when Hedin walked down the dried-up Kuruk Dariya. It was as though nothing had changed and as if not a drop of water had flowed down the Kuruk Dariya between 1921 and 1976.

In 1976, the Kuruk Dariya dried up once again after its brief awakening from its 1,600-year sleep. There was no rebirth of Lou Lan's ancient city. The two lakebeds of Lop Nur, to the east and to the south of Lou Lan, have both dried up and Hedin's prophecy of a green hinterland has come to naught.

Following in the footsteps of Sven Hedin, our expedition found Lop Nur surrounded once again by 'drought and the silence of death'. The fish had long since disappeared and the wild boar had fled. The Kuruk Dariya was totally dry and the poplar trees that had flourished along its banks for the brief space of fifty years were withered and dead. It was a total reversion to Hedin's memory of the river as he first saw it just before the turn of the century.

Paradoxically, the only beneficiary of this geographical upheaval is the wild Bactrian camel. Had the desert bloomed as Hedin predicted, the camel would have been driven away from the area and hunted out of existence. However, the drying up of both lakes is a direct cause of environmental change in the desert and the spread of desertification. A large lake, 140 miles in length and fifty miles wide, full of snowmelt water that is replenished annually, must give off a significant amount of vapour into the atmosphere. This has not been the case for the last twenty-eight years. With the other lakebed also completely dry, little wonder that water points are drying up and that the desert is encroaching on once-fertile farming land.

On an earlier expedition, I unexpectedly came across a huge dam, the Dashi Hazi. This was the dam that had been constructed to cut off water from entering the Kuruk Dariya. The Somme-like dead and dying remains of mature desert poplars were a depressing testimony to the dam's contribution to desertification further south. The severing of seasonal water flow to these rivers was the sole reason for both the ancient lakebeds of Lop Nur now being totally dry.

Later on that expedition, I visited a village called Aksupe in a fertile area 150 miles to the west of Lou Lan. The headman of Aksupe, a gauche young, non-Uighur-speaking Chinese man with thick-rimmed spectacles, a wisp of a beard and pimples, greeted us with deference. He was very different in outlook and demeanour to the autonomous, 'big, burly and dignified' Uighur headman, Sali Beg, who administered Aksupe's village life in Sven Hedin's day. The language barrier, his ignorance of Islam and Uighur customs had clearly isolated him from the local villagers. He seemed a typical, imposed stooge, cut off from the people, lonely and anxious, and was clearly delighted to have visitors from the outside world to relieve him from the daily tensions of his mundane existence.

'He was elected by democratic means,' commented Professor Yuan when I queried his credentials. 'There were four candidates selected by the government. The people had a good choice.'

'Were any of the candidates Uighurs?' I asked.

'Oh, no,' said the Professor looking askance at my question, 'they were all Chinese.'

At our request, the headman assembled a group of worthy Uighur oldies in the communal village hall. As soon as I broached the subject of Sven Hedin and staff that he had recruited at Aksupe a fierce argument broke out.

'I remember a Russian who came here at that time,' said one sightless old man. 'He gave me money.'

'Nonsense,' asserted another. 'What a lie. You're only a youngster. You weren't even born. I was ten years old at the time. I remember my father saying . . .'

'You! What are you talking about?' Another ancient with a finely-chiselled face, embroidered skullcap, flowing gown and pointed beard shook a finger at the blind one. 'My uncle was a boatman for the European, and the white man wasn't a Russian, he was from another tribe.'

The argument blazed. It became impossible to sift fact from fiction. But I did learn that they remembered Ordek, the man who was sent into the desert to look for Hedin's lost spade; he had become a village hero.

We later visited the Aksupe dam with the headman and some of the old men. Smaller than Dashi Hazi, the water smelt foul and leaked from the dam walls in countless places.

'When I was a boy,' said the man whose uncle had been Sven Hedin's boatman, 'it didn't get as hot as it does today. The Bengal tiger was found near here, there were wild pig and plenty of gazelles. Nowadays, except for a very few gazelles, they've all disappeared.'

'We didn't have the diseases that we get today,' another ancient worthy interjected. 'When the water was flowing down the Konche Dariya, it was clean and fresh. Look at this,' He extended his arm towards the dam, 'it's filthy. This is our drinking water.'

I stared at the stagnant, murky water and understood why hepatitis, a disease unknown to them before, was common now.

9

The Secrets of the Sands

The worms were hallow'd that did *breed the silk,*
And it was dy'd in mummy which the skilful
Conserv'd of maidens' hearts.

William Shakespeare, *Othello*

In a smart new museum in Urumqi, there is a collection of mummies that lie at the centre of another ancient Gobi mystery. Some of these Urumqi mummies have recently been carbon-dated to 2000 BC. This makes them the contemporaries of Egyptian mummies. Surprisingly, they are not Chinese or Mongolian in origin but Caucasian, tall, large-nosed and in some cases blond, with round, possibly blue eyes.

Few artefacts were placed with them in their graves and this makes it difficult for archaeologists and researchers to identify any cultural connections from the clues that might have been revealed by buried pottery or tools. One possible indication lies in their clothing, which, thanks to the extreme dryness of the desert environment, had been preserved – in some cases with hues as bright as the day that they were buried.

The earliest discoveries of mummies were made by the teams that accompanied Sven Hedin and Aurel Stein on their expeditions at the end of the nineteenth century and later in the 1930s. In 1914, when Stein explored and excavated the site of Lou Lan, he began tracing the Middle Silk Road to Dun Huang. He came across ruined forts and cemeteries for about fifteen miles and then discovered:

> A small ruined fort . . . on the top of a precipitous mesa [*an ancient isolated land formation made of clay, sculpted over millennia by severe winds and sandstorms. There are hundreds of* mesas *or* yardangs *to the north of Lop Nur and to the west of Dun Huang*] fully a hundred feet high and commanding a distant view over the desolate waste ground. The elevated position, together with the absolute aridity of the climate since ancient times, has assured here a truly remarkable state of conservation to the bodies of men and women found in graves outside what was evidently a look-out post occupied by indigenous Lou-lan people. Several of the bodies were wonderfully well conserved, together with their burial deposits. The peaked felt caps decorated with big feathers and other trophies of the chase, the arrow shafts by their side, the coarse but strong woollen garments, the neatly woven small baskets holding the food for the dead etc., all indicated a race of semi-nomadic herdsmen and hunters, just as the Han [*Chinese*] Annals describe the Lou-lan people when the Chinese found them on the first opening of the route through the desert.
>
> It was a strange sensation to look down on figures which but for the parched skin seemed like those of men asleep . . . The characteristics of the men's heads showed close affinity to that Homo Alpinus type which, as the anthropometrical materials collected by me have proved, still remain the prevailing element in the racial constitution of the present population of the Tarim Basin.
>
> The distant view gained from this elevated point made it certain that we were here near the eastern proximity of the ground once reached by the life-giving water from the river. Beyond to the east there lay the boundless expanse of shimmering salt, marking the dried up Lop sea-bed.

Stein remarks that one edge of a shroud had been formed into a pouch that held twigs of ephedra, a plant prized as a stimulant today and an important compound in the relief of asthma. In fact, nearly all of the known graves found over the years near Lou Lan and on the perimeter of the Taklamakan desert contained ephedra. What is so special about ephedra that the dead seemed to require it when they were buried?

Ephedra, a shrubby plant that grows primarily in desert regions, contains a stimulant that is today called ephedrine. Chinese ephedra, *Ephedra Sinica*, is still exported by the lorry-load for medicinal purposes from Xinjiang where it is called *ma huang* – yellow hemp. Taken in large quantities, ephedra can also bring on hallucinations. In some cultures the dead are buried with artefacts, food stuffs or drugs to help them reach and remain happily in an after-life and to ensure that they do not return to plague or disturb the living. It would seem that ephedra was used by the people of Lou Lan and the Taklamakan for this purpose. They realized that ephedra was both a stimulant and had hallucinatory properties and that both these factors would assist in ensuring the comfort and well-being of the deceased.

What is fascinating about these discoveries by Stein is that they seem to be contemporary to approximately 100 BC. As the burial methods and the items that were put into the grave are strikingly similar in all cases, it suggests that we are dealing with people whose nomadic habits and dress changed little over a period of 2,000 years. Such extreme conservatism seems to be startling, since great cultures to the east in China and to the west in Greece and Rome were, during the period, changing rapidly. Maybe it was their nomadic practices and remoteness that kept their habits and dress unchanged.

Stein continues:

The graves were marked by rows of small posts placed close together and sticking out above the gravel surface. They were found in two small groups, at a distance of about twenty yards from each other . . . The corroding force of wind-driven sand and gravel was strikingly illustrated by the abraded appearance of the rough wooden posts marking the individual graves. Their tops emerging only a few inches above the surface of the soil, had the side facing to the north and east invariably scooped and splintered . . . How high the posts had risen from the surface is impossible to say. But like the wooden enclosures of the graves found at Lou Lan which they at once recalled by their arrangement, they were much higher.

In 1934, on his return trip to the Desert of Lop, when the wandering lake of Lop Nur had swung back to its original basis, Sven Hedin canoed down the Kuruk Dariya to the new lake. During the first week of May, Hedin had reached Lop Nur. The depth was no more than two feet and his paddles touched the bottom at every stroke.

At 1 p.m., having entered a canal, he spotted some strange-looking tree-trunks near the shore. He landed and discovered the remains of an ancient house, at least 1,600 years old. There was a fireplace in one corner with traces of coal in it. In one room, which may have served as an outhouse, there was a quantity of sheep's dung. Hedin found fragments of clay utensils, cattle horns, fish bones, a wooden card, a knife blade, the base of a cooking pot, scraps of close-woven cloth and the bottom of a wicker basket and other items.

These items were all similar to the artefacts that we unearthed at Tu-ying in 1996. However, in addition we found nuggets of jade. Intriguingly, the nearest jade mines are over 300 miles to the south at Khotan, south of the Taklamakan desert. We also found a quantity of beads, amulets and arrowheads.

After the discovery of the ancient house, Hedin and his team returned to the lake and paddled on. They stopped to explore a monumental *mesa* and meanwhile several of his boatmen had jumped ashore and disappeared among the reeds on the bank and the surrounding rough ground. Two of them reported that they had found an old grave. The government in Beijing, no doubt alarmed and aggrieved at the treasures that Aurel Stein had exported by camel from China over thirty years earlier, had forbidden Hedin to take with him more than one spade. Hedin commented ruefully that during the hours that followed he would gladly have been equipped with ten spades.

Some of his boatmen began to excavate the shallow grave using their bare hands or tree stumps that lay scattered on the ground. The grave, which was on a little balcony, or smooth terraced surface, was evidently a mass grave, for when Hedin arrived, the men had laid out on its edge three skulls and numerous other parts of skeletons and pieces of clothing. By mid-afternoon, his boatmen had arrayed fifteen skulls, four little food tables with legs, two bows, three wooden combs, eight round or oval wooden bowls, hair pins, slippers and some beautiful pieces of silk. A few small silk purses with delicate chain-stitch embroidery were especially pretty.

Two of Hedin's hawk-eyed boatmen then discovered another grave on top of a *mesa*. Further digging was started and after reaching a depth of two feet three inches they struck a wooden lid. This consisted of two very well-preserved boards just under six feet long. By digging around the coffin, they managed to loosen it from the clay wall in which it was entrapped, and at last managed to move it up to the top of the *mesa*.

When the lid was raised they were confronted with a shroud that covered the corpse completely from head to toe. It was so brittle that at the slightest touch it crumpled to dust. Hedin's men moved the part that concealed its head and then they saw, in all her beauty and wealth, the mummified girl that Hedin movingly describes as the mistress of the desert, Queen of Lou Lan and Lop Nur.

Death had surprised her young, and loving hands had enshrouded her and borne her to the peaceful mound within which she had rested for 2,000 years. The skin of her face was like parchment but its shape and features had not been changed by time. She lay with eye-lids closed over eyeballs that had fallen in hardly at all.

About her lips a smile still played that the centuries had not extinguished and which rendered the mysterious being still more attractive and appealing. But she did not betray her secrets of her past, and her memories of Lou lan, the spring green about the lakes, river-trips by boat and canoe, she had taken with her to the grave.

She wore on her head a turban-like cap and round it a simple band. Her body was covered with a linen cloth, and under this were two similar coverings of silk. Her breast was covered by a square piece of embroidered silk with, under it, another short linen garment. The lower part of the body was wrapped in a silk skirt that formed a continuation of the yellow silk and linen. Her waist was encircled nearest the body by a kind of girdle.

For one single night in over 2,000 years, the Queen of Lou Lan was left in her coffin in the starlight. The night breezes caressed her long hair. Then, next day she was placed carefully back in her coffin and let down into the grave, which was then filled as completely as possible. Having taken a last farewell to their unknown discovery, Hedin returned to his five double canoes and the Kuruk Dariya river.

The day after Hedin and his party had set off down the Kuruk Dariya for Lop Nur, Bergman, one of Hedin's Swedish colleagues, had left Hedin's base camp in search of a burial site that Ordek had discovered when he found Lou Lan. About thirty miles south of the Kuruk Dariya, Bergman found a watch-tower dating from the time of Lou Lan. It was visible from a long way round thanks to a regular copse of upright posts, possibly monuments to the dead. A few of the posts bore very primitive sculptures. Bergman discovered 120 graves.

Many of the corpses lay shattered and skeletons were exposed. Some, however, were still well preserved as mummies. Beyond doubt, they were not Chinese. They were wearing pointed caps of a shape that used to be found among nomadic people in the steppes of Central Asia and which can be seen in the 1930s photographs taken by the Swiss explorer, Ella Maillart. The coarse shrouds in which the dead had been wrapped suggested that they belonged to a primitive people, perhaps living mainly by hunting and fishing. These people were dressed in cloaks of coarse wool and a girdle was wound round their waists. There was no silk used at all at this burial site.

The dead rested in coffins of heavy curved boards fashioned after the size of the bodies that they supported. The different parts of the coffins were not joined together by nails but were held together by ox hides placed on top of the lid and wrapped around the upper section of the coffin. There were no bottoms and due to the extraordinary dryness of the climate the corpses were mummified, the features in some cases being wonderfully well preserved. Once again, the coffins contained ephedra twigs as well as grass, feathers and animal sinews. The curved coffins containing ephedra were clearly similar to those that Aurel Stein had discovered.

West of the little river on which the burial mound was situated were three smaller burial places. These were partly exposed and this time there was silk in these graves. One female corpse was clothed in a peculiarly decorative dress.

Bergman had been with Hedin during his expeditions in the 1920s and 1930s and had concentrated mainly on mapping prehistoric sites, investigating burials and collecting objects. For example, in the Lop Nur area eight sites belonging to prehistoric sites were discovered and investigated by Bergman. In all 1,510 objects were found. Publishing his finds in the Lou Lan area in 1941, Bergman admitted that he still had no idea how to date anything not tied to Chinese artefacts of that historical period. So his Central Asia material falls into two categories: objects cross-datable to Chinese artefacts (the Chinese arrived just before 100 BC) and objects that date from an earlier period.

One can see how the process of carbon-dating revolutionized archaeology. In late 1940, Walter Libby, an atomic physicist, discovered that archaeologists could use the steady rate of decay of radioactive carbon in ancient objects of organic wood, cloth or grain to calculate how old the objects were. Over a period of roughly 5,700 years, half the radioactive carbon left in a particular sample decays. If we know that, we only have to see what percentage of the radiocarbon in a dead organic sample has decayed in order to learn how long ago the organism died. As radiocarbon in the atmosphere fluctuates over millennia there is usually a plus or minus factor of about 100 years.

Carbon testing on the Lou Lan mummies and on other mummies found to the east in the Taklamakan desert has established that the oldest could be dated to 2000 BC and that their ages vary between that date to the Chinese presence in the area in 100 BC. It is a very long period of time, and it appears that their nomadic way of life hardly changed during those 1,900 years.

So who were these people who predated the arrival of the Chinese in the Lou Lan basin by almost 2,000 years? Elizabeth Wayland Barber, a noted expert on textiles, has attempted to trace the origins of these Lou Lan nomads by discerning the type of weave in their cloth garments. She was particularly taken by the weave that was shown in the cloth from mummies buried further to the north near Hami. It seemed to show a distinct resemblance both in pattern and in weave to cloth that had been found among Celts who had been buried in salt near Salzburg in Austria.

During the first millennium BC, Celtic communities grew rich exporting salt and salted meat to the growing civilizations in Greece and Rome, importing wine and other luxuries in return. In an investigation of cloth remnants from the area in Austria where these Celtic salt mines were so productive, Barber comes to the conclusion that the striking similarities between the plaid twills from Hami and Salzburg mummies strengthen the case for both the Celtic and Hami weavers coming from the same tradition. Though lying approximately 4,000 miles apart, they parallel each other, according to Barber, too closely for mere chance. The people of Lou Lan spoke a language called Tokharian, as deduced from tablets and manuscripts unearthed by the early explorers. It has been discovered that there are language similarities that link Celtic and Tokharian speakers.

So, cloth and language are two mediums that suggest that the inhabitants of Lou Lan, Hami and the Taklamakan may in part be there on account of successive waves of Celtic migration. In other words, the people of Lou Lan originated from the west and not from the east.

One of the most striking mummies discovered near Cherchen in the perimeter area to the south of the Taklamakan is the mummy known as Cherchen man. Easily the most impressive of the mummies on view in Urumqi, Cherchen man is six foot six inches tall, a veritable giant to his compatriots, and he died at the comparatively old age of 55 years. His face is at rest; eyes closed and sunken, lips slightly parted; his hands lie in his lap, while his knees are tilted upwards. A two-inch beard covers his face. What is so remarkable about Cherchen man is his brown/red hair, his aquiline nose and round eyes. In no way does he bear any resemblance to a Chinese person. His clothes, too, are of great interest. His legging wraps are highly coloured blue/yellow and red/brown. On one leg there is a deer-skin boot which reaches to his calf.

In 2005, a team of Chinese and American researchers working in Sweden tested DNA from several Xinjiang mummies, including the mummy found by Sven Hedin that he called the 'Queen of Lou Lan'. By genetically mapping the mummies' origins, the researchers confirmed the theory that these mummies were of West Asian descent. In an interview with Al Jazeera, the Arabic language news source, Victor Mair, a University of Pennsylvania professor and project leader for the team that did the genetic mapping, commented that these studies were: '. . . extremely important because they link up eastern and western Eurasia at a formative stage of civilization (Bronze Age and early Iron Age) in a much closer way than has ever been done before'.

This evidence corroborated the earlier link made by Barber between the textiles found with the mummies and early European textile and weave types from Salzburg. There is also the superficial observation that the mummies seemed to have blond and red hair. In trying to trace the origins of these peoples, Victor Mair's team suggested that they may have arrived in the region by way of the forbidding Pamir Mountains about 5,000 years ago.

Needless to say, this evidence is considered controversial. It refutes the contemporary nationalist declarations of the Uighur people, who claimed to be the indigenous people of Xinjiang, rather than the Chinese. In comparing the DNA to the modern-day Uighur people, they found some genetic similarities with the mummies, but no direct links. About the controversy, Mair has stated that:

> The new finds are also forcing a re-examination of old Chinese books that describe historical or legendary figures of great height, with deep-set blue or green eyes, long noses, full beards, and red or blond hair. Scholars have traditionally scoffed at these accounts, but it now seems that they may be accurate.

However, Chinese scientists have been reluctant to give up the mummies for DNA sampling because they are sensitive about nationalist Uighur claims on Xinjiang. The Chinese government has appeared to have delayed making public the new research out of concerns of fuelling Uighur Muslim separatism.

'It is unfortunate that the issue has been so politicized because it has created a lot of difficulties,' Victor Mair said. 'It would be better for everyone to approach this from a purely scientific and historical perspective.'

But China's concern over its rule in restive Xinjiang has widely been perceived as impeding faster research into the mummies and greater publicity of the findings. The desiccated corpses have not only given scientists a look into their physical biologies, but their clothes, tools and burial rituals have given historians a glimpse into life in 2000 BC.

Mair, who played a pivotal role in bringing the discoveries to Western scholars in the 1990s, has worked tirelessly to get Chinese approval to take samples out of China for definitive genetic testing. One expedition in recent years succeeded in collecting fifty-two samples with the aid of Chinese researchers, but later Mair's hosts had a change of heart and only let five of them out of the country.

'I spent six months in Sweden last year doing nothing but genetic research,' Mair said from his home in the United States. 'My research has shown that in the second millennium BC, the oldest mummies, like the Queen of Lou Lan, were the earliest settlers in the Tarim Basin. From the evidence available, we have found that during the first 1,000 years after the Queen of Lou Lan lived on earth, the only settlers in the Tarim Basin were Caucasoid.'

'East Asian peoples only began showing up in the eastern portions of the Tarim Basin about 3,000 years ago,' Mair said, 'while the Uighur peoples arrived after the collapse of the Orkon Uighur Kingdom, largely based in modern-day Mongolia, around the year AD 842.' He added that, 'Modern DNA and ancient DNA show that Uighurs, Kazakhs, Krygyzs, the peoples of Central Asia are all mixed Caucasian and East Asian. The modern and ancient DNA tell the same story.'

China has undertaken its own genetic studies on the mummies only in the last few years. A 2004 study carried out by Jilin University found that the mummies' DNA had European genes, further proving that the earliest settlers of western China were not East Asians. In the preface to the 2002 book, *Ancient Corpses of Xinjiang*, written by Chinese archaeologist Wang Huabing, the Chinese historian and Sanskrit specialist Ji Xianlin soundly denounced the use of the mummies by Uighur separatists as proof that Xinjiang should not belong to China.

'What has stirred up the most excitement in academic circles, both in the East and the West, is the fact that the ancient corpses have been excavated,' Ji wrote.

'However, within China a small group of ethnic separatists have taken advantage of this opportunity to stir up trouble and are acting like buffoons, styling themselves the descendants of these ancient "white people" with the aim of dividing the motherland.'

Further on, in an apparent swipe at the government's lack of eagerness to acknowledge the science and publicize it to the world, Ji Xianlin wrote, 'A scientist may not distort facts for political reasons, religious reasons, or any other reason.'

By displaying the mummies more prominently in a new museum in Urumqi, the Chinese have clearly become more relaxed in the face of mounting evidence that the origin of people dating back to 2000 BC, the people living at Lou Lan and in the surrounding area for centuries, could be of Celtic stock.

10

Greater Than Anyone Thinks

Where shadows pass gigantic on the sand

James Elroy Flecker, 'The Golden Journey to Samarkand'

My first introduction to camels was in the early 1960s, when I learnt that a camel will not walk up a ramp into the back of a truck. You have to position the truck so its tailboard is level with the ground. Only then will a camel walk into the vehicle. This knowledge came about when I was cast as a provincial marshal in the independence durbar in northern Nigeria. This involved trekking with 900 horsemen and twenty camels 300 miles to Kaduna, the then capital of the north. I learnt a great deal about camels, horses and people during that remarkable journey. Among other things, I marvelled that camels could carry huge ceremonial drums on either side of their hump and still retain their wonderful equanimity when the drums were exuberantly thumped.

It was that trek that taught me just how biddable a camel can be. During the magnificent durbar spectacle – which took nearly three hours for the procession of tribal chiefs (Muslim, Christian and

Pagan), footmen, horsemen, camel men, archers, jesters and ju-ju men to pass the royal box – some of the emirs appeared mounted on camels. Huge, coloured, elaborately tasselled umbrellas were continually twirled above the emirs' turbanned heads to protect their distinguished personages from the sun. In spite of the blowing of horns, the thumping of drums, the excitable horses and the revolving umbrellas, the magnificent camels took everything in their formidable stride.

There was one unforgettable incident that occurred during this great trek to the northern capital. Our horsemen and camels were advancing through the suburbs of Kaduna in an area called Kawo Village. The streets were narrow, yet we were managing to ride six abreast, filling completely the untarred, pot-holed road. All at once a taxi started to move towards us, the driver hooting loudly on his horn. He forced his way right into our massed ranks of steaming horseflesh.

'Out of the way,' someone shouted at him in Hausa. 'Go back,' another called out. But the Ibo driver from the south of Nigeria either had no knowledge of Hausa or a supreme contempt for horses and camels. He paid no heed and continued to edge his way through the advancing cavalry. Soon the shouts turned to yells of rage and one infuriated horseman reached for the scabbard at his side. In a flash he had plunged his sword through the yellow metal roof of the vehicle leaving the point of the sword positioned just above the head of the driver.

A scream of sheer terror erupted as the driver flung open the car door and bolted into one of the mud and thatched houses that lined the road. As we flowed past the stalled vehicle, horseman after horseman and even a cameleer or two reached for his sword and thrust it into the taxi's roof until it looked like a brutally assaulted sardine tin.

Many years later, while based in Nairobi I undertook a number of walkabouts with Jasper Evans' camels in the northern districts of Kenya to escape from city life and office tedium. It was then that I began to gain a deep respect for the camel's stoic qualities, its ability to continue under the most trying conditions, when temperatures hovered in the Suguta valley in the high 40s Celsius and when fodder and water were in short supply.

Recently I trekked again with camels in Kenya, this time around Lake Turkana in the far north of the country. The northern tip of that lake enters Ethiopia and the camels had to cross the fast-flowing river Omo, whose width exceeded three football pitches. By strapping each camel to the side of a boat, we managed to get the team of twenty across the Omo in five hours. Again, the camel's common sense, adaptability and unflappable stoicism impressed me enormously. Little wonder that Tuaregs consider camels to be superior to every living thing – except Tuaregs.

I am neither a qualified naturalist nor a scientist but have always had the instincts of an explorer. I marvel at the links in the chain of events that have enabled me to visit the four enclaves in the Gobi in China and Mongolia where the wild Bactrian camel still survives.

The camel trail for me began in neither of those two countries but in Moscow where, in 1992, I had arrived to stage an exhibition of environmental photographs in the Polytechnic Museum. In 1992, Moscow had diverse attractions for an adventurer. At night the city was a dangerous place. Both communism and law and order had collapsed. I witnessed the torching of private enterprise wooden shops and heard the sounds of street shoot-outs. The KGB still stood in hotel and office lobbies reading their newspapers upside down, my room telephone was bugged, and I couldn't persuade a persistent caller that my name was not Roger. Taxi drivers were as likely to rob you as to take you where you wanted to go, and the metro – though still a model of efficiency – had been turned into a market-place. I watched chickens being killed, plucked, eviscerated and sold at the top of the premier metro station's escalator and scanned the sad faces of women, young and old, who lined the station environs and offered for sale anything from a toddler's shoe to a cucumber. I also survived a rather frightening confrontation with a rough Muscovite, full to the brim with vodka, who thankfully slumped to the ground at my feet before he could relieve me of my wallet.

It was at the post photographic exhibition party sponsored by the United Nations Environment Programme for whom I was working, that I turned to the burly Russian dressed in an ill-fitting brown serge suit who sported a Stalin-esque moustache and asked him how he was managing to survive in lawless Moscow. At that moment, camels, the desert and the Gobi could not have been further from my mind. However, the man had soft blue eyes with a far-away look, which should have given me a clue.

'I work for the Russian Academy of Sciences,' Professor Peter Gunin replied in hesitant English. 'I lead the joint Russian/Mongolian expeditions to the Gobi desert. That takes me away from Moscow every year and so I manage to survive.'

He said this as though it was of absolutely no significance. He might have been telling me that he was a lottery-seller in the Moscow metro who occasionally managed to take a day off. This was clearly no longer a moment for small talk. 'Do you ever take foreigners on your expeditions?' I asked. 'I'd give my right arm to go with you.'

Peter Gunin stroked his bushy moustache. 'There's no market in Moscow for a foreigner's right arm,' he said with a smile, 'even the Mafia aren't interested in them. However, if you could find some foreign exchange . . .' Since the collapse of communism, the Russian Academy of Sciences' finances had clearly reached crisis levels. 'What can you do?' he continued. 'Are you a scientist?'

'Unfortunately, not,' I replied, searching desperately for something relevant to say. 'I could take photos. I could come as your cameraman.' My ability as a photographer is very modest, but Canon, the sponsor of the photographic exhibition, had recently presented me with a new camera. I had yet to learn how to use it.

'My brother, Anatoly, is coming on the next expedition as the official photographer,' Peter replied.

'I could publicize the work that you are doing in Mongolia. I could take a video?'

'That would be a help, but it's not really enough. Is there nothing that you can do that has a scientific background? I will have to justify your inclusion to the Academy.'

I realized that I was at the bottom of a barrel being scraped and that Professor Peter Gunin must be very short of funds.

'Do you use camels on your expeditions?' I asked. 'I've had experience working with camels in Africa.'

Gunin's face lit up immediately. 'That's it!' he cried.

'I don't understand.'

'Camels! We need a camel expert. We need someone to undertake a survey on the wild Bactrian camel population in the Mongolian Gobi.'

'I know nothing about the wild camel,' I said. 'Nothing at all. I didn't even know there was such an animal.'

'You will learn all about the wild Bactrian camel if you come with us,' Peter Gunin said. He gave me a broad wink, 'provided that you can get the foreign exchange.'

'How much do you want?'

'Fifteen hundred dollars plus your air-fare.'

'I'll find it,' I said, without the slightest hesitation. I had no idea how I was going to or whether I would get leave of absence from my job. I only knew that this opportunity was too good to miss.

'Good,' said Peter, bursting into laughter. 'To the Gobi!' he shouted, holding up his glass of vodka.

'To the Gobi,' I echoed as we tossed the vodka down in one.

'To the wild camel.'

'To Mongolia.'

'To the Sciences of Russian Academy.'

'To the joint Russian/British expedition to the Gobi.'

'What about the Mongolians?'

'The Mongolians,' we solemnly intoned.

'To . . .' Our bonhomie blossomed on an ocean of vodka.

Peter needed that foreign exchange. Two weeks later an invitation reached me in Kenya, signed by the very distinguished academician Sokolov of the Russian Academy of Sciences. I accepted, even though I still had to find the money and, more importantly, the time. Peter wanted me to arrive in Ulan Bator in less than six months, on 3 August.

I managed to arrive on an Aeroflot flight only one day late. I had found the foreign exchange by tapping an unallocated resource in a friendly bureaucrat's budget and the time, in spite of a hostile boss, by taking the trip out of unspent leave.

The expedition with the Russians to Mongolia was a huge success and I learnt a great deal about the wild Bactrian camel. I was particularly fortunate that George Schaller, the distinguished American naturalist, had hitched a lift with the expedition when he found himself stranded on the Mongolian Steppe without petrol. George taught me a great deal about the habits and the habitat of the wild camel. However, he had never visited the wild camels' habitat in China and he fired me with enthusiasm to attempt to get there. How I was to achieve this I had absolutely no idea.

Two weeks after my return from the expedition in Mongolia, I was stunned to receive an invitation to present a paper to a bio-diversity conference in Ulan Bator on the wild Bactrian camel in Mongolia. The invitation was totally unexpected and unwittingly provided me with the chance that I was waiting for. In the audience, listening intently to my fifteen-minute presentation, sat a serious-looking, bespectacled Professor surrounded by Chinese scientists. By this time I had learnt that the wild Bactrian camel survived in China, partly in the region of Lop Nur, China's former nuclear test area.

I took a deep breath and turned to look round at the impassive faces of the Chinese delegation. What were they thinking? Had they understood my paper? Were they asleep? One of them obviously did understand English. His paper on 'Economic Reform on the Nomadic Way of Life in the Xinjiang Province of China' had not set the conference alight, but it had certainly been delivered in passable English. I turned away. At the back of the hall, I saw a microphone being pointed in my direction. I had to do it now.

'As you will have gathered,' I began lamely, 'the wild camel situation in Mongolia is extremely serious and a cause for great concern. Unfortunately, we have no knowledge of the current status of wild Bactrians across the border in China.'

I looked round the crowded conference hall and then turned again towards the three bespectacled, dark-suited Chinese who sat motionless with crossed arms three rows to my left.

'We therefore appeal to our Chinese colleagues to allow us to visit the four areas of Xinjiang Province where the wild Bactrian camel is still thought to survive. If we can do this, then we can ascertain . . .'

The three Chinese applauded politely. At least they weren't asleep, I thought, as I sat down. But whether my coded appeal had been clearly understood I had not the slightest idea. After all, the Lop Nur area had been closed to foreigners since it became a nuclear testing area in 1950. Why should a foreign wild camel freak be allowed to enter the area in 1994?

My paper had been the last to be delivered. The chairman of the conference on 'Bio-Diversity and Sustainable Development in Central Asia' stood up, summed up and bid us a safe journey home. The Chinese delegation filed out of the Children's Palace Conference Hall in Ulan Bator.

At ten o'clock that night there was a hesitant knock on my hotel room door. I opened it cautiously. A young member of the Chinese delegation was standing nervously in the corridor.

'Professor Yuan would like to meet with you,' he said softly. 'Are you free to come to his room?'

I nodded and followed him up the flight of carpetless stairs to room 302 on the floor above. The Bayan Gol Hotel was not the most prestigious hotel in the world, but at that time it was the best in Mongolia. Engineer Cai knocked loudly on the Professor's door.

'Come in, come in,' a cheerful voice called out. The door was flung open and I was ushered into Professor Yuan Guoying's bedroom. A television set flickered in one corner of the fusty room, which had tightly locked windows, partially covered with strips of frayed, crimson cloth. For some reason, the room reeked of coal dust. The sound on the TV was set at full volume. Japan was invading Mongolia and bombs and shells were exploding everywhere. Professor Yuan made no attempt to stop the noise of war. He was dressed in a sleeveless string vest and a vivid, pink towel was wrapped round his waist. Sharp, bright eyes twinkled behind rimless spectacles. I shook his outstretched hand.

'I liked your paper on the camel,' he began. 'Very interesting.'

'Thank you.'

'I have a great interest in the wild camel. Last year I saw one from the new oil road that is under construction in the Taklamakan desert. Unfortunately, it cuts right through their west-to-east migration routes.' He handed me a colour photograph that showed a camel disappearing rapidly over the top of a huge sand dune.

'You're very lucky,' I said. 'I have never seen one.'

'Sit down, sit down,' said the Professor propelling me towards his bed. He pulled out a tattered map of Xinjiang Province and spread it out on the bed beside me. Four circles had been drawn on the map. One of them encircled the Lop Nur nuclear testing area.

'We believe the camels are here, here and . . .' The Professor pointed at the four areas with a stubby finger. 'In the Taklamakan they are under great threat from oil development. But here and here and here,' he pointed to Lop Nur, the Arjin Mountains and the Mongolian border area, they still survive.'

'Have you any idea how many there are?'

'Maybe 800, maybe 1,000. I'm not sure. The last scientific research was carried out in the early 1980s.'

'By Professors Gu and Gao.'

Professor Yuan's face lit up. 'You know them?'

'I've seen their report,' I replied. 'UNEP has a copy.'

'I'm glad that you've read it. Their findings will be useful to us on our expedition.'

'Our expedition, Professor?'

Professor Yuan grinned boyishly. 'I would like to invite you to come to Xinjiang next year to join a team of scientists from my institute to research the status of the wild Bactrian camel in China.'

I stared at him in disbelief. 'Have you the authority to issue this invitation?' I asked.

'Yes, of course,' he said abruptly, showing his annoyance at my tactless question. 'Otherwise, I would not be doing so.'

There was a loud explosion behind me. The Professor adjusted his glasses, which had slipped to the bottom of his nose. 'I like old war films,' he said with a laugh, 'especially when the Japanese are being beaten.'

Another explosion was overlaid with terrified screams and shouts. I ignored the compulsive call of the TV. If I had understood Professor Yuan correctly, he was extending not only an invitation to visit the three restriction-free areas where the wild Bactrian still roamed, but also to the forbidden fourth – Lop Nur.

'Is it safe to go in there?' I queried.

'Yes. Lao Zhao, who will be our guide, went in there last year with a Geiger counter. Radiation levels were well below danger levels. Anyway, all the nuclear tests are carried out underground these days, so don't worry. Have a beer.'

I declined and the Professor turned his whole attention to the flickering screen. The meeting was at an end. I was too excited to think straight. It had worked, I had been given the invitation to go to China to follow up on our camel findings in Mongolia.

'Thanks, Professor, I can't tell you how grateful I am.'

'It's nothing. I liked your paper. I will send the invitation to UNEP. The expedition will take two months and we will set off in March or early April next year. That's the best time to go because it's neither too hot nor too cold, even though it is the season of sandstorms.' He paused for a moment. 'Will UNEP give you permission to go?'

I didn't hesitate. 'Yes, my contract finishes in March. There won't be a problem.' I moved towards the door.

'We will provide the food, vehicles, petrol, equipment. We will organize everything.' He paused and smiled. 'You will find the money.'

'How much?'

'Thirty thousand US dollars.'

I looked at his beaming face and twinkling eyes. $30,000 was a lot of money. Far, far in excess of the amount my friends in UNEP's desertification department had scraped together for my Mongolian expedition.

'I'll try my best, but I'll need a formal invitation in writing as soon as possible.'

'The invitation will be sent from the Xinjiang Environmental Protection Institute. I am the vice-director. It will come under my signature and will be sent through the State Environment Protection Agency in Beijing.'

SEPA was a partner of UNEP, and they had a representative in Nairobi. An invitation cleared by SEPA would help considerably to obtain UNEP funding and support.

And that was how my long collaboration with Professor Yuan Guoying, which has lasted for over fourteen years, began. We have undertaken six major expeditions of wild camel research – four of them in Lop Nur.

During those expeditions, my admiration for the camel, whether single or double-humped, domestic, wild or feral has grown. To my mind, there is no creature so wonderfully adapted to its desert environment. Its popular image as a fractious, dirty, mean-minded creature is far from reality. When properly handled, the camel is the most amenable of creatures with, I believe, an intelligence superior to that of the horse.

During the three and a half month Sahara crossing that we undertook in 2001/2, my camel Pasha followed me about like a dog, nudging my trouser pocket to see if it contained dates and allowing me to utilize his body as a windbreak when I needed sleep.

When the Przhevalsky horse died out in Mongolia and China in 1969, there were hundreds of captive wild horses in zoos around the world. It was not difficult to collect sufficient numbers from these zoos and establish a captive wild Przhevalsky Horse Breeding Programme. This was not the case with the wild Bactrian camel. There were only approximately fifteen in captivity, caught over the years by Mongolian herdsmen. These have formed the basis of the successful captive wild Bactrian camel breeding programme established by our charity, the Wild Camel Protection Foundation. The numbers of wild Bactrian camels bred in captivity have increased so dramatically that a programme which will release a small herd back into the Gobi is now underway.

Since the discovery of the wild Bactrian camel by Przhevalsky in 1873, many critics have alleged that the wild camel is feral, a runaway from the thousands of Bactrians that travelled the Silk Road. Like Dromedary camels in Australia, it was alleged that they were camels that had escaped from domesticity and adjusted to living in a wild state. Our DNA tests are proving this allegation to be inaccurate.

Unfortunately, the wild Bactrian camel now only survives in the wild in the Gashun Gobi, the Desert of Lop, the Arjin Mountain foothills, the Taklamakan, the Tarim River basin in Xinjiang, China, and in an isolated corner of south-western Mongolia. It is on the very edge of extinction.

In deserts as disparate as the Gobi and the Sahara, my personal survival has been linked on a number of occasions to the survival of this magnificent animal. When one sees a camel among the greens of a European spring, or standing wet and muddy in a relentless downpour thousands of miles from its natural habitat, one is tempted to wonder how God permitted such an extraordinary creature to evolve. When, however, one observes the camel in its true environment, amidst desert sands and rolling dunes, then one realizes that this creature has been designed to perfection.

For example, the camel's long eyelashes are not there to enhance its looks but to protect its eyes from driving sand. In addition, the camel can induce its tear ducts to flow in order to wash out sand from its eyes. In the acclaimed film, *The Story of the Weeping Camel*, a female camel, which initially rejected its young calf, is shown emotionally affected and crying when she finally allows the young calf to suckle. But camels do not cry with emotion, they just wash their eyes as a reflex action to expel excessive dust, dirt and sand.

A male camel's urine dribbles down the back of its legs. The casual observer will remark that the designer must have slipped up when he caused it to behave in this way. However, the casual observer is wrong. Water trickles down its back legs to cool its body. Its urine forms a black crust to trap liquid underneath, thereby prolonging the cooling period. The Mongolians use camel's urine as a cure for toothache. But proceed with caution: if the liquid is not administered with great care and is accidentally applied to sound teeth and gums, then the Mongolians believe that all the affected teeth will be loosened and fall out. In addition, the Romans thought that camel urine was an excellent medium for washing clothes; especially if the camel had been fed cabbage leaves beforehand.

A camel can digest and survive on the roughest and toughest vegetation. It can even chew the sharp thorns that protect the numerous species of acacia shrubs or trees. The wild or domestic Bactrian camel can grow a massive woolly coat to protect it from the temperatures of -40 °Celsius that it might encounter. The Bactrian sheds this coat in the summer months when the temperatures rise to +55 °Celsius. Wool obtained from one camel has been known to exceed a weight of sixty pounds. No designer could come up with any creature more suited to survive in its utterly harsh and barren natural habitation. As for travel, hardened desert travellers have been known to cover seventy or more miles a day on a camel's back. In particular, the wild Bactrian camel must be one of nature's most astonishing survivors. Its ancestry dates back from three to four million years and only about 600 are thought to have survived in China and 450 in Mongolia. It has been recognized by the Zoological Society of London as the eighth most endangered large mammal species in the world.

The wild Bactrian camel differs from the domestic Bactrian in a number of ways – smaller, more conical humps, a flatter skull (*havtagai*, the Mongolian name for a wild Bactrian camel, means 'flat-head'), a different shape of foot – but the outstanding difference is genetic. Its DNA varies from that of the domestic Bactrian by 3 per cent. Our genetic variation from a chimpanzee is 5 per cent.

However, the appeal of the wild Bactrian camel to conservationists and scientists goes beyond genetics and curiosity value. All camels have the ability to recycle their urine until it becomes extremely concentrated. It is able to do this because it has a very long series of loops in the kidneys where water is reabsorbed. Although all mammals, including man, have these loops, they are especially effective in the camel. This ability to concentrate and refilter urine allows the camel to drink water that has a very high salt content.

Besides drinking salty water, wild camels can survive on salt bushes or plants that would be inedible to most other mammals. It appears that the wild Bactrian camel has developed in such a way that it is able to tolerate a degree of salt that would be unacceptable to the domestic camel, whether double or single humped. With the possibility of a world water shortage in the twenty-first century, and forecasts of future wars being fought over water, it is increasingly important to discover how the wild Bactrian camel can tolerate this high level of salt.

All camels have an immune system unique among mammals. The camel, whether a Dromedary or a Bactrian, is extremely resistant to many deadly viral and microbial contagions, such as tetanus, foot-and-mouth disease and mad cow disease. Camel antibodies are smaller than any other mammalian antibody and are about two-thirds to one-tenth of the size of human antibodies. This means that they can enter tissues and cells that other antibodies cannot. Antibodies act as red flags for the immune system by recognizing hostile germs and triggering methods to overcome any malign influence. Camel antibodies consist of only simple chains of heavy proteins, missing the additional lighter protein chains that other species' more complicated antibodies use to repel germs.

Nevertheless, simple as they are, camel antibodies are very effective. In fact, many camel antibodies demonstrate the remarkable ability to render germ molecules inactive, reaching inside malign enzymes and adhering to the active portions that toxins use to invade cells. This prevents them from working effectively. The large number of antiviral antibodies frequently found in camel milk and blood serum shows that they have been exposed to disease but not infected – further proof that camel antibodies have the power to neutralize viral enzymes.

Camel antibodies may prove important in cancer therapy. When doctors want to treat cancer they seek out a targeting method that can penetrate tumours and label cancer cells while leaving healthy tissue unmarked. Simple small cancer antibodies may prove to be critical in this research. Because of their remarkable immune system, it begins to appear more credible that the wild Bactrian camel was able to withstand the horrific effects of the sustained nuclear experimentation in Lop Nur.

In addition, there are recent discoveries that demonstrate that the consumption of camel milk in type-1 diabetes results in a significant reduction in the dose of insulin required to maintain long-term control. Based on results, camel-milk consumption may be considered as a useful adjunct to insulin administration. The antibodies and the properties of camel milk apply to Dromedary as well as Bactrian camels.

Furthermore, if one looks at the week-old embryo of a Dromedary camel, one can see the remains of a second hump. So it is quite possible that the Dromedary single-humped camel of the Sahara, Africa and the Middle East is a mutant from the double-humped Bactrian, which could make the wild Bactrian camel the ancestor of all camels, whether single or double humped.

How did this mutation occur? Camels are thought to have originated in the Arizona desert; one-foot-high camelids that were found there are displayed in the Natural History Museum of New York. Some of these camels wandered south, and over the millennia developed into the llamas, guanacos and alpacas of South America. Others crossed over the Bering Strait, which in those days joined North America to Asia. They entered an extremely cold region and developed humps (some scientists say one and others two) to store fat for use as supplementary food. The camel also developed the ability to go for many days without drinking water.

During a further development period, they changed into the double-humped camel that we are familiar with today. Some of these camels remained in this cold and hostile region and developed long shaggy coats to protect them from climatic extremes. Others continued to wander south and entered warmer parts of the world where they no longer needed shaggy coats and two humps. Some people believe that it was at this time that they mutated into single-humped Dromedary camels. One hump for fat storage was all they had need of in a hotter climate.

At some stage in its development, the wild ancestor from North America separated from a similar double-humped species. About 4,000 years ago man caught the wild camel and taught it to carry loads and to carry him. We believe that the earlier and more timid double-humped species that was more elusive and difficult to catch remained in the wild. This species is what we now call the wild Bactrian camel, which has a genetic make-up distinct from its domestic cousin.

Why is the double-humper called a Bactrian? During the time of Alexander the Great, when his soldiers advanced into Afghanistan, the northern part of that country was called Bactria. It was here that foreigners had their first sighting of a double-humped camel. They dubbed it – the Bactrian camel.

New discoveries are becoming known that add to the mystery surrounding the evolution of the camel. In 2003 Swiss researchers discovered the 100,000-year-old remains of a previously unknown giant camel species in central Syria. The single-humped camel's shoulders stood nine feet high and it was around twelve feet tall – as big as a giraffe or an elephant. Previous to its discovery, nobody knew that such a species had existed.

Since 1999, Dr Tensorer, the scientist who discovered the giant camel, had been undertaking archaeological excavations at a desert site in Kowm, Syria. He explained that the first large bones were found some years ago but were only confirmed as belonging to a camel after more bones from several parts of the same animal were discovered. A group of humans apparently killed the camel while it was drinking from a spring, said Dr Tensorer, adding that 100,000-year-old human remains were also discovered nearby.

Kowm, the site where the remains were discovered, is a fourteen-mile-wide gap between two mountain ranges that had a number of springs. The site, which was first surveyed in the 1960s, and where evidence of a million-year-old human settlement has been found, attracted migrating herds, such as antelopes. Archaeological layers covering a period of several hundreds of thousands of years were discovered.

'It was savanna,' Dr Tensorer said. 'The giant camels probably ate then what they eat today.'

The Bactrian camel, both wild and domestic, has taught me a great deal. It has shown me that it is the only mammal equipped to survive in its hostile and fragile environment. It has taught me to respect its stoic qualities and its ability to stay alive on the minimum of forage and water for long periods of time. Above all, it has taught me personally how to survive in one of the harshest deserts in the world. Even after 4,000 years of domestication, man is still discovering the secrets of the camel and its potential benefits. Scientists acknowledge that they still have much to learn.

In the same way, I believe that there are many unresolved mysteries waiting to be revealed by the Gobi. Amid other, as yet undiscovered, ancient cities buried under drifting sands there are more mummified figures lying in a 3,000-year sleep and coffins that are shrouded from view by the desert. Tucked away in the mountains, there are still isolated areas waiting to be mapped and explored. Maybe these mountains conceal the existence of wild man? The Professor believes so and so did Lao Zhao. But no one should attempt to undertake any expedition of discovery lightly. The desert gives up her secrets reluctantly and exacts a hard price. Over the years, many have died in attempts to discover the Gobi's hidden secrets, one of the latest casualties being our highly knowledgeable and competent guide, Lao Zhao.

I have been extremely fortunate and privileged to have been given the opportunity to penetrate into the heartland of this great desert and to glimpse a few of the many mysteries that lie there. I have no doubt whatsoever that deep in the sands of the Gobi there are more astonishing secrets waiting to be revealed to the archaeologist, the scientist and the adventurer.

'Lost and waiting for you . . . go!'

Appendix 1

The Current Situation of the Uighurs in Xinjiang

With the break-up of the USSR and the recent rise in Islamic extremism, Beijing once again keeps a wary eye on far-flung Xinjiang. In the wake of the 11 September attacks on the United States, China launched its own 'war on terror' against the Uighurs. Beijing now labels as terrorists those who are fighting for an independent state in Xinjiang, which the Uighur separatists call 'Eastern Turkestan'. The government considers these activists part of a network of international Islamic terror, with funding from the Middle East, training in Pakistan and combat experience in Chechnya and Afghanistan.

In fact, separatist violence in Xinjiang is neither new nor driven primarily by outsiders. The Uighurs, most of whom practise Sufism and speak a Turkic language, have long had their nationalist ambitions frustrated by Beijing. The latest wave of Uighur separatism has been inspired not by Osama bin Laden but by the unravelling of the Soviet Union, as militants seek to emulate the independence gained by some other Muslim communities in Central Asia. The Chinese offer no future for their minority peoples, except eventually to become Chinese. In June 1952, Dr Zhu Zhia-hua, a former vice-premier of Nationalist (not Communist) China could still write from exile in Taiwan to a Uighur leader, Mohammed Min Burg, who was a refugee in Istanbul:

> Not only Xinjiang [*the Western Dominion*] itself lies in China but even much territory beyond, once formed part of the Chinese Empire. That is why all the Chinese people consider it as a sacred inheritance . . .
>
> The Chinese blood is a mixture of many stocks . . . The concept of One-Family-Under-Heaven is not a mere rhetorical flourish . . . but serves as a criterion of our daily conduct.
>
> In the 'Lives of Eminent Monks', there is an interesting account of how Jumolosh, a Xinjiang monk, went to the court of one of the short-lived kingdoms in the age of the barbarian invasions and how the king of that period presented him with ten beautiful Chinese girls in order to perpetuate the best qualities of mind through their descendants . . . Jumolosh's descendants, if any, by his pretty wives must have been absorbed into Chinese society and formed part of the Chinese stock . . . The modern Chinese race is the offspring of many racial elements, which accounts for the brilliance of the Chinese civilization and the continued vigour of the Chinese people . . .

Mohammed Emin Burga replied that:

> the language, religion, script and other characteristics of Uighur, Mongolian and Tibetan peoples now under Chinese domination have nothing in common with Chinese . . . Xinjiang lies beyond the natural boundary of China in a distinct geographical area with the majority of its population being Uighur. Consequently it should be independent.

For the past fifteen years, demonstrations, bombings and political assassinations have rocked Xinjiang. According to a recent government report, Uighur separatists were responsible for 200 attacks between 1990 and 2001, causing 162 deaths and injuring more than 440 people. In the largest single incident, in 1997, as many as 100 people may have been killed during a pro-independence uprising in the town of Ili, with the government and the separatists blaming each other for the fatalities.

These incidents have occurred despite the best efforts of the Chinese authorities to suppress them. As part of their continuing 'strike hard' campaign against crime, for example, Chinese police recently reported the arrest of 166 separatist 'terrorists' and other 'major criminals' in a series of raids carried out in Urumqi. The separatists have accused the Chinese government of resorting to arbitrary arrest, torture, detention without public trial, and summary execution. The Chinese government, meanwhile, has alleged that members of a shadowy 'Eastern Turkestan Islamic Movement' have obtained funds and training from al-Qaeda.

The million-strong Uighur community provides support for several separatist political organizations. Located across the globe, these organizations are not all radical; indeed, many do not advocate violence at all. The Washington, DC-based Eastern Turkestan National Freedom Centre, for instance, lobbies members of Congress on behalf of the Uighur cause and publishes books and tapes on pan-Turkic nationalism for circulation inside Xinjiang. Meanwhile, the leader of the Europe-based Eastern Turkestan Union, Erkin Alptekin, prefers to organize conferences and work with Tibetan émigré groups seeking autonomy for their own homeland. In truth, whether or not they support the use of violent methods, the Xinjiang separatist groups both at home and abroad are too small, dispersed and faceless to constitute a threat to Chinese control over the region. Beijing fears them nevertheless, because the mere possibility that they may cause disruption creates an impression of social instability in Xinjiang and dampens foreign investment and exploration for the province's rich natural resources. Beijing also realizes that acquiescing to Uighur demands will only embolden separatists in Tibet and Taiwan.

The Chinese government has alleged that more than 1,000 Xinjiang separatists have received terrorist training in Afghanistan, and it claims to have arrested 100 foreign-trained terrorists who have made their way back to Xinjiang. But only one Uighur separatist organization, the Eastern Turkestan Islamic Party of Allah, appears conclusively to have operated in Afghanistan. Its identity was exposed when its putative leader, Alerkan Abula, was executed by the Chinese authorities in January 2001.

Other groups, such as the East Turkestan Opposition Party, the Revolutionary Front of Eastern Turkestan, the Organization for Turkestan Freedom, and the Organization for the Liberation of Uighurstan, have links to small guerrilla cells based in the oasis towns of Xinjiang's Taklamakan desert. The guerrillas have raided government laboratories and warehouses for explosive materials, and have manufactured various types of bombs. The Turkey-based Organization for Turkestan Freedom, for example, claimed responsibility for the bombing of a bus in Beijing on 7 March 1997 that injured thirty people. The Chinese government also suspects this organization of attacks on the Chinese embassy in Ankara and the Chinese consulate in Istanbul that same year.

Despite the separatists' efforts, China is unlikely to relinquish control of the province. With a population of eighteen million people, Xinjiang Province produces one-third of China's cotton, and exploration in the Tarim River basin has revealed the country's largest oil and gas reserves. The region borders Mongolia, Russia, several Central Asian republics, Pakistan and India, making it of strategic military importance to China and a useful springboard for projecting Chinese influence abroad.

The government has also invested a great deal in Xinjiang. As part of a grand scheme to develop China's western areas, Beijing plans to spend more than 100 billion yuan ($12 billion) on seventy major projects in Xinjiang, mostly to improve infrastructure. Major roads and highways have been built and the government has completed a railway linking the remote western city of Kashgar to the rest of Xinjiang. And the regime is considering proposals for using foreign investment to build oil and gas pipelines from Central Asia across the Taklamakan desert.

However, material advancement and massive investment are only a partial solution to the simmering violence in Xinjiang.

Appendix 2

The First Published Account of the Wild Bactrian Camel by Colonel Nikolai Mikhailovich Przhevalsky

I have managed to acquire the first written foreign account, an English translation from the Russian, on the wild Bactrian camel, published by Przhevalsky in 1879. It is an account that relates how Przhevalsky had startled the St Petersburg scientists when he had returned in 1874 from Central Asia with three wild Bactrian camel skins.

At the start of our expedition to Kum Su, I showed the Professor this prescient account of Przhevalsky's discovery. It is extraordinary how his thinking and understanding of the wild Bactrian camel coincide with what we are able to confirm through scientific research almost 150 years later. For Przhevalsky, the wild camel was certainly not a feral creature. Here is his account:

> According to the unanimous testimony of the Lob-nortsi [*the inhabitants who at that time lived around Lop Nur. Today they have virtually disappeared, having inter-bred with the Uighur. In 1996 in the village of Tikar, north of the*

Gashun Gobi, I was shown a one-year-old baby that had extraordinarily long ear lobes. 'This is a characteristic of the old inhabitants who lived near Lop Nur,' the mother told me], the chief habitat of the wild camel at the present day is the desert of Kum-tagh, to the east of Lake Lob; the animal is also occasionally found on the Lower Tarim, in the Kuruk-tagh mountains [*north of the Lop Nur Wild Camel National Nature Reserve*], and more rarely still on the sands bordering with the Cherchen-dariya; beyond the town of Cherchen, in the direction of Khoten, its existence is not known. [*As described, this is the habitat of the wild camel in China today.*] Twenty years ago, wild camels were numerous near Lake Lob, where the village of Chargalik [*Charkhlick or Ruoqian*] now stands, and farther to the east along the foot of the Altyn-tagh [*Arjin Mountains*], as well as in the range itself. Our guide, a hunter of Chargalik, told us that it was not unusual in these days, to see some dozens, or even a hundred of these animals together. He himself had killed upwards of a hundred of them in the course of his life (and he was an old man), with a flint and steel musket. With an increase of population at Chargalik, the hunters of Lob-nor became more numerous and camels scarcer. Now, the wild camel only frequents the neighbourhood of Lob-nor and even here in small numbers. Years pass without so much as one being seen; in more favourable seasons again the native hunters kill their five and six during the summer and autumn. The flesh of the wild camel, which is very fat in autumn, is used for food, and the skins for clothing. These fetch ten tengas or a ruble and thirty copecks at Lob-nor.

The hunters of Lake Lob assured us that all the camels came from, and returned to, the Kum Tagh deserts [*as we believe to be the case today*]. But these are entirely inaccessible, owing to the absence of water. At all events, none of the Lob-Nortsi had ever been there. Some had made the attempt starting from Chaglyk spring; but after struggling for a couple of days in loose sand-drift, where men and pack animals sank knee-deep, they became exhausted, and returned home unsuccessful [*we know the tribulations of travel in this area only too well*]. Total absence of water, however there cannot be in the Kum-tagh; for if this were the case, camels could not live there; probably springs may be found which serve as drinking-places [*for example, Kum Su which we found in 1999*]. These animals, like their domestic congeners, are not particular as to food, and can, therefore, safely inhabit the wildest and most barren desert, provided that they are far removed from man [*quite true*].

During the excessive heats in summer, the camels are attracted by the cool temperature of the higher valleys of Altyn-Tagh [*Arjin Mountains*] and make their way thither to an altitude of 11,000 feet, and even higher, for our guides informed us that they are occasionally found on the lofty plateau on its southern side. Here the chief attraction for them are the springs of water, to say nothing of the greater abundance of camel's thorn (calidium) and their favourite, but less plentiful hedyasarum. In winter the wild camel keeps entirely to the lower and warmer desert, only entering the mountains from time to time [*this is true today*].

Unlike the domestic animal, whose chief characteristics are cowardice, stupidity and apathy [*I do not agree with this*], the wild variety is remarkable for its sagacity and admirably developed senses. Its sight is marvellously keen, hearing exceedingly acute, and sense of smell wonderfully perfect. The hunters told us that a camel could scent a man several versts off, see him, however cautiously he might approach, from a great distance, and hear the slightest rustle of his footsteps. Once aware of its danger, it instantly takes to flight, and never stops for some dozens or even hundreds of versts. A camel I fired at certainly ran twenty versts without stopping, as I saw by its traces, and probably farther still, had I been able to follow it, for it turned into a ravine off our line of march. One would suppose that so uncouth an animal would be incapable of climbing mountains; the contrary, however, is actually the case, for we often saw the tracks and droppings of camels in the narrowest gorges, and on slopes steep enough to baffle the hunter. Here their footprints are mingled with those of the mountain sheep (*Pseudo Nahoor*) and the arkari (*Ovis Poli*).

So incredible did this appear, that we could hardly believe our eyes when we saw it. The wild camel is very swift, its pace being almost invariably a trot. In this respect, however, the domesticated species will, on a long distance, overtake a good galloper. It is very weak when wounded, and drops directly it is hit by a bullet of small calibre, such as the hunters of Lob-nor use.

The wild camel pairs in winter, from the middle of January nearly to the end of February. At some times the old males collect troops of some dozens of females, and jealously guard them from the attentions of their rivals. They have even been known to drive their wives into some secluded glen, and keep them in it as long as the rutting season lasts [*I have known a wild Bactrian camel cripple a female by biting its tendons to ensure that she stays in the 'glen' to be mated]*. At this period too, frequent fights take place between the males, often terminating in the death of one or other of the combatants. An old male, when he has overpowered a younger and weaker antagonist, will crush his skull between his teeth [*I have never heard of this but I have seen a domestic camel crush and eat the skull of a wild camel*].

Females bear once in three years, the period of gestation being rather over a year; the young camels are born one at a time, early in spring, i.e. in March. They are much attached to their dams. Should one of these later be killed, the young camel takes to flight, returning, however, again later to the same spot. When caught young, wild camels are easily tamed and taught to carry a pack [*I have never experienced this*].

Their voice, very rarely heard, is a deep, lowing noise; in this way the dams call their young; males, even during the rutting, find their consorts by scent.

We were unable to learn the duration of a camel's life; some are known to live to a great age. Our hunter-guide once chanced to kill a he-camel, with teeth completely worn down, notwithstanding which the animal was in good condition. [*On the 1997 expedition we found such a wild bull camel's skull. Jasper Evans said that he thought that it was 15 years old.*]

The Lob-nortsi, who hunt the wild camel in summer and autumn, never go expressly in search of it, but kill them whenever they get the chance.

This sport is generally difficult, and only three or four hunters in the whole district of Lob-nor engage in it. The ordinary mode of killing camels is by lying in wait for them at the watering-places, not by following on their fresh tracks [*as the Uighurs do today*]. The hunters I sent out in search of this animal did not return to Lob-nor before the 10th March, but they were successful. On the border of the Kum Tagh they killed a male and a female, and quite unexpectedly obtained a colt, by taking it from the dead mother's womb. This young camel would, in the natural course, have been born on the following day.

The skins of all three specimens were excellent, and had been prepared in the best way, by the hunters, to whom we had given lessons in the art of skinning and dressing. The skulls were also perfect. Some days afterwards I received another skin of a wild camel (male), killed on the Lower Tarim. The specimen was a little inferior to the others, because the animal from which it was taken came from a warmer climate, and had already begun to shed its coat, besides having been unscientifically skinned. I need scarcely say how glad I was to procure the skin of an animal about which Marco Polo had written [*this is a mistake, Marco Polo makes no mention of the wild Bactrian camel*], but which no European had hitherto seen.

From a zoological point of view there is little to distinguish the wild from the domesticated camel, and as far as we could judge from a superficial glance, the differences are the following, viz.: (a) there are no corns on the forelegs of the wild specimen; (b) the humps are half the size as compared with those of the tame breed, and the long hair on top of the humps is shorter; (c) the male has no crest, or a very small one; (d) the colour of all wild camels is the same – a reddish sandy hue; this is rare with domestic animals; (e) the muzzle is more grizzled, and apparently shorter; (f) the ears are also shorter. In addition to these peculiarities, wild camels are generally remarkable for their medium size; huge brutes such as are sometimes seen among their domestic brethren are never found in a wild state.

Now as to the question – are the camels found by us the direct descendants of wild parents, or are they domesticated specimens which have wandered into the steppe, become wild, and multiplied in a state of nature? Each of these questions can be answered in both the affirmative and the negative. In South America we find an instance of domesticated specimens running wild and multiplying, as where a few horned cattle and horses have escaped from the Spanish colonies and increased on the free pasture-lands into great herds. A similar instance, on a smaller scale, attracted my attention in Ordos, where, after the Dungan insurrection, in the course of some two or three years cows and bulls had become as wild and difficult to stalk as antelope. But with regard to the multiplying of camels which had obtained their liberty, a difficulty arises in the circumstance of there being very few males of the domesticated kind fit for the stud, and lastly, the acts of breeding and birth are for the most part performed with the assistance of man. Assuming that the latter of these difficulties may disappear when leading a free life, the other nevertheless remains, i.e. the irremediable injury produced by castration. Few chances, therefore, remain of camels capable of breeding escaping; one exception must, however, be made in the case of interbreeding of wild male with female domesticated camels [*this is still all too prevalent today*].

On the other hand, the localities fit for human habitation in the basin of Lob-nor are particularly ill-suited for camels, owing to the damp climate, insects, and bad food [*Przhevalsky is here referring to the 1874 position of Lop Nur, which at that time was situated 100 miles north of Ruoqian. He was unaware of the pendulum-like movements of Lop Nur.* Hence the population could hardly at any time have kept many, and now the Lob-nortsi keep none at all.

Turning to the other proposition, i.e. that the wild camel of the present day is directly descended from wild ancestors, more weighty evidence may, I think, be adduced in support of this theory. It is true that besides the peculiarities we have already enumerated, this animal in its wild state possesses those qualifications developed in the highest degree which should enable in its struggle for life to have every chance of preserving itself and its young. The admirable development of its external senses save it from enemies; moreover these are very few in number in the localities that it inhabits – man and wolves being the only ones it has to encounter. Even wolves are rare in the desert, and would scarcely be dangerous to a full-grown camel. Besides being habitually wary, it will resort to the most inaccessible spots to avoid man, and it is probable that the sandy wastes to the east of Lake Lob have served time out of mind as its settled abode. Of course in earlier ages the limits of its distribution may have extended much farther than at the present time, when all that remains for it is the most remote corner of the great desert of Central Asia. [*We now have the advantage of DNA testing, which consistently shows that there is a substantial base difference between the domestic and the wild Bactrian camel.*]

On comparing the above mentioned data, it seems to me possible to arrive at the conclusion that the wild camel of the present day is the direct descendant of wild parents, but that from time to time escaped domestic animals probably became mixed with them. The latter, or rather such as were capable of begetting stock, left offspring, and these in after-ages could not be distinguished from wild camels. But in order to decide this point finally it will be important to compare the skulls of the two varieties.

Sven Hedin, who travelled through the Desert of Lop almost twenty years after Przhevalsky, was sceptical of this account. He asserted that wild Bactrian camels were most likely descended from Silk Road runaways. However, he illustrates with his own hand a wild Bactrian camel skull and a domestic camel skull in his book, *Through Asia*, volume 2, pp 828–9. The skull of the wild Bactrian camel is shown to be much flatter than the more rounded skull of the domestic camel. Today, we have the benefits of genetic testing which is tending to confirm some of Przhevalsky's perceptive observations.

Appendix 3

Spies Among the Kazakhs

During research for Chapter 4 on the Kazakh exodus, interesting facts emerged concerning the two Americans who met up with the Kazakhs in Timurlik. These were Douglas Mackiernan, the American vice-consul in Urumqi, and Frank Bessac, an itinerant Fulbright scholar with an anthropological bent, who linked up with Mackiernan in Urumqi. It is fairly obvious that Mackiernan's consular appointment was probably used as a strategic listening-post for American interests and a cover for work on behalf of the CIA; Bessac had worked for the CIA just before the end of the Second World War. In addition to his possible secret work, the vice-consul's personal life was equally ambiguous, involving a string of relationships with women.

Bessac, at the behest of the CIA, had met the Mongolian, Prince De. The prince was a direct descendant of Genghis Khan, through thirty-one recorded generations. The Mongolians say that from the time of Genghis Khan to the arrest of Prince De by the Chinese in 1950, they as a people had been united by the great Khan's descendants under one tribe and banner. At various times in his life Prince De's political strategy for survival had been to negotiate, openly or secretly, with the Japanese army, the Chinese Nationalists and Communists, and the American secret service. He strived for one objective – the national survival of the people of Inner Mongolia. Bessac had been one of his American secret service contacts.

In the summer of 1949, Xinjiang was experiencing great turbulence. The American consul John Paxton had fled from the capital Urumqi on 13 August 1949 and Mackiernan had been left behind to 'maintain rearguard operations'. To assist Mackiernan, consular cash and other assets had been handed over to him when Paxton left.

Meanwhile, Bessac – allegedly travelling on Fulbright scholarship resources – was, according to his account, attempting to reach Torgut Mongol settlements in the Tien Shan. His aim, as he put it, was to travel 'over the Pamirs to the Karakorums to Afghanistan or Kashmir'. Whether the Fulbright scholarship had at this time been turned into a cover for further CIA employment is not made clear by Bessac. His travel plans after Urumqi seemed to be nebulous and vague. It is hardly surprising that after he met up with Mackiernan in Urumqi in September 1949, he jumped at a proposal to travel with the American vice-consul to the north of Hami to meet Usuman Batur, the famed Kazakh leader. Mackiernan had told Bessac that he wanted to give the Kazakhs 'material assistance'.

The news of a successful Soviet nuclear test in an area very close to Xinjiang in what is now called Kazakhstan on 29 August 1949 had been announced on 23 September and Mackiernan had convinced himself that a third world war would shortly break out. Mackiernan felt that in the event of a major war, the minority peoples in Central Asia, notably the Kazakhs, would be a strategic force on the side of the West against the Communist forces from Soviet Russia. Usuman Batur was the acknowledged leader of all the Kazakhs in their struggle to survive as an independent people, free from either Chinese or Russian domination. Mackiernan, whose position in Urumqi was becoming more untenable by the day, had resolved to give Usuman what help he could.

In his revealing book, *Into Tibet*, Thomas Laird explains that when the atomic bomb had been dropped on Hiroshima, the Americans were extremely concerned that the Russians would acquire their own nuclear device. The Soviet spies Fuchs, the Rosenbergs and Ted Hall had successfully sent valuable atomic secrets to the Communists. It had been common knowledge for some time that the Russians were preparing to conduct a nuclear test in Kazakhstan and that, thanks to the information gleaned from the spies, their bomb would be identical to the one that the Americans had dropped to such devastating effect on Hiroshima.

Based in Urumqi, Mackiernan would have been in an ideal position to collect information on Soviet plans to conduct such a nuclear test. However, what the Russians desperately needed for their nuclear programme was uranium, and the United States was determined to maintain their monopoly of it for as long as possible. The Soviet (now Kazakhstan) border is only 150 miles north of Urumqi. This northern section of Xinjiang had, by 1949, been overrun by the Russian Communists. Because of its prospective mineral wealth – not only uranium but also oil and gold – north-west Xinjiang was of great interest to the Russian Communists.

When the northern part of Xinjiang had fallen under Russian control, they had established the Eastern Turkestan Republic (ETR) in an attempt to gain Kazakh and Uighur support for the Russian Communists. Mackiernan received disturbing information that the Russians, in addition to exploiting a uranium mine at Kotogai in the Altai Mountains in today's Kazakhstan, were also mining uranium at Peitaishan in the ETR. This no doubt increased the pressure on him to obtain more detailed and accurate information about the Kotogai mine. Before the Soviet nuclear explosion in 1949, Mackiernan, apparently responding to covert instructions from the United States, contacted five White Russians living in Urumqi and asked them to obtain uranium samples from the Altai. Four of them were killed in the attempt but one did return with uranium samples.

Mackiernan was also allegedly involved in assisting Usuman Batur in the battle against the Russian Communists at Peitaishan in the ETR. It appears that a major part of Mackiernan's mission as vice-consul was to find out as much information as he could about the uranium mine and the Russians' access to it.

At about this time, Vasili Zvansov, a White Russian, was also working for Mackiernan. Zvansov had extensive knowledge of the Altai region, having helped the Kazakhs resist the advancing Russian Communists before he was forced to flee to Urumqi in 1944. He and hundreds of other White Russians who had fled from Russia during the Communist Revolution had taken refuge on the Soviet–Chinese border. The arrival of Soviet troops in the Altai region forced these émigrés to flee yet again.

Some of them joined Usuman Batur and his Kazakh freedom fighters in the mountains, others joined the Chinese Nationalist army. A few of these White Russians had been born in the city of Semipalatinsk in what is now called Kazakhstan. It was at Semipalatinsk that Soviet Russia tested its first nuclear bomb in August 1949. These former inhabitants of Semipalatinsk were of great interest to Mackiernan.

Prior to the Soviet nuclear test, Mackiernan appears to have been busy installing Hegenberger sonic detectors that were capable of identifying and picking up sensitive information when a nuclear device was detonated. Hegenberger was a US general in charge of a secret project whose mission was, among other things, the development of equipment for the detection of nuclear explosives. However, to be of any use, these devices had to be placed within 600 to 1,200 miles of a test site. Within 100 miles they could accurately pinpoint the location of an atomic explosion and determine the precise size of the explosive device.

There was only one American facility within 1,200 miles of a potential test site of a Soviet atomic explosion: the American consulate at Urumqi. It appears that Mackiernan was instrumental in overseeing the installation of these Hegenberger detectors in or near Xinjiang's capital city. It is also thought that he ensured that the information obtained was relayed to a 'weather station' that Mackiernan had had installed at his family home in the United States. The 'weather station', manned by members of his family, relayed information directly to Washington.

The political situation at this time in Xinjiang was utterly confusing, with many groups fighting for control of the province. The Chinese Nationalists were fighting the Chinese Communists for ultimate supremacy in China. The Russian Communists had territorial designs on northern Xinjiang because of its mineral wealth and strategic location. In addition, White Russians who had fled the advance of the Russian Communists had ended up in the Xinjiang capital in considerable numbers.

Amidst this turmoil, the Kazakh nomads were caught in the cross-fire, as they switched allegiance from one side or the other. Having fought for or against all factions, they tried to gauge who would ultimately be successful. It was inevitable that eventually they would find themselves without any support; everyone's hand was against them. The Kazakhs had no political agenda, they wanted the freedom to pursue their traditional nomadic way of life. They had always had scant regard for international borders or mutually antagonistic political ideals. Sadly, their days of uninhibited freedom to roam had passed away forever.

When Mackiernan and Bessac contacted Usuman Batur north of Hami, Mackiernan gave him gold to buy weapons. Then, apparently acting under orders obtained by wireless link, the vice-consul and the Fulbright scholar allegedly left Hami and after a month's travel arrived on 29 November 1949 in Timurlik, where Hussein Tajji and Qali Beg were encamped.

It would have been foolhardy and almost impossible to attempt to reach Lhasa during the winter months and their time spent during the winter of 1949/50 in Timurlik is briefly described in an earlier chapter of the book.

At the onset of spring, on 15 March 1949, they set out to cross the Chang Tang plateau with three White Russians, Vasili Zvansov,

Stephan Yanuishkin and Leonid Shutov, together with the flesh-eating camels and horses. During the crossing the travellers suffered extreme hardship. Due to the lack of vegetables some of the party developed scurvy, leaving them with bleeding gums and loose teeth. They were all plagued with boils and were constantly short of water. Game shot by Vasili was their main source of food and the frozen hunks of meat had to be chopped up with an axe.

There is no human habitation in the Chang Tang. Few local people and only a handful of foreigners have ever attempted to walk or ride across it, the most notable being Sven Hedin in 1901. An outstanding feature of this 16,000-foot plateau is the wind, which blows – as it does in the heart of the Gobi – from dawn to dusk. The strength of the wind, as we found when we were in the Desert of Lop, inhibits conversation for much of the day and one can only shout at one's colleague to be understood.

For a reason that remains a mystery to me, before they reached the first border post where Tibetan guards were stationed, Mackiernan suggested to Bessac – according to Bessac's own account – that they part company. It is alleged that Mackiernan dramatically halted the caravan and ordered everyone to dismount and form a circle round about him. He then approached Bessac and made the following speech.

'I have decided, Frank, that there is no need for you to go to Lhasa with me. You can head off and take a western route across Tibet with Stephan and Leonid. I'll take Vasili with me to Lhasa.'

Bessac says that he does not know what prompted Mackiernan to make this very unusual and potentially dangerous suggestion. Without Mackiernan's map-reading expertise, it is extremely doubtful whether the three men would have found their way to safety. That he should have asked Bessac to leave in this manner when they were in one of the remotest and most barren regions in the world is inexplicable.

Relationships between the two men must have become completely fractured, because Mackiernan's order amounted to a virtual death sentence. One possible explanation is that the altitude and the harshness of their journey had affected Mackiernan's mental stability. Whatever the true reason, Bessac flatly rejected the decision. He turned to Mackiernan and replied, 'Wherever the radio goes, I go.'

Mackiernan grimaced but said nothing more. They remounted their camels, rode on and, according to Bessac, Mackiernan never mentioned the matter again.

Eventually, on 29 April 1950, six weeks after they had left Timurlik, the party reached the Tibetan border post of Shegar-Hungling and their first sight of Tibetan nomads. It was here that an extraordinary incident occurred. In Bessac's words, written as a journal:

At 1100 on April 29th, Tibetan tents on hillside to SSE seen through glasses. Mac and I (armed) proceeded ahead of main party which was to follow slowly. After about one hour Tibetans saw us. Mac proceeded about quarter of a mile ahead of me waving white flag. Tibetans sent delegate (girl) to meet Mac. They grinned at each other and tried to speak to each other. The girl left with us following slowly behind. The girl met a man at the top of the hill and talked for a few minutes. The man unlimbered gun and both disappeared over hill. We followed slowly. Upon reaching top of hill Tibetans were seen reinforcing a small family fortification with rocks and with guns ready for use. I went half way back to them waving white flag until Mac stopped me and told me to come back.

Mac's idea was to put up camp, make a fire and act as peacefully as possible hoping thus to convince Tibetans that we could not be Kazakhs because Kazakhs wouldn't act in such a fashion and that in any case we were friendly and not after sheep and property. At about this time the rest of the party appeared and we pitched camp on east bank of above-mentioned stream. Immediately after pitching camp six men on horseback were seen approaching us from W or NW. In this general direction was a Tibetan tent and two men with a flock of sheep.

It was decided that I, unarmed with a small gift of raisins, tobacco and cloth, waving white cloth would go to two men and try and make friends. Mac then changed his mind and told me to go to see people in rock formation . . . I made my presentation, convinced them that I was an American and a friend, and started to return to camp. Just before reaching top of rise, before our tent could be seen, shots were heard to my immediate front. I assumed that the six men had fired on tent.

. . . Four men with hands above head left our tent and approached the Tibetans who also approached our men. Just before the two groups met two shots, Mac shouted 'Don't shoot' and another shot was heard. Three men fell to the ground. The fourth was running to the tent. A fusilade of shots were heard and when about half of the way to the tent the left leg of the person running doubled under him, but he managed to make it to the tent.

Mackiernan, Stephan and Leonid were killed. Vasili was wounded in the leg and Bessac remained unharmed. A communication sent by runner from Lhasa explaining that the party consisted of friendly Americans and Russians had allegedly not arrived in time. The guards, who were on the look-out for Kazakh bandits, did not ask questions when the strangers appeared and shot on sight.

Bessac continues:

I went to the three objects on the ground. They were men all right — very dead. Mac was lying on his back with his legs crossed. He looked not uncomfortable and was smiling, perhaps slightly ironically. I had a strong emotion of envy which lasted until one of the Tibetans while going through Mac's pockets came across some dried biscuit. He offered me a piece which I refused. He laughed, put the biscuit to Mac's teeth and then in his own mouth. Mac's lower jaw relaxed and his mouth fell wide open . . . I felt a little sick in the stomach and walked away. The Tibetans realized by now that they had made a mistake and although some seemed sorry about the incident the leader and to some extent all were flushed with victory. They were also more or less interested in looting.

On reading Bessac's account it would appear that he and Vasili has a miraculous escape. His account is full of anomalies and unanswered questions. How is it that the guard who allegedly proffered Mackiernan a biscuit, joked with Bessac when the dead man's jaw fell open? Why was extreme hostility turned in a few minutes into a semi-jocular relationship? Bessac and Vasili apparently 'kowtowed' to the Tibetans, but in view of the action meted out to the other members of the party, the fact that Bessac was left unharmed and the wounded Vasili was not killed seems odd.

Bessac and Vasili Zvansov made it under escort to Lhasa and eventually reached India and from there the United States. The heads of Mackiernan and the two Russians were cut from their bodies and accompanied Bessac and Zvansov to Lhasa in a sack.

On 30 July 1950, the *New York Times* reported:

U.S. Consul, Fleeing China, Slain by Tibetan on Watch for Bandits

Douglas S. MacKiernan, forced to flee his post as United States vice consul at Urumchi in Northwest China last September, was accidentally shot and killed by Tibetan border guards at the Tibet border on his way out of Communist China.

Ten months after Mr. MacKiernan's hasty departure from the capital of Sinkiang Province, now held by the Chinese Communists, the State Department announced today that the vice consul who was 37 years of age, had been shot last April 13. The guards, according to the department, had apparently mistaken the party, at that point travelling by camel, for bandits or Communist raiders.

. . . Mr MacKiernan was accompanied by Frank Bessac, a scholar from Lodi, Calif., who had been studying in Northwest China. Mr. Bessac was not hurt, and is now making his way to New Delhi. Two native servants, however, were killed in the shooting and another was injured.

. . . While he was still believed to be in China, Mr. MacKiernan had been charged in Communist propaganda, recently re-broadcast by Moscow, with organizing bands of Chinese for resisting the advancing Communists. The State Department had denied that the Vice Consul had undertaken such a task and a spokesman described the charges today as 'absolutely untrue.'

. . . The vast distances separating westernmost China from the outer world have made the brief consular career of Douglas S. MacKiernan somewhat vague and indistinct.

Bessac is still living, in Montana; Vasili, who became a successful businessman after his arrival in the States, is living in Hawaii. Both men are now well into their eighties.

Their journey across the Chang Tang was a formidable undertaking. Although Bessac treats it modestly in his account, *Death on the Chang Tang*, the difficulties and hardships of travelling at high altitudes with flesh-eating camels should not be underestimated. However, much of the story remains hidden and many questions remain.

This incident occurred just prior to the Chinese Communist invasion of Tibet. Mackiernan, who was, according to Bessac, in almost daily wireless contact with his masters could, it has been suggested, have been part of a ploy to arrange undercover support for the Tibetans. It certainly seems that he was ordered to end his parleying with Usuman Batur north of Hami and head directly for Lhasa. Bessac claims to have been unaware of the Tibetan project and had no idea of any covert plot. Hence the instruction from Mackiernan to cut loose and travel across Tibet as a separate party seemed bizarre to him. Whatever the true motive behind the arduous crossing to Lhasa, it was thwarted unintentionally by the Tibetans who had not received instructions in time to allow the Americans and Russians free access to their capital city.

The Korean War and the opening rounds of the Vietnam crisis had broken out and whatever American intentions had been with regard to covertly supporting the Tibetans, enthusiasm for this particular strategy had rapidly cooled as the Korean conflict worsened. As a gesture of goodwill, the Americans had assured Chiang Kai-shek that they recognized China's sovereignty over Tibet. This policy played straight into the hands of Mao Tse-tung. After he had gained power in China, he asserted that the United States had recognized Chinese sovereignty and that their invasion of Tibet was entirely an internal Chinese affair and not a colonial adventure against an independent country. There was no difference in the Chinese government's policy towards Tibet under either the Nationalists or the Communists.

Tibet sought help, but America turned aside appeals to secure Tibet's admission as an independent country into the United Nations. The United States asserted that:

Any Tibetan effort to obtain United Nations membership at this time would be unsuccessful in view of the certain opposition of the USSR and of the Chinese delegations . . . The Tibetan plan to dispatch a special mission to obtain United Nations membership may at this time serve to precipitate Chinese Communist action to gain control of Tibet.

The powerful 'China Lobby' in Washington had for years applied pressure on America policy-makers not to countenance an independent Tibet. Consequently, both Chinese Nationalist and Communist governments had in turn been assured that America recognized Chinese sovereignty over Tibet.

In 1950, the Chinese invasion of Tibet brought about a slight modification of this policy insofar as the United States might be prepared to offer support to Tibet covertly but not openly. In the winter of 1950, the State Department told the British Foreign Office that: 'Should developments warrant, consideration could be given to recognition of Tibet as an independent country.'

Fifty-seven years later, conditions have never, in the eyes of the United States, warranted the recognition of Tibet.

It is conceivable that Mackiernan's mission to Tibet could have been part of this earlier covert American policy of recognizing Tibetan policy. He may have been working on a plan to drop American weapons into Tibet before the invading forces of Chairman Mao reached Lhasa. It could explain why he asked Bessac not to come with him to Lhasa but to make his own way by a different route to India. If Mackiernan had felt during their travels over the Chang Tang that Bessac might be more of a hindrance than a help in a clandestine operation, he could have convinced himself to present this extraordinary proposition to Bessac. Bessac sensibly refused to do this, otherwise he might not have survived.

This is, however, pure speculation. Mackiernan's instructions, the motives of his masters and his true intentions died with him in that fatal shoot out in the Chang Tang.

There are many mysteries still unsolved. Many parties were playing their own political games, many nations interested in acquiring spheres of interest, while the outcome of the Chinese Communist and Nationalist battles were undecided. Like the fortunes of the Kazakhs, political fortunes changed daily.

Then there is mystery of Bessac's survival and the unanswered question of how far he was involved in Mackiernan's intrigues and machinations. The United States records remain sealed to this day.

Bibliography

Wild Bactrian Camels

Bannikov, A. (1976). 'Wild Camels of the Gobi', *Wildlife Magazine*. New York, pp 398–403.

Littledale, S. (1894). *Field-Notes on the Wild Camel of Lob-Nur*. Proceedings of the Zoological Society, London, pp 446–8.

Grill, P. (1980). *Introducing the Camel*, UNEP, Nairobi.

Gu, J. and Gao, X. (1985). *The Distribution of theWild Camel*. Chinese Academy of Sciences and Mammal Society of Japan, Osaka, pp 117–20.

Hare, J. (1997). 'The Wild Bactrian Camel, Camelus Bactrianus Ferus, in China: The Need for Urgent Action', *Oryx*, Vol. 31, No 1, pp 45–8.

Hare, J. (1998). *The Lost Camels of Tartary*. Little Brown, London.

Hare, J. (2003). *Shadows across the Sahara*. Constable, London.

Kozlov, P. (1899). *Proceedings of the Expedition of the Imperial Russian Geographic Society to Central Asia in 1893–1896 under the Leadership of Roborovsky*. St. Petersburg.

Prejevalsky [Przhevalsky], N. (1879). *From Kulja across the Tian Shan to Lob Nur*. Sampson Low, Marston, Searle and Rivington, London.

Tulgat, R. and Schaller, G. (1992). 'Status and Distribution of Wild Bactrian Camels, Camelus Bactrianus Ferus', *Biological Conservation*, Vol. 62, pp 11–19.

Zhirinov, L. and Ilyinsky, V. (1986). *The Great Gobi National Park – A Refuge for Rare Animals of the Central Asian Deserts*. Centre for International Projects, Moscow.

Mongolia

Bulstrode, B. (1920). *A Tour of Mongolia.* Methuen, London.

Blunt, W. (1973). *The Golden Road to Samarkand.* Hamish Hamilton, London.

Carpine, J. (1961). *Histoire des Mongols,* translated by P. Schmitt. Paris.

Lamb, H. (1928). *Genghis Khan: The Emperor of All Men.* Thornton Butterworth, London.

Lattimore, O. (1942). *Mongol Journeys.* Travel Book Club, London.

Maclean, Sir F. (1974). *To the Back of Beyond. An Illustrated Companion to Central Asia and Mongolia.* Jonathan Cape, London.

Rossabi, M. (1988). *Kublai Khan: His Life and Times.* University of California Press, Berkeley and Los Angeles.

Rubruck, W. of (1900). *The Journey of William of Rubruck to the Eastern Parts of the World,* translated by R. Rockhill. Hakluyt Society, London.

Severin, T. (1991). *In Search of Genghis Khan.* Hutchinson, London.

Xinjiang

Barber, E. (1999). *The Mummies of Urumchi.* Macmillan, London.

Bessac, F. and Bessac, S. (2006). *Death on the Chang Tang.* University of Montana, Missoula.

Cable, M. and French, F. (1942). *The Gobi Desert.* Hodder & Stoughton, London.

Hedin, S. (1898). *Through Asia.* Methuen, London, vols 1 and 2.

Hedin, S. (1903). *Central Asia and Tibet.* Hurst and Blackett, London, vols 1 and 2.

Hedin, S. (1926). *My Life as an Explorer.* Cassell, London.

Hedin, S. (1936). *Big Horse's Flight. The Trail of War in Central Asia.* Macmillan, London.

Hedin, S. (1940). *The Wandering Lake.* George Routledge and Sons, London.

Holgate, W. (1994). *Arka Tagh. The Mysterious Mountains.* Ernest Press, London.

Hopkirk, P. (1980). *Foreign Devils on the Silk Road.* John Murray, London.

Laird, T. (2002). *Into Tibet.* Grove Press, New York.

Lias, G. (1956). *Kazak Exodus.* Evans Brothers, London.

Maillart, E. (1934). *Turkestan Solo.* Putnam, London.

Paula, C. (1994). *The Road to Miran.* HarperCollins, London.

Polo, M. (1903). *The Book of Ser Marco Polo,* translated and edited, with notes by Sir Henry Yule. London, vols 1 and 2.

Prejevalsky [Przhevalsky], N. (1879). *From Kulja across the Tian Shan to Lob Nur.* Sampson Low, Marston, Searle and Rivington, London.

Stein, Sir A. (1912). *Ruins of Desert Cathay.* Macmillan, London, vols 1 and 2.

Acknowledgements

Professor Yuan Guoying has been an invaluable supporter of all my expeditions into China. Without his support, I would never have set foot in the Desert of Lop and the Gashun Gobi. His son, Yuan Lei (Leilei) has accompanied me on each expedition and has been a constant friend and colleague, as has the late Lao Zhao.

In Mongolia, Bilgee, Tuya, Mijjidorj, Adiya and Dovchin have all given me great assistance and I am particularly grateful to the late Tsoijin, guide, ranger, and all-round Gobi expert. The late Dr Sarantuya, who worked in the Mongolian Ministry of Nature and the Environment, has also been an enormous help in many ways, as has Enkhbat, also of the MNE.

Peter Hall of Hunter Hall single-handedly provided the finance to establish the Zakhyn Us captive wild Bactrian camel breeding centre and it is largely due to his foresight and commitment that so much has been achieved.

National Geographic magazine, the Royal Geographical Society, the Royal Scottish Geographical Society, the Royal Society for Asian Affairs, the Explorers' Club of America, Arysta LifeScience, the Grocers' Livery Company, Shell China, UNEP/GEF, Nancy Abraham, Jennifer Bute, Pam Dunn, Mike Davies and the late Ann Savage all provided funding or other valuable support for my various expeditions, as did the Transglobe Expedition Trust and its executives – Peter and Anton Bowring, Simon Gault and Ranulph Fiennes. Without their collective financial and moral support there would have been no story to tell.

Dr Jane Goodall, DBE, the patron of the Wild Camel Protection Foundation, has given me consistent encouragement and advice. Over a number of years, Matthew Parris has provided financial support and encouragement as well as contributing a more than generous Preface to this book. In addition, Sylvia Howe made many constructive suggestions for the opening chapters.

My deep and heartfelt thanks go to Kate Rae, WCPF co-trustee, who has given me generous amounts of her time, energy and detailed knowledge and in particular for the trouble she had taken in making so many constructive suggestions for this book.

Fellow co-trustee Jasper Evans gave the Zoological Society of London's training team and the Mongolian and Chinese participants so much help and hospitality in Kenya.

John Skermer of Brackley Proof Reading Services constructed an excellent index and, lastly, great thanks are due to the design and editorial staff of I.B. Tauris and in particular to my editor Tatiana Wilde, who put in so much time and effort to ensure this book remained coherent and consistent.

Index

35 Tuan (Regiment) 10–14, 16
36 Tuan (Regiment) 16, 18, 20

Abdu Sadik 12
Adam, slave descendant 101
Adiya 100, 151; expedition in Gobi
  'A' [Ulan Bator–Bayan Toroi] 94–6;
  expedition in Gobi 'A' [Bayan
  Toroi–Zakhyn Us] 102–17; second
  expedition to Kum Su 118–50
Aksai 54, 75, 76, 77, 126
Aksupe 171, 172
Al Jazeera 181
Ali Abutalerp 54, 55, 75, 87, 123, 125
alpacas, connection to camels 199
Altai Mountains 76, 78, 79, 85, 87
'Angel Dado' 19
Annanba 54, 55, 76, 87, 144, 145
Annanba Nature Reserve 57
Anshi 67
Aqike valley 73–4
Argali, herdsman 136
Argali sheep, wild 32, 48, 114, 115,
  132, 133, 154
Arjin Mountains 2, 4, 9, 27, 28, 30, 33,
  34, 36, 37, 38, 49, 54, 72, 73, 75,
  77, 80, 82, 87, 129, 134, 135, 139,
  192, 195; yeti sighting 46
Arysta 118
ass, wild (kulan) 103, 115
ass, wild Tibetan (Kiang) 133, 141,
  145; reappearance at Kum Su 154

Atis Mountains 92, 103, 110
Aural SA 133

Bactrian camels, domestic 47–8, 119,
  120, behaviour and treatment 21–2,
  cannibalism 33; intelligence 35–6;
  endurance 43; shape 45; Shadrak
  46–7; threat to wild Bactrian
  camels 57; trained to eat meat 83,
  84; loading 101–2; eat snow 104;
  treatment of feet 108–9; hobbling
  140–1; qualities 187, 194–201;
  cancer therapy & type-1 diabetes
  antibodies 198; origin of name 199
Bactrian camel, wild (havtagai) 6, 14,
  29, 34, 40, 41, 42, 44–5, 48, 49, 52,
  54, 72, 74, 77, 91, 92, 103, 111–13,
  115, 120, 128, 132, 145, 151, 156,
  170, 190; survival in radioactive
  fall-out 6, 198; first discovery 18;
  survival in temperature extremes
  & scarcity of water 28; ticks on 31;
  wolf as predator 32–3, 47; shape
  45; threat from domestic Bactrian
  camels 57; shot by Tikar villagers
  70; aerial surveys forbidden 144;
  migration routes 146, 151, 192;
  reappearance at Kum Su 154; man
  as predator 157; qualities 187,
  194–201; habitats 196; cancer
  therapy & type-1 diabetes antibodies
  198; origin of name 199

Barber, Elizabeth Wayland 180
Bayan Gol Hotel 191; table-turning
    123
Bayan Toroi 94–6, 117
bear, Gobi (*ursus gobiensis*) 103–4
Beijing 67, 78, 98, 154, 159, 176; Zoo
    71; conference 91; airport 119
Belgrade 133
Bengal tiger 14, 172
Bergman (in Hedin's team) 178, 179
Bering Strait 199
Bessac, Frank 82–5; F & Susanne
    Bessac, *Death on the Chang Tang* 84;
    spy amongst the Kazakhs 213–24
    (Appendix 3)
Bilgee course in Kenya on tracking
    wildlife 88–91; expedition in Gobi
    'A' [Ulan Bator–Bayan Toroi] 94–6;
    expedition in Gobi 'A' [Bayan
    Toroi–Zakhyn-Us] 102–17
Bogd Khan, ruler of Mongolians 106
Bogd Ola (Mount of God), China 72
Bogd Ula Mountains, Mongolia 106
Bogt Sagaan Spring 107–8
bones, divination by 105–6
Buddhism 13, 60–1, 76; shrines 19,
    127, 164
Burrin Hayar hills 114
Branson, Sir Richard 144

Cable, Mildred 8
Canon 188
carbon-dating 173, 179–80
Caucasian mummies, *see* mummies
Caves of a Thousand Buddhas (Ch'ien
    Fo-tung) 60–4, 80
CC (Zhao Honglin) (of CCTV)2
    second expedition to Kum Su
    129–50
Celts 180, 184
Central China Television (CCTV) 120,
    129. *See also* CC, TV
Charkhlick *see* Ruoqian
Chen (in Hedin's team) 164–5
Chen Zhirven 129, 148–50
Cherchen 181; Cherchen man
    (mummy) 181
Chiang-Ssu-yeh 61, 162
Chien Lung 66

Chin Shu-jen 67
Chinese Central Television 7
Chinese Gobi 10
Chinese Nationalists 27, 53, 54, 78, 81
Chinese Red Beards 78–9
chung-chi (grape-drying halls) 69
CIA (US Central Intelligence Agency)
    82, 85
Communists 77, 78, 79, 80–3, 85, 86,
    87; communism 188
Cultural Revolution 11, 13, 62, 68

Danube 133
Dashi Hazi (dam) 171, 172
del (cloak) 94, 124
Deng Xiaoping 159
Desert of Lop 1, 16, 32, 58, 61, 79,
    80, 85, 92, 121, 144, 155–72, 176,
    195
DNA 161, 181–3
dog farm 65–6
Dorgotov 116
Dovchin 96, 151; expedition in Gobi
    'A' [Bayan Toroi–Zakhyn-Us]
    102–17; second expedition to Kum
    Su 118–50; incident with glass door
    151–3
Dromedary camels 136; behaviour
    and treatment 21–2, cannibalism
    33; endurance 43; predators 141,
    qualities 187, 194–200; cancer
    therapy & type-1 diabetes antibodies
    198
Dun Huang (Blazing Beacon) (also
    Shachow) 56, 57, 58–60, 64, 74,
    80–2, 121, 161, 163, 174
dust devils (*kwei*) 156–7
Dzungaria 66

Eastern Turkestan 66, 77, 86
Endrigen Nuru hills 100
ephedra (*ma huang*) (*Ephedra Sinica*)
    168, 174–5, 179
Evans, Jasper 33, 36, 42, 140–1, 186;
    course in Kenya on tracking wildlife
    88–91, 115, 119; trodden on by
    camel 110–11

Fan Yao-nan 154

fragmitis grass 31, 49
French, Francesca 8

Gandharan 162
Gansu Forestry Bureau 150
Gansu Province 54, 67, 76, 80–1,
    133–5, 150, 151
Gao, Professor 192
'Garland Dado' 19
Gashun (Bitter) Gobi desert 1, 11, 15,
    19, 30, 32, 44, 49, 68, 71, 76, 79,
    85, 99, 121, 155–72, 195; ticks 31
gazelles 89, 90, 103, 109, 115, 129,
    141, 172
Genghis Khan 76, 119
ger 95, 103, 108, 115, 124, 128
gerbils 98
Ghaz Kol (lake) 80–1, 85, 86, 87
giraffe 90
Gobi desert 14, 45, 66, 82, 94–117,
    173, 187, 188, 201; temperatures
    28; Mongolian ticks, absence of,
    31; expedition 94–117; *see also*
    Great Gobi Specially Protected Area
    Reserve 'A'
GPS 41, 89–90, 115
Great Gobi Specially Protected Area
    Reserve 'A' (Gobi 'A') 90, 94–117
Grocers' Livery Company, London 118
Gu, Professor 192
guanacos, connection to camels 199
Gunin, Professor Peter 188

Halle-Bopp comet 12
Hami (oasis – I-ku; district – Kumul)
    56, 57, 64–7, 69, 82, 120–1, 180;
    melons of 64–6
Han Dynasty 19, 58, 61
Hare, John, ('Ye Tuzi') diary entries,
    on Korla 10, on ticks 42, on
    sighting camels 52, 109–10, on Atis
    Mountains 103–4, on Mongolian
    sleeping-bag 128, on Hartabar
    valley 129, on dangerous journey
    143; bitten by dog 22–3; first phase
    of expedition [Hongliugou–Qui
    Kin Kan Sayi] 28–35; rendezvous
    at Qui Shi Kan Sayi 35; second
    phase of expedition [Qui Kin Kan

Sayi–Lapeiquan Spring] 37–53;
    explanation of Ye Tuzi 40; anti-rabies
    injections 55–7; eating dog 66; *The
    Lost Camels of Tartary* 76; on maps
    96–7; expedition in Gobi 'A' [Ulan
    Bator–Bayan Toroi] 94–6, expedition
    in Gobi 'A' [Bayan Toroi–Zakhyn-
    Us] 102–17; trodden on by camel
    110–11; second expedition to Kum
    Su 118–50; pirated book 151; 1992
    expedition 189–90; first meeting
    with Professor Yuan 191–4
Harrer, Heinrich, *Seven Years in Tibet* 76
Hartabar valley 129, 131
Hedin, Sven 9, 11, 16, 38–40, 64,
    70–1, 74, 135, 161–5, 170, 171–2,
    174, 179, 181; theory on silting of
    rivers proved 168–70; discovery of
    Queen of Lou Lan 176–8
Himalayas 67
Hindu Kush 162
Hong Gu valley 141
Hongliugou 4, 9, 14, 17, 20–4, 42, 54,
    72, 158; mosquitoes 22
Horner (in Hedin's team) 164–5
horses 158, 185–6; *see also* Przhevalsky
Hui Hui (Chinese Muslims) 125
Hsuan-tsang 1, 60, 116
Hussein Tajji 80–3, 86, 87
Hwang Wen-pi 164

ighiz kum (high sand) 40
impala 90
India 58, 60, 67, 83, 85, 87
Islam *see* Muslims

jade 176
Jamin Khan 86
Japan and Japanese 62, 78, 95, 125–6;
    Rape of Nanjing 126
jerboas 98
Ji Xianlin (historian) 183
Jiangsu Province 160
Jilin University 183

Kaduna 185
kang (raised area) 70–1
karez (irrigation system) 69
Karokoram mountain range 162

Kashgar 16, 19, 61, 67, 162
Kawo Village 186
Kazakh people, Kazakhstan 20, 22,
    46, 51, 54, 55, 57, 58, 75, 76,
    121, 144, 147, 183; sighting of yeti
    46; persecution of 77–87; second
    expedition to Kum Su 128–50;
    exodus across Lop Nur 123
Kenya 33, 88–91, 101, 109, 115, 119,
    123, 141, 186–7, 190
Kharoshti 163
Khotan 176; kingdom 19; texts 61
Kiang *see* ass, wild Tibetan
Konche Dariya 161–2, 172
Korea 95
Korla 9, 10, 15, 16, 18, 79, 156
Kowm, Syria 200
Krygyzs 183
Kum Bulak 140
Kum Kulak 129
Kum Su (Desert Spring) 50–2, 72,
    128, 140; secrecy regarding 51, 122;
    poisoning of 132–6, 145, 151, 154;
    clean-up 154
Kum Tagh 2, 34, 36, 37, 38, 40, 49,
    112, 128, 129, 145, 158
Kunlun Mountains 20, 120; yeti 46
Kuruk Dariya 161, 163, 168–70, 176,
    178
Kuruk Mountains (Dry Mountains) 2,
    79, 85, 155, 169

Laikipia 89
Lanzhou 80–1, 127, 150–1
Lao Zhang 54; shaman 26; first phase
    of expedition [Hongliugou–Qui
    Kin Kan Sayi] 28–35; rendezvous at
    Qui Shi Kan Sayi 35; second phase
    of expedition [Qui Kin Kan Sayi–
    Lapeiquan spring] 37–53; lost in
    desert on return to Ruoqian 72–3
Lao Zhao 3, 4, 7, 9, 14, 15, 30, 61,
    64, 70–1, 161, 164, 167, 193, 201;
    ill-treatment of camel 21; second
    phase of expedition [Qui Kin Kan
    Sayi–Lapeiquan spring] 37–53; death
    120–1

Lapeiquan spring 5, 35, 53, 143;
    ambush at, 27, 28; check-point
    144–5
Lawrence T.E. (Lawrence of Arabia),
    Seven Pillars of Wisdom 41
Le Coq, Albert von 158
Leilei 4, 5, 7, 18, 19, 150, 154,
    157; ambush at Lapeiquan spring
    27–8; first phase of expedition
    [Hongliugou–Qui Kin Kan Sayi]
    28–35; rendezvous at Qui Shi Kan
    Sayi 35; second phase of expedition
    [Qui Kin Kan Sayi–Lapeiquan
    spring] 37–53; course in Kenya on
    tracking wildlife 88–91; second
    expedition to Kum Su 120–50;
    table-turning 122
Lhasa 18, 58, 76, 85
Libby, Walter 179
Li Weidong 7, 24, 63; rendezvous at
    Qui Shi Kan Sayi 35; second phase
    of expedition [Qui Kin Kan Sayi–
    Lapeiquan spring] 37–53
Lias, Geoffrey 78, 81, 83, 123
Life magazine 85
llamas, connection to camels 199
Lop Desert *see* Desert of Lop
Lop Nur (dried-up lake) 2, 5, 7, 11,
    18, 19, 38, 40, 52, 77, 79–80, 145,
    155, 161, 169, 174, 177, 179, 192;
    nuclear test site 70, 170, 190–1,
    198
Lop Nur Wild Camel National Nature
    Reserve (Lop Nur Reserve) 68, 72,
    74, 76, 79, 90, 118, 120, 144
Lou Lan 5, 11, 15, 162–8, 174, 175,
    178, 180, 184; as Kroraina 163;
    Queen of Lou Lan 177–8, 181, 183

Ma (manager, Government State Melon
    Cooperative) 64–6
Ma Chongyu 150–1
Ma Chung-Ying 67–8
Mackiernan, Douglas 82–5; death 85;
    spy amongst the Kazakhs 213–24
    (Appendix 3)
Maillart, Ella 178
Mair, Victor 181–3
Mama Feng and daughter 16–17

Mamil 57, 87; second expedition to
Kum Su 123–50
Manchuria and people 58, 76, 78
mao-tai spirit 24, 147
Mao Tse-tung 127; badges 81–2; Great
Leap Forward 127
Marco Polo 1, 7, 158; sheep (*ovis poli*)
48
mesas, see yardangs
Mijjidorj (Mijji) 96, 100, 102, 114,
116, 150; course in Kenya on
tracking wildlife 90–1
Milky Way 41
miners and mining (coal, gold, jade)
73–4, 132–6, 140, 144, 151, 154,
155, 159, 176
Miran 16, 18–20, 61
Mongolian people, Mongolia 57, 58,
67, 76, 78, 89, 118–50, 183, 188–9,
195; example of resourcefulness
92–3; excellent eyesight 102–3;
Bogd Khan 106
mosquito, white 22, 36
mummies 173, 180–4, 201; Caucasian
173, 183
Muslims 13, 66, 67, 68, 71, 123–5,
182, 185; Hui Hui 125

Nairobi 186
Nanjing (Nanking) 125–6
National Geographic Magazine 6, 154
National Geographic Society 6, 21, 29
nature reserve, wild camel 4
New Aksai 121, 123, 144
New Delhi 19
New York National History Museum
199
Niazhan 12
Nigeria 185

Oates, Captain Lawrence 159
Omo river 187
Ordek 11, 12, 172, 178; grandson
Abdu Sadik and granddaughter
Niazhan 12, 71; grandson Torde
Ahun 70–1
oryx 89

Pamir Mountains 161, 181

Peng Jiamu, Professor, 159–61
People's Daily, The, 160
pika 7
poachers 114
Populus diversifola (desert poplar) 64,
156, 169–71
potassium cyanide 133–5, 151, 154
Przhevalsky, Nikolai Mikhailovich
16, 18, 135; discovers wild
Bactrian camel 18, 195; horse 4,
195; Przhevalsky Horse Breeding
Programme 195; first published
account of wild Bactrian camel
206–12 (Appendix 2)

Qali Beg 79–83, 85, 86
Queen of Lou Lan *see* Lou Lan
Qui Shi Kan Sayi (valley) 4, 26, 33, 34,
36, 43
Qi Yun 7, 24, 27; rendezvous at
Lapeiquan 52–3

Rae, Kate, course in Kenya on tracking
wildlife 88–91
Red Guards *see* Cultural Revolution
Romania 133
Runic Turkish manuscripts 61
Ruoqian 11, 14, 16, 17, 18, 20, 72,
156, 162
Russia and people 67, 76, 78, 79, 92
Russian Academy of Sciences 188, 189

Sadiq (relative of Torde Ahun) 71; fined
for shooting wild camel 71
Saka texts 61
Sali Beg 171
Salzburg 180, 181
Sanskrit manuscripts 61
Schaefer, Ernst, *Geheimmis Tibet* (Secret
or Mysterious Tibet) 84
Shachow *see* Dun Huang
Shandung Province 160
Shanshan kingdom 19
shorr (salt-bearing clay) 168
Siberia 58; sighting of yeti 46
Silk Road 166; old 58; southern 158;
Middle 2, 163, 169, 174
snow leopard 141
Sogdian manuscripts 61

Sokolov 190
Sringar 70
St Petersburg 18
Stalin 68, 75
State Environment Protection Agency
    (SEPA) 74, 154, 194
Stein, Aurel 9, 16, 18, 19, 61–3,
    162–4, 174–5, 176, 179
stones, divination by 105–7
stupas 19
Suguta valley 187
sum (local government) 96
Sykes monkey 88

table-turning 121–3
Ta-shi 77
Taipei 76
Taiwan 11
Taklamakan desert 11, 15, 38, 161,
    175, 176, 192, 195
Tan Shao Hong 55–6
Tangut people 58
Tarim River and Basin 161, 183, 195
Ternsorer, Dr 200
Tibet, Tibetan people 16, 18, 58, 76, 83,
    84–5, 86, 144; sighting of yeti 46;
    manuscripts 61; Tibet Plateau 156
Tibetan ass, wild 32, 48
Tibetan brown bear 43–4
Tibetan mastiff 55
ticks 30–1
Tien Shan (Heavenly Mountains) 7, 9,
    10, 72, 78, 79, 156, 161
Tiger River 13, 14
Tikar (Last Prayer) 68–72
Times, The 154
Timurlik 80, 82, 83, 85
Tisza river, Hungary 133
Toacharish texts 61
Tokharian 180
Torde Ahun 70–1
Torgut clan (Kalmuks) 76
Tsaidam 76, 77
Tsenker Mountains 103
Tserenbataa Tuya 150, course in Kenya
    on tracking wildlife 90–1
Tso Tsung-tang 67
Tsog Erdene, expedition in Gobi 'A'
    [Bayan Toroi–Zakhyn-Us] 102–17

Tsoi Spring 110–13
Tsoijin 100; expedition in Gobi 'A'
    [Ulan Bator–Bayan Toroi] 94–6;
    expedition in Gobi 'A' [Bayan
    Toroi–Zakhyn-Us] 102–17; divining
    by stones 105–7; discovered spring
    110
Tuareg 136, 137, 187
Turfan 58, 68, 69, 71–2, 155
Turkana, Kenya 109, 187
Tu-ying 2, 163–4, 176; as T'u-ken 164
TV (Liu Dong) (of CCTV) second
    expedition to Kum Su 129–50

Uighur people, 10, 11, 13, 15, 34,
    67–8, 70, 71, 78, 124, 171, 182–3;
    slums 8; manuscripts 61; slaughter
    and torture of 6,000 68; moved
    to Tikar from Sringar 70; current
    situation of Uighurs in Xinjiang
    202–5 (Appendix 1)
Ulan Bator 92, 95, 190; Black Market
    93–4, 117
Ungern-Sternberg, Baron 107–6
United Nations Development
    Programme (UNDP) 95
United Nations Environment
    Programme (UNEP) 188, 192–4
UNESCO 62
Urumqi 4, 7, 8, 56, 57, 68, 72, 73, 78,
    82, 86, 119, 120, 144, 150, 173,
    181, 184
USA 85, 181, 183
Usuman (cameleer) and wife 22–4,
    54, 72, 75, 87; treatment of dog-
    bite 23–4; first phase of expedition
    [Hongliugou–Qui Kin Kan Sayi]
    28–35; rendezvous at Qui Shi Kan
    Sayi 35; second phase of expedition
    [Qui Kin Kan Sayi–Lapeiquan
    spring] 37–53
Usuman Batur (leader of Kazakhs) 82,
    85; capture, torture and death 86

Volga region 76

Wacher, Tim, course in Kenya on
    tracking wildlife 88–91

Wang Huabing *Ancient Corpses of
  Xinjiang* 183
Wang Tao-shih, Abbot 61, 63
Wang Wanxuan 159
Wangkidan 76
wazungus (white men) 90
White Russians 62, 68, 82, 84–5, 106;
  see also Zvansov, Vasili
Wild Camel Protection Foundation
  (WCPF) 89, 117, 195
wolves 32, 106, 139–40
World Bank 120
Wutong (Wild Poplar Spring) 30, 33,
  43

Xia Xuncheng 160
Xinjiang 7, 8, 54, 58, 64, 67–8, 77, 78,
  86, 124, 159, 175, 182, 191, 192,
  195
Xinjiang Environmental Protection
  Bureau 3, 5, 153

yak 83, 84
Yakub Beg 67
yaman kum (hateful sand) 37, 42
yamen (municipal centre) 165
Yang Tseng-hsin 67, 153–4
yardangs (*mesas*)166–7, 174, 176, 177

yeti 43, 46; sightings in Siberia,
  Kazakhstan, Tibet, North America 46
Yingpan, ancient city 13, 14
Yuan Guoying , Professor 3, 7, 13, 16,
  17, 20, 24, 26–7, 30, 38, 46, 51,
  55, 65, 139, 150, 167, 171, 201;
  acupuncturist 23–4; ambush at
  Lapeiquan spring 27–8; rendezvous
  at Qui Shi Kan Sayi 35; rendezvous
  at Lapeiquan 52–3; on cultural
  relics 63–4; on maps 96; second
  expedition to Kum Su 120–50;
  table-turning 121–3; anti-Japanese
  126, 192; first meeting with John
  Hare 191–4
Yuan Lei *see* Leilei
Yuli 10, 11, 12, 14

Zakhyn Us 102, 113
Zhang, Deputy 118, 119; course in
  Kenya on tracking wildlife 90–1;
  second expedition to Kum Su
  128–50
Zhang, Dr, Director 119–20, 147–9,
  150, 153
Zhang Ying 119–21, 145; table-turning
  122; jeep driving at camels 146–7
Zhao Ziyung *see* Lao Zhao
Zoological Society of London (ZSL) 89
Zvansov, Vasili 85